MONTH-BY-MONTH GARDENING

NEW ENGLAND

Quarto is the authority on a wide range of topics.

Quarto educates, entertains and enriches the lives of our readers—enthusiasts and lovers of hands-on living.

www.quartoknows.com

First published in 2015 by Cool Springs Press, an imprint of Quarto Publishing Group USA Inc., 400 First Avenue North, Suite 400, Minneapolis, MN 55401 USA. Telephone: (612) 344-8100 Fax: (612) 344-8692

quartoknows.com
Visit our blogs at quartoknows.com

Cool Springs Press titles are also available at discounts in bulk quantity for industrial or sales-promotional use. For details contact the Special Sales Manager at Quarto Publishing Group USA Inc., 400 First Avenue North, Suite 400, Minneapolis, MN 55401 USA.

10 9 8 7 6 5 4 3 2

ISBN: 978-1-59186-641-1

Library of Congress Cataloging-in-Publication Data

Nardozzi, Charlie, author.
  New England month-by-month gardening : what to do each month to have a beautiful garden all year / [Charlie Nardozzi].
     pages cm
  Includes index.
  ISBN 978-1-59186-641-1 (pb)
  1. Gardening--New England. 2. Plants, Ornamental--New England. I. Title.

  SB453.2.N3N373 2016
  635.0974--dc23

                                                                                          2015023858

Acquiring Editor: Billie Brownell
Project Manager: Alyssa Bluhm
Art Director: Cindy Samargia Laun
Layout: Danielle Smith-Boldt

Printed in China

MONTH-BY-MONTH GARDENING

NEW ENGLAND

**What to Do Each Month to Have
a Beautiful Garden All Year**

CHARLIE NARDOZZI

COOL
SPRINGS
PRESS™

Home and Garden Experts™

MINNEAPOLIS, MINNESOTA

Dedication

To all the Master Gardeners, Garden Club members, and home gardeners in New England who take the time to help other gardeners be more successful.

Acknowledgments

I'd like to acknowledge the Master Gardener organizations and Extension Services in each New England state (Connecticut, Maine, Massachusetts, New Hampshire, Rhode Island, and Vermont). Their websites are filled with specific information on gardening in these areas, including pest controls, how-to information, and monthly calendars.

I'd also like to thank Billie Brownell, Tracy Stanley, Brad Springer, and the whole Cool Springs Press staff for once again making this book a straightforward and clear process. Thanks also to the horticulture editor, Katie Elzer-Peters, for her care and expertise. It helps to have a plan, and Cool Springs Press has a good one for this book.

Contents

Introduction

Welcome to gardening in New England. If you are new to gardening or new to gardening in New England, you'll see that our climate, soil, and seasons can be very conducive to amazing gardens. We seem to have just the right amount of sun, rain, and warm temperatures to grow beautiful annual and perennial flower gardens, vegetables, berries, bulbs, shrubs, and trees.

We all know a beautiful garden and landscape when we see one, but keeping it looking good may be a mystery. Whether you inherited an established landscape and garden when you purchased your home or condo or you've been building the gardens yourself, proper maintenance is essential. I often feel sad when I see a beautifully designed flower garden, shrub border, or edible garden looking overgrown, messy, and unkept because the owners didn't have the time or knowledge to maintain it. As a garden consultant, that's the number-one issue I see in home landscapes. How do you maintain and improve what you have and keep it looking good? While I can't help you find more time in your day to weed, fertilize, prune, and water, I can help you know what to do when in your garden. I also can take you step by step through how to do some of the basic chores in the landscape, such as pruning shrubs, controlling pests, and planting a tree.

That's the purpose of this book. This month-by-month guide arms you with the information you'll need to improve upon your existing landscape, and more importantly, maintain it well. It's always surprising that once you have a plan for what to do when, your garden maintenance doesn't feel so overwhelming. Also, the better organized you are, the less time your yard and garden will take to maintain.

DIVERSE GEOGRAPHY

Geographically, New England isn't that large when compared to other parts of the country, but it is diverse. The coastal areas are moderated by the Atlantic Ocean. This makes for less severe cold in winter and a longer growing season. However, the down side of coastal gardening is that sometimes poor soil, salt spray, harsh winds, and storms wreak havoc on plants. The rivers of New England are historic and were used by Native Americans and early settlers as transportation highways and food sources. It's along the Connecticut, Merrimack, and Kennebec and many other, smaller waterways that the best soils for growing are often found. But these rivers can quickly swell in spring, causing flooding and damage. The mountain areas, such as the Green Mountains of Vermont, White Mountains of New Hampshire, and inland areas of Maine, have a short growing season with long, cold winters. New Englanders are traditionally hardy people, so even here we scratch out some amazing gardens. In fact, clients of mine in Stowe, Vermont (a mountain ski community), have amazing perennial and annual flower gardens even with their three-month-long growing season.

PLAN

Every garden needs a well-thought-out plan. Start with a map of what you have in your yard, including permanent structures such as the house, garage, fences, rocks, walls, and large trees. Then dream a little. Think about the potential uses for various parts of your yard and the plants that would be best suited there. Consider the light, water, soil, and space requirements of your plants. Winter is a good time to put all this information down on paper and get ready to act come spring.

It's also a time to plan on changes to existing gardens based on your notes from the summer and fall. But before you start moving and digging, remember the soil. The soil is the foundation of your garden, and having healthy, fertile soil will reduce overall maintenance. With healthy soil you'll grow stronger plants that will better withstand insect, disease, and animal attacks and produce fruits and blooms in more abundance. While this book is filled with information on how

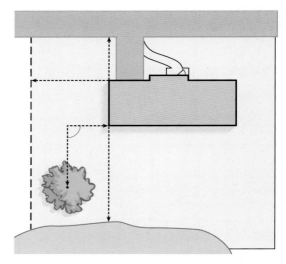

■ *Make a sketch of your yard showing the location of major permanent features such as the house, driveway, walkway, road, large trees, walls, and fences. You can add in your garden beds later.*

to plant, weed, fertilize, water, prune, and problem solve, always start with making better soil.

It's good to know your type of soil to get started. Soils in New England range from sand to clay. Sand has few nutrients and is well drained, while clay is usually nutrient rich but doesn't drain water well. The solution to make both of these soils healthier is organic matter. Organic matter sources come in many forms, such as hay, straw, untreated grass clippings, manure, shredded bark, leaves, peat moss, and compost. These break down into nutrient-rich humus. Organic matter not only makes sandy soils hold more water and nutrients and clay soil easier to work, it feeds the soil microbial life. Soil microbes are important for creating an ecological balance in the soil and in your garden. A soil with a broad range of soil microbes can make water and nutrients more readily available to your plants and help ward off insect and disease attacks.

PLANT

Once you have your soil-building plan in place, it's time to turn your attention to the plants. A wide range of plants can grow in New England. With hardiness zones ranging from 7 along the southern

HERE'S HOW

TO DETERMINE YOUR SOIL TYPE

■ *Take a handful of soil and dampen it with water until it is moldable, almost like moist putty.*

■ *Roll the soil into a ball, as if working with cookie dough.*

■ *Using your thumb and forefinger, gently press the soil until the ball begins to roll out of your closed hand. The ribbon will begin to form, and will eventually break under its own weight. If the soil crumbles and doesn't form a ribbon at all, you have sandy soil.*

■ *If a ribbon more than 1 inch long forms before it breaks, you have silty soil. If a ribbon 2 to 3 inches long forms before it breaks, you have clay soil.*

New England shore to 3 in the mountains of Vermont and New Hampshire, the spectrum of shrubs, trees, and perennial flowers is broad.

When selecting perennial plants, shrubs, and trees for your yard always remember the "right plant for the right place" rule. Understand the ultimate size and shape of the plant and if it will fit in your location. Think about the sun and soil requirements. Planting the right plant in the right place will save you many headaches down the road.

For annual flowers, herbs, and vegetables, timing is *everything*. Planting these too soon into cold, wet soil can lead to rotting seeds and transplants. Waiting too late during our sometimes short summers can mean crops won't mature or flower much before frost. You can extend the season with frost protection and plastics to heat the soil, but getting plants out at the right time is essential.

A good way to minimize problems with growing plants in the wrong location, dealing with pests

■ *When planting a tree, dig a hole that is two or three times the diameter of the rootball or container and just as deep.*

on plants, and having plants not survive is to grow native plants. I like to think of native plants as those plants indigenous or naturalized to a given area over a long period of time. This includes plants that have grown in an area for thousands of years and ones that have naturalized in New England over the last few centuries. The key is that native plants have developed a balance with other plants, insects, and animals in the ecosystem. They fill a niche for wildlife and insect life without crowding out other plants.

The native plant movement is going strong in New England, and many garden centers and nurseries promote growing natives because they're good for the ecological habitat and easy to maintain. These are plants that you know won't get out of hand in your yard, and many are very attractive additions.

Whatever perennial flower, shrub, or tree you plant, dig a large enough hole to accommodate the roots. The hole should be two to three times wider than the rootball and as deep. Use the native soil to fill the hole. This will encourage the roots to get established faster and get the tree off to a good start.

CARE

It would be nice if all the flowers, vegetables, bulbs, trees, and shrubs that you just planted would fend for themselves. While some plants *are* lower maintenance than others, all will benefit from some care. Beside the watering, fertilizing, and pest-control techniques I mention in these sections and in each monthly chapter, mulching is a good way to reduce work and keep your plants healthy. Organic mulches such as straw, bark, and wood chips reduce the amount of weeding and watering, while slowly decomposing to provide nutrients for your plants. Even crushed stone works to prevent weed growth and watering, even though it doesn't add organic matter to the soil.

Pruning is *essential* for some plants to produce the best flowers and fruits. Annual flowers benefit from deadheading the spent blossoms. Not only do they look better, but the snipping also encourages more flowering. Fruit bushes and trees need annual pruning to keep their shape and prevent overcrowding. This will result in better production. Ornamental trees and shrubs can always benefit from the removal of dead, diseased, and broken branches each spring to help keep the plant healthy.

Dividing overcrowded perennial plants and harvesting vegetables promptly help keep the flowers and veggies coming. By dividing perennials, such as iris and daylilies, you can create more plants for yourself and friends. With many vegetables, the more you pick, the more they will produce, so staying on top of harvesting is key to optimum production.

WATER

There's nothing worse than working hard to plant your garden only to have it dry up with the first summer drought. Although New England tends to

HERE'S HOW

TO DIVIDE PLANTS

■ *Dig up the plant that you want to divide. Dig all the way around the plant clump, about 4 inches away from the edge of the plant. If you water the plants you're planning to dig up and divide the night before you're dividing them, they'll be easier to dig up.*

■ *Divide the plant with either a spade or two gardening forks. Gardening forks work well for plants like daylilies because they have relatively small roots. Hostas have large roots, and ornamental grasses are often so dense that it is impossible to pry pieces of the plant apart with the forks, so you might have to use a spade to chop the plant apart.*

■ *To divide with two forks, put the forks back to back in the center of the plant clump, push both down, and pry apart.*

■ *Water new plants thoroughly after planting so the rootball is well-soaked.*

get plenty of rain to water our landscapes, it may not come when we want it or in the quantities we need. Young transplants and newly planted shrubs and trees especially need a constant supply of water to survive.

Check young transplants and germinating seeds almost daily to make sure the soil stays moist. Deeply water perennials, shrubs, and trees so the moisture seeps 6 to 8 inches into the ground.

This will encourage deeper rooting and lessen the chance of the plant succumbing to drought. Use mulches to conserve moisture on all landscape plants and as a way to prevent weeds from competing with your plants for water.

FERTILIZE

Starting with healthy soil is essential to a productive garden, but sometimes you'll find the need to add fertilizer. Before you automatically add any fertilizer, you should do a soil test in spring or fall. This test will give you a snapshot of what's lacking in your soil and what to do to correct the deficiency. Perform a separate soil test for each type of garden or planting. Soil labs mentioned in the appendix offer testing services for our region.

For healthy plants growing in healthy soils, adding a layer of compost in spring may be enough to keep them growing strong. For fast-growing, more demanding annual flowers, vegetables, and roses, adding an organic balanced fertilizer, such as 5-5-5, early in the growing season helps give them a boost. These plants may need additional doses of fertilizer, or a sidedressing, during the spring and summer to keep them flowering and producing fruits.

■ *Choose a fertilizer that is appropriate for your plant. Organic types are slow-release and healthier for the plant and soil.*

Organic fertilizers are preferred in most cases because they release nutrients slowly. This allows the plants to take up the food as needed and reduces the risk of some nutrients leaching out to pollute waterways.

Sometimes young plants will need a boost of a specific nutrient to get them growing strong. Nitrogen is a key chemical to help keep leaves green and vibrant. A young struggling seedling or transplant that has pale-colored leaves may need a dose of a soluble nitrogen fertilizer, such as fish emulsion, to just give it a boost.

PROBLEM-SOLVE

While there can be many problems in the garden, most of us think of weeds and pests as our biggest concerns.

Many plants in New England are not natives. These have arrived on purpose or by accident. While most exotics have adapted to our climate and soils without harming the native vegetation, some have become a problem and are considered weeds. Some plants, such as goutweed or bishop weed (*Aegopodium*), were originally brought here as ornamental plants. Unfortunately, these plants were too happy in New England, and without any natural insect and disease predators to keep them in check, they have spread to take over gardens and forests. When this happens, the exotic plant is now considered an invasive weed. Some invasives continue to be spread inadvertently by people. The water weed, Eurasian water milfoil, is spread when boaters go from pond to pond with their boats, unknowingly bringing pieces of the plant along.

Some invasives are obvious in our New England gardens and woods. For years I've driven one of the major north–south interstates in New England (I-91), and once I reach Massachusetts and Connecticut from Vermont I start seeing signs of Oriental bittersweet (*Celastrus orbiculatus*). This vine will grow aggressively to cover, choke, and kill healthy trees. I've seen 70-foot-tall trees along the highway swallowed up by bittersweet vines. For an extensive list of invasive plants that might be in

■ *Avoid planting invasive plants, such as Oriental bittersweet, in your yard. It can quickly become a weed that will last for years.*

INTEGRATED PEST MANAGEMENT

I'm an organic gardener, and most of the recommendations in this book reflect that fact. I like to follow the integrated pest management (IPM) approach to controlling pests. In this approach, you first make sure you're growing the right plants in the right places on healthy soil. Once pests arise, IPM strategies lead you through the least-invasive practices. Spraying pesticides of any kind, organic or not, is always a last resort. Here are some of the steps of IPM to follow.

KEEP PLANTS HEALTHY

Just like humans, when plants are healthy they're less likely to succumb to insect and disease attacks. Proper watering, fertilizing, weeding, and mulching, as well as healthy soil conditions and placement in the right light levels, will ensure that your plants grow strong. Also, growing plants

your yard and need to be removed, check the state-by-state resources in the appendix.

Some of these invasive weeds are obvious, while others are less conspicuous. Laws in some states, such as Connecticut, prohibit the sale of plants on the invasive list, but you still should be careful not to unknowingly introduce an invasive into your yard from a neighborhood plant swap or a division from a friend or family member. Not only will it be harmful to your garden environment, you may be battling it for years to come.

The tricky part about controlling invasives is they can spread easily by roots or seeds. Herbicides sprayed in spring and summer can provide some relief and are one of the few places I can see using them to combat a real problem area. Otherwise, you'll have to be diligent about hand weeding, mowing, and uprooting the invasives wherever they're found.

While invasive weeds are pests in New England, most gardeners are more concerned with controlling insects, diseases, and animals that can make a hard-worked garden look like a battlefield. In this book, I cover what pests to watch for when and on which plants. This is where some education really helps in your work to have a healthy garden. Identifying the pest and knowing its habits will help you prevent damage or minimize it.

■ *Encourage beneficial insects, such as ladybugs, into your yard by growing a diverse selection of plants.*

■ *Praying mantis is a natural predator of many insects in the garden.*

■ *Be on the lookout for exotic invasive insects such as the Asian longhorned beetle. This beetle has been found in the New England region and is devastating to maples and many hardwood trees if it's not controlled.*

a beetle on the adult leaf with a large hole, you might think the beetle is eating the leaves, but chances are the damage was caused days ago by the slug. Using resources such as the Internet and the Master Gardener organizations in your area, you can properly identify the damage and know if it's insect, disease, or animal related.

While many pests, such as Japanese beetles, are annual problems in the garden, new exotic pests have invaded our region in recent years and are really cause for concern. The Asian longhorned beetle has killed thousands of maple, elm, willow, birch, and other hardwood trees from the Great Lakes to New England. In our region it is presently confined to areas in Massachusetts and is being actively monitored to reduce its spread. The emerald ash borer is another exotic, invasive tree insect that kills a variety of ash trees in our forests and landscapes. It found its way into New England and has spread to Connecticut, Massachusetts, and New Hampshire. Like the Asian longhorned beetle, it has no natural predators and so can quickly spread from tree to tree, killing this important forest and landscape tree. The hemlock woolly adelgid is a pest of hemlock trees and is presently in all New England states, reducing wild and planted stands of this beautiful evergreen tree. By carefully monitoring your trees and being able to properly identify these insects you can help alert state authorities about these pests to help slow their spread.

that are hardy and adapted to your part of New England and ones that fit in the space without overcrowding will also lessen the chances of pests causing serious damage. Look for varieties with specific insect and disease resistance to reduce the need for further pest controls. Remove dead, diseased, and insect-ridden plants when you find them to prevent their spread.

Growing a variety of different types of plants also helps create an ecological system that will take care of itself. Mix and match vegetables, herbs, flowers, shrubs, and trees together in the landscape. The greater the variety of plant types, the less likely your garden will be overrun with pests. This should include having water sources and shelter nearby for beneficial insects and creatures such as frogs and birds.

IDENTIFY THE PESTS

Not all insects and diseases are considered pests. In fact, the vast majority of insects and diseases are either neutral or beneficial toward your plants. The first step is to properly identify the problem. Some plant problems aren't even caused by pests. Damage may be from hail, frost, wind, water, or even herbicide drift if you live near a farm. The insect you see on leaves may not be the culprit causing the damage. For example, slugs will often eat holes in hosta leaves when the plant is young. As the leaf grows, so does the hole. If you find

MECHANICAL CONTROLS

Once you know the pest, you can start controlling it. The best control is prevention. By blocking insects from laying eggs, diseases from spreading from leaf to leaf, or animals from chewing on branches, you will be able to stop damage before it becomes a problem. In this book, I talk about floating row covers, mulches, spacing plants properly, netting, fencing, and repellent sprays as ways to prevent damage.

The other aspect of mechanical controls is handpicking. By continually monitoring your plants you will be able to identify eggs and young stages of insects and early signs of diseases. Then you can crush eggs, handpick young insects, and pick off diseased leaves before they start spreading.

You can also use traps, such as apple maggot traps or the yellow sticky cards that lure and trap whiteflies and aphids, to reduce the population of specific, harmful insects.

BIOLOGICAL CONTROLS

Mother Nature has many ways to keep your garden pests in check. Beneficial insects and animals thrive in a healthy organic garden so no one pest can get out of control. You can help this process by creating habitats for beneficials to live. For example, placing an upside-down, broken clay pot in a garden provides a nice hiding place for frogs and toads. They *love* to eat insects and slugs.

You can go a step further for pests that are getting out of hand. Biological sprays have become that latest trend in pest controls. These sprays use naturally occurring bacteria to control insects and fungus. They are less disruptive to the environment and are safe for pests and children. *Bacillus thuringiensis* (Bt) is probably the most common type. There are forms of Bt that kill cabbageworms, Colorado potato beetles, fungus gnats, and mosquito larvae. There is even research on a form of Bt that will kill Japanese beetle grubs.

Bacillus subtilis is a type of bacteria that attacks common fungal diseases such as blackspot on roses,

blight on tomatoes, and scab on apples. When looking for sprays, start with these.

ORGANIC SPRAYS

The final line of defense should be an organic spray. Insecticidal, soap, Neem oil, diatomaceous earth, kaolin clay, horticultural oil, acetic acid (weed control), and pyrethrum are some of the organic sprays available. Be aware that even though these are organic, they still kill, sometimes indiscriminately, so use them cautiously. Spray on calm days, following the label directions.

Some sprays, such as pyrethrum and spinosad, are toxic to bees and should not be sprayed on plants in bloom. It's best to spray these later in the day, when bees are less active. Others, such as acetic acid, can be harmful to frogs and toads and should mostly be used to spot-treat weeds on patios and decks. With careful use, sprays can be just one of the tools in your garden basket to curb an out-of-control infestation.

Just knowing all these tasks isn't enough. The key is to know when to do them. When to water, when to prune, when to look for pests . . . that's what this book is all about. By knowing how and when to do these gardening tasks you'll be able to be most effective with the least amount of work.

■ *New England is known for its magnificent fall foliage color.*

INTRODUCTION

HOW TO USE THIS BOOK

New England Month-by-Month Gardening is a handbook to help you know what to do when in your garden, every month of the year. It's a great companion to another book of mine, *New England Getting Started Garden Guide* (Cool Springs Press, 2014). This book provides more than just reminders, though. It has recommendations for types and varieties of plants and many step-by-step how-tos to guide you through some of the more common maintenance topics.

I've tried to make this pretty simple and straightforward. Each month is broken into six task categories. These are Plan, Plant, Care, Water, Fertilize, and Problem-Solve. Within each of these tasks are plant categories, which include Annuals, Bulbs, Edibles, Lawns & Groundcovers, Perennials & Vines, Roses, Shrubs, and Trees. The tasks that are important to perform for each of these types of plants are then explained for that month. Some months won't have any tasks to do, so that category will be blank.

Scattered throughout the book are Here's How sections that will help you dig a little deeper into how to do the tasks recommended for that month. Some of the Here's How topics include pruning a shrub, planting a container tree or shrub, building a raised bed, seeding a lawn, and planting bulbs. And there's so much more.

So, let's get started taking care of and improving your yard and garden.

USDA HARDINESS ZONE MAP

The USDA Hardiness Zone Map gives gardeners a key tool for selecting hardy plants in their region. It's based on the *average* annual minimum temperatures during a thirty-year period in the past, not the lowest temperature that has ever occurred in the past or might occur in the future. Therefore, it should be used as a guide, not the absolute final word about which perennial, shrub, or tree is hardy in your area. Other factors that will contribute to plant hardiness are wind exposure, soil, sun, and the age of the plant.

The USDA hardiness zones were recently changed to reflect the warming climate. Many zone designations shifted northward because of warmer conditions of the last thirty years. This has tempted gardeners to grow more tender plants in their area, but it's important to remember that the hardiness zones are only the *average* winter minimum temperatures. There are sure to be winters that will be colder than the average and may harm your plants.

Microclimates can be created that will protect plants so more tender species can grow in your area. A microclimate is any area that provides a plant with protection from the cold or enhances the accumulation of heat. Some examples are a building or wall that blocks cold north and west winds in winter, or a courtyard that has a southern exposure so it stays warmer in winter from retained heat.

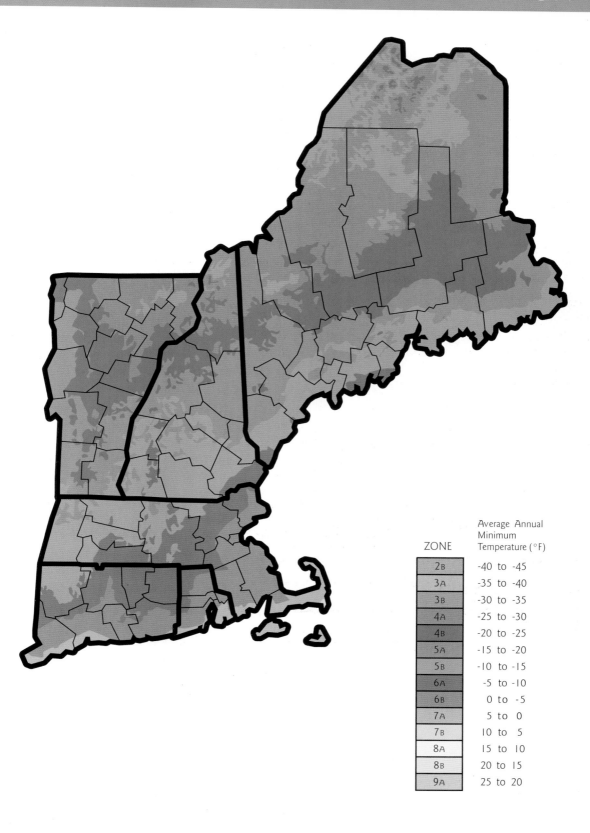

ZONE	Average Annual Minimum Temperature (°F)
2B	-40 to -45
3A	-35 to -40
3B	-30 to -35
4A	-25 to -30
4B	-20 to -25
5A	-15 to -20
5B	-10 to -15
6A	-5 to -10
6B	0 to -5
7A	5 to 0
7B	10 to 5
8A	15 to 10
8B	20 to 15
9A	25 to 20

January

It's funny how a change in the calendar can change our attitudes about our gardens and landscapes. Hope springs eternal at the beginning of the new year. Come January, energy and enthusiasm starts to return and we start imagining new and healthier vegetables, flowers, trees, and shrubs.

It's good that New England gardeners are so enthusiastic because January is a quiet month in the garden. It's a time for gathering ideas, getting inspired, and looking forward to the longer days and warmer temperatures that will eventually arrive.

January is also a time of lists. This is one area where we can do a better job. I seem to have memory loss when it comes to what worked and didn't work in my garden the past year. I gloss over the hard parts and the plants that didn't do well and embellish the good parts. That's why I often sit down in January with my wife, Wendy, to discuss what worked and didn't work the past year. We talk about flower or vegetable varieties that performed well, or not so much. We talk about expanding or consolidating gardens, which gardens need more mulching, fertilizing, and care, and what plants need to be moved. Most important, we write all this down so during the spring gardening rush, we have a list of priorities to follow and aren't swayed too much by the latest and greatest plants we find at the garden center.

January is a great time to look at the "bones" or hardscapes of our gardens, those elements that are fairly permanent. These include stone walls, outbuildings, large trees, fences, pergolas, arbors, and walkways. Of course, if everything is buried under a classic New England snowstorm, it may be hard to see all these elements. But often there is a January thaw and the landscape opens up enough for us to appreciate and reflect on any changes with these hardscape pieces. It's good to look at the garden without all the plants in full glory to see how these bones support the overall landscape. Before you know it, flowers will be decorating our yards once again.

PLAN

ANNUALS

Annuals give your garden a splash of color. The beauty of annual flowers is they bloom all season. Now is a good time to start thinking about what annual flowers you'll either start from seed or purchase as transplants for planting in May.

When planning your annual flower garden you can design it a number of ways. You can plant a flower bed that's just annuals, mixing colors, heights, and sizes of different flowers. Or you can mix annual flowers in among perennials, under shrubs and trees, and even in with edibles, to add color during times of the year when it might be lacking.

If you are planting a whole bed of annuals remember that different colors will have different effects on the viewer. Bold colors, such as red, yellow, and orange, are best viewed from a distance. Their brightness pops in the yard and can feel overwhelming if you're looking at a whole bed of red salvia close up. Some of my favorite bold annual flowers for beds include large-flowered marigolds, dwarf sunflowers, and red 'Profusion' zinnias. Pastel colors, such as violet, blue, and pink, are best viewed close up and get overlooked when viewed from a distance. Some good pastel annuals for close viewing are 'Johnny Jump-Up' violas, clown flowers (*Torenia*), and blue fan flowers (*Scaevola*).

Planting the right height of annual flower in the right location is important as well. Plant low-growing annuals, such as lobelia and alyssum, in the front of the annual garden where they won't get shaded. Plant taller cosmos and sunflowers in the back of the garden as a beautiful backdrop.

Match the right annual with the right sun conditions. Grow shade-loving annuals, such as begonias, impatiens, and clown flowers, under tall shrubs and trees that allow part sun to reach the ground. Save full sun-loving annuals, such as lantana, verbena, and moss rose (*Portulaca*), for those spots that bathe in sun all day.

BULBS

Unless you remember the areas where you planted spring-flowering bulbs in fall, it's always a surprise where your bulbs pop up in spring. This year, plan to mark where your tulips, daffodils, hyacinths, and other spring-flowering bulbs are growing once they're up so you'll know where you can plant annuals and other flowers without harming those bulbs. You can make a map of the garden showing where these bulbs reside or place metal or wooden markers, or even golf tees, in the soil.

Plan on adding other summer-flowering bulbs that you'll plant this May, such as Asiatic and Oriental lilies.

EDIBLES

Sketch out your vegetable and herb garden beds from last year, filling in where you planted each vegetable and herb. Evaluate how the plants grew in each bed and decide which you'll plant again and which you might replace. Note which vegetables you planted too much or not enough of. Adjust your planting plan based on what you like to eat.

Make a list of the vegetables and herbs you'll be growing this year, and on a new piece of paper, start filling in the beds in the new garden. Remember to rotate crops. Don't grow plants from the same

PLANT FAMILIES

Amaryllidaceae—chives, garlic, leeks, onions

Brassicaceae—broccoli, Brussels sprouts, cabbage, cauliflower, collards, kale, kohlrabi, radish, mustard

Chenopodiaceae—spinach, beets, Swiss chard

Compositae—endive, escarole, artichoke, lettuce, sunflower

Cucurbitaceae—cucumbers, summer squash, zucchini, winter squash, melons, watermelons, gourds

Leguminosae—peas, beans

Solanaceae—tomatoes, potatoes, eggplant, peppers, tomatillos

Umbelliferae—celery, carrot, dill, parsnip, cilantro, parsley, fennel

family for three years in the same bed. For example, tomato family crops, such as peppers, tomatoes, eggplant, and potatoes, shouldn't be planted in the same bed on continuous years. See the sidebar on plant families to decide which crops to rotate. This will reduce problems from insect and disease attacks.

If you're short on room, vegetables and herbs grow well in containers, so you can grow some of your edibles in pots. This saves space, and certain vegetables, such as eggplant, appreciate the added heat that comes from growing in a container (because the soil in containers warms up more and faster).

Plant a few berry bushes or fruit trees in your yard this year. While many berries and fruits are self-fertile, meaning you only need one plant to get fruit, it's usually best to plant a few of each. For example, if you want to plant blueberries, plant an early-, mid-, and late-season variety to extend the fruiting season. Most fruit trees produce better or may even need another variety for proper pollination. Do a little research on the fruits you'd like to grow to understand how many to plant.

Select fruits and berries that fit in your landscape. While a tall apple tree may seem too big for your yard, dwarf trees or columnar apples will fit in a smaller space. Always look for varieties that are hardy in your area. Check the hardiness zone map on page 17 to see what is your zone. Select plants whose hardiness range is at or below that zone.

PERENNIALS & VINES

If you're tired of replanting your flower gardens with annuals each spring, consider expanding or creating new perennial beds in your yard in April. Find locations that have fertile, well-drained soil to start. Watch the sun levels in those locations. Plant sun-loving perennials, such as iris, peony, Shasta daisy, and tall phlox, in full-sun areas, and shade-loving perennials, such as hosta, astilbe, ferns, and lungwort (*Pulmonaria*), in part- to full-shade areas.

Look for walls or trellises near which to plant perennial climbing vines. Choose the right vine for the sun and exposure conditions. For sunny spots select vines such as clematis, honeysuckle, and wisteria. For shady spots consider climbing hydrangea, Boston ivy, and Virginia creeper.

LAWNS & GROUNDCOVERS

There's not much planning happening with lawns until the snow melts, but start thinking about groundcovers where the grass doesn't grow well. You probably remember the thin or bare spots in your yard. Maybe it was under some trees or close to a rock ledge. Plant groundcovers instead. Shade-loving groundcovers include sweet woodruff, lily-of-the-valley, and vinca. Groundcovers that thrive with a little more sun include pachysandra, mint, and ivy.

ROSES

Everyone loves a rose bush in full bloom, but many New England gardeners shy away from roses because they think they're too hard to grow or have too many problems. Reconsider planting roses in your yard this spring, especially if you have a sunny spot with well-drained, fertile soil. To avoid the disappointment of dead roses in spring, look for varieties that are hardy for your area and varieties with disease resistance. Some of my favorites are the rugosa roses and their hybrids and the landscape roses such as the 'Knockout' series.

Roses look great planted in their own garden, mixed with perennial flowers and shrubs, and even used as a hedge. Some roses are low growing and act like sun-loving groundcovers. Select the best type for your usage and location. Look at flower traits that you want, such as everblooming versus once blooming, single versus double flowers, and scent versus no scent. Selecting the right rose variety will help you avoid problems during the growing season. Find out if the rose of your dreams spreads by suckers or is more contained. Always make sure your rose variety is hardy for your area.

SHRUBS

Planting evergreen or deciduous shrubs this April and May is a great way to dress up the area around your home. Shrubs planted around your home are called "foundation plantings" because they hide a cement foundation. When choosing a shrub, always consider the plant's ultimate size. Often, I've seen the wrong shrub planted under a window or near a walkway. In a few years, the owner has to continually cut the shrub back to keep it in bounds. The result is an awkward-looking shrub trimmed into a square or lollipop shape.

Shrubs are also good choices for mixed plantings with perennials and as hedges. Do some research during these down days of January into what shrubs will look best in your location. Always check the hardiness zone rating for that shrub and grow it in the right light and soil conditions. Consider the role it will play in your landscape. Do you want a plant that is green year-round (evergreen) or a shrub that loses its leaves in fall (deciduous)? When do you want it to flower? Do you want berries on the shrub? What about fall foliage color or winter bark color?

TREES

A tree is a long-term and sometimes expensive commitment. As with shrubs, if planted in the wrong location it will struggle or need to be severely pruned when older. Always avoid planting under overhead power lines or in areas where workers may have to prune the tree to get to your home.

Think of the purpose of the tree. Do you want a shade tree? Is this a specimen tree that will be a highlight of your yard? Do you want an evergreen that will help block a view? Do you want edible fruit? Is fall color important to you?

PLANT

ANNUALS

While it's too early to plant most annual flowers this time of year, it's not too early to get ready. Once you have your list of flowers, decide which will be grown from transplants and which from seed. Purchase seed locally or online. It's good to understand what a seed packet tells you about the plant. The information it offers, such as germination rates, right conditions for growing, and plant size, will help you get the plant off to a good start.

Clean and inventory your indoor seed-starting equipment. Check the amount of seed-starting mix left over from last year and plan on buying more if needed. Don't get just any potting soil; buy one specifically designed for seed starting. Replace broken plastic pots and seed trays. Experiment using peat pots or cow pots, which can be planted into the soil with the seedlings and decompose over time. Cow pots are made from dried, compressed manure

TO PERFORM A SEED GERMINATION TEST

If you have leftover seeds from past years, it might be a good idea to do a germination test to see if those seeds are still viable to plant. Generally, the germination percentage of most flower and vegetable seed decreases dramatically after two to three years. Some decrease even after one year. If you do the test and have a germination percentage lower than 70 percent, it's time to buy new seeds. A germination percentage higher than that means you can sow the seeds, but just plant more seeds than normal.

1. Wet a paper towel so it's moist, but not soaking.

2. Choose a sampling of the seeds to test. Usually at least ten seeds is best, but it may be less if you don't have that many seeds remaining.

3. Place the seeds on one-half of the paper towel and fold the other half over them.

4. Place the paper towel in a clear plastic bag. Mark the bag to identify the variety you're testing.

5. Place the bag in a warm, dark location out of sunlight.

6. Remove the towel after a few days and check the results. Rotten seeds count as non-germinating. Return the towel to the bag. Check every day for more germination, keeping a tally.

7. After ten to fourteen days, calculate your germination percentage.

HERE'S HOW

TO READ A SEED PACKET

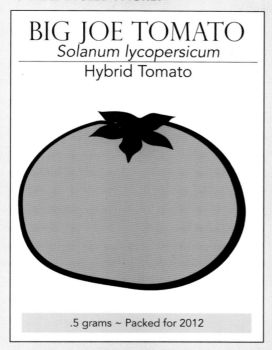

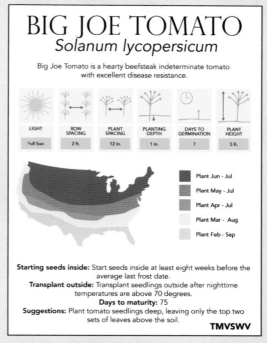

Usually when we purchase seed packets we look at the variety name and the color photo. However, there is more information on the packet that might be helpful in growing your flower, vegetable, or herb.

1. **Botanical Name:** The botanical, or Latin, name will help you purchase the correct plant. Common names can be misleading. Sometimes there are different common names for the same plant. Botanical names are more accurate and unique to that plant.

2. **Growing Information:** Most seed packets have detailed growing information for that flower, vegetable, or herb. This may include when to sow (indoors or outdoors), where to sow, seed depth and spacing, and sun requirements.

3. **Days to Maturity:** This number is almost always included. It's important to note that the days to maturity may be from direct seeding in the ground (lettuce, carrots) or from when a seedling is transplanted in the ground (tomatoes, peppers). Choose varieties that will mature within the frost-free days you have in your area. See the map in the appendix for frost-free days in New England.

4. **Germination Percentage and Date:** Check to be sure you're buying this year's seed. There should be a packing date on the packet. Packets may also include days to germination. This, of course, will vary depending on the weather. Cool weather will slow germination.

5. **Disease Resistance:** Next to the variety name there may be letters such as *V, F,* and *N*. These mean Verticillium wilt, Fusarium wilt, and Nematodes. These letters indicate that your variety is resistant to these problems. *F1* means this variety is a hybrid and you can't save the seeds from it because it won't come true to seed the next year.

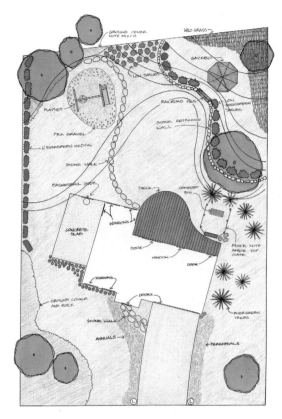

■ *Having an overall landscape design will help you phase in projects, pacing your landscape work one step at a time.*

and add fertilizer to the soil as they break down. This way you won't disturb the seedling's roots when transplanting. Check your grow lights to be sure they work. Purchase a timer so your lights will turn on and off automatically, giving your seedlings the required fourteen hours of light per day.

Start viola and pansy seeds near the end of January in warm areas of our region such as southern New England and along the coast. These will be ready to transplant into large containers in about eight to ten weeks. In ten weeks it will still be too cold to plant outside in the ground. However, you can move large containers into a warmer area if extreme cold weather or our occasional late winter snowstorm strikes.

BULBS

Plant paperwhite narcissus and amaryllis bulbs to force indoors to ensure some color and fragrance

in a month or so. Some people dislike the scent of paperwhites, but I think they smell great.

EDIBLES

Decide what you'll start from seed and what you'll purchase as transplants. Get your seed-starting supplies ready for the big indoor sowing in a month or so.

Check the germination rates of old seeds. See Here's How To Perform A Seed Germination Test on page 22.

In warmer areas of our region, start alliums, such as leeks and onions, from seed at the end of January. These plants need eight to ten weeks of indoor growing before they can be transplanted into the garden.

PERENNIALS & VINES

Some perennial flowers can be started from seed indoors. Decide which ones you'll be growing from seed, purchase those packets, and get your seed-starting equipment ready in order to plant at the appropriate time in the next month or so.

ROSES

Beware of the bare-root roses you'll find in stores late this month. These roses are dug and shipped

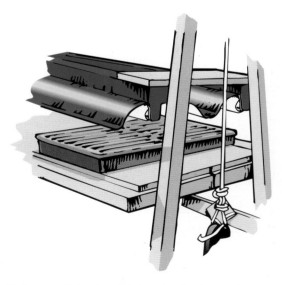

■ *Keep grow lights suspended about 6 inches above seedlings. Raise the lights as the seedlings grow.*

from warmer climates such as California and sometimes show up in stores as early as the end of January. Don't be seduced into buying them now because you'll have nowhere to plant them until the ground thaws. Even if planted in containers, they'll need a warm location and sunny window to thrive. In about a month they will probably outgrow the spot and you'll have a leggy rose bush.

CARE

ANNUALS

For those seeds you've already started indoors, keep grow lights suspended a few inches above the germinating seeds and keep the soil evenly moist. Don't overwater or the seeds may rot. Raise the lights higher as the seedlings grow to keep them about 6 inches from the tops. They will get the right amount of light duration and intensity, and the seedlings will stay short and stocky. A short seedling has less transplant shock than tall, leggy seedlings that were light deprived.

BULBS

Once any amaryllis bulbs that were potted up earlier in winter have finished blooming, cut back the flower stalks to the base of the bulb, but allow the leaves to grow. Keep the plant well watered and fertilize monthly, growing in a sunny window.

Spring-flowering bulbs given as holiday gifts that have been forced into bloom, such as tulips, hyacinths, and daffodils, rarely come back to flower a second year after being forced indoors. You can try keeping these bulbs alive in their pots until spring and then plant them in the garden, but chances are it will take a few years for a bulb to rejuvenate enough to reflower. If you go this route, cut back the flower stalk to the bulb, leave the leaves, and grow it in a sunny, cool location. Otherwise, compost these bulbs after flowering and force new bulbs each winter.

EDIBLES

Check any windowsill herbs you're growing. Cut back leggy stems of thyme, oregano, and rosemary and use these in cooking. Finish harvesting old parsley plants you may have brought indoors last fall. This herb is a biennial and will soon send up a flower stalk and have off-tasting leaves. Keep the

plants away from cold windows and drafts, but in a location where they get the most sunlight. Water sparingly, adding just enough moisture so the soil doesn't dry out. Unless they're growing under artificial lights, they probably won't be growing very much.

Check stored winter squash, potatoes, and carrots. Compost any that are soft and rotten.

PERENNIALS & VINES

Check the mulch around tender perennials, such as hardy hibiscus and lavender. Replenish the mulch that is protecting them if it has blown away. Holiday evergreen boughs can be used as mulch around tender perennials. They will also collect snow, and that acts as an insulator.

LAWNS & GROUNDCOVERS

Avoid piling snow that is laden with de-icing salts on your lawn. As it melts in spring, the salt will kill the lawn grass roots. Using sand or kitty litter as de-icers is gentler on lawn grasses than commercial de-icers.

ROSES

Check your rose protection to be sure it's still in place. Add more mulch if needed to cover the rose crown. Secure rose cones that might have been blown partially off the plant during storms.

■ *Some seed-starting kits come complete with bottom trays for watering and lids to maintain moisture.*

SHRUBS

Check any windscreens placed around tender evergreen shrubs, such as rhododendrons or shrubs growing along the coast. The salt air can damage the shoots and roots. Refasten the burlap or mesh that you're using to block the cold and salty winds. On days above 40 degrees Fahrenheit, consider applying an anti-desiccant spray to protect the evergreen leaves.

TREES

Place fresh-cut holiday trees in your yard as a resting place for birds near feeders where the birds can hide.

WATER

ANNUALS

This month, lightly water any annual flowers, such as geraniums, fuchsia, and coleus, that are overwintering indoors in a sunny window. With the short days and low light levels and intensity, plants won't need much water to survive. By adding too much water, you'll risk rotting the roots.

Keep any seedlings started under grow lights watered. Bottom watering is better than top watering. Look for seed-starting systems that have a water reservoir and wicking mat. Place the seed trays on top of the wicking mat and fill the reservoir with water. The pots will soak up the water from the bottom, and you won't harm young seedlings with an overhead spray.

BULBS

Keep paperwhite narcissus and amaryllis bulbs well watered, especially as they start growing and come into flower. Keep watering the amaryllis after flowering if you intend to keep it each year.

EDIBLES

As with annuals, keep vegetable seeds, such as leeks and onions started the end of the month, well watered in their trays. Lightly water windowsill herbs, keeping the soil barely moist. Too much water can cause herbs to rot.

PERENNIALS & VINES

There's little need for watering perennials this time of year since the ground is most likely frozen. Check container-grown perennials and roses stored in the basement or garage and keep the soil barely moist.

SHRUBS & TREES

As with container-grown perennials, any shrubs or small trees growing in containers stored in an unheated garage or basement should be kept barely moist through the winter.

FERTILIZE

ANNUALS & PERENNIALS

Lightly fertilize annual flower seedlings growing indoors once their true leaves form. Consider using a mild organic fertilizer such as seaweed mix. If you use fish emulsion, look for a deodorized version and dilute it well or your house will smell like fish.

Flowers growing in a sunny windowsill, such as geraniums and fuchsia, don't need fertilizing this month. If you fertilize too much when the light levels are low, the plant will respond with leggy growth and weak branches. Wait until the longer days come in the months ahead to start fertilizing.

BULBS

Keep amaryllis bulbs that were forced into flower earlier this winter lightly fertilized every month after they finish flowering.

EDIBLES

Lightly fertilize any vegetable seedlings as described for the annual flower seedlings (see above).

PROBLEM-SOLVE

ANNUALS

Check young seedlings for signs of damping-off disease. This fungal disease can wipe out young seedlings seemingly overnight. The disease attacks the thin stems, causing them to shrivel and die. It thrives on wet soil and with poor air circulation around the plants. To prevent this disease, don't overwater seedlings; use a well-drained, seed-starting soil, and place a small fan on the seed-starting set-up to help keep the air moving. If you have damping-off disease, quickly remove any diseased seedlings and destroy them. Luckily it's still early in the seed-starting calendar, so you probably can replant. If you do replant, thoroughly clean the pots with a 10 percent bleach solution to kill any fungus before reseeding.

BULBS

Check overwintering dahlia, gladiolus, tuberous begonia, and canna lily bulbs in your dark, cool basement or storage area. Any bulbs that are soft and rotting should be removed and composted. If your dahlia and canna lily bulbs are shriveling, mist them lightly with water so they don't dry out.

EDIBLES

Check young edible seedlings for damping off as described in the annuals section.

Watch for whiteflies on windowsill herbs. These small, white insects will fly around your herbs when the leaves are brushed. They live on the underside of the leaves, and their feeding can cause leaves to die back. Spray any herbs infected with whiteflies with insecticidal soap to kill them. Since whiteflies hatch their eggs periodically over time, you may need to spray a number of times to get them under control. Consider moving the herbs into a warm garage to spray.

Aphids are soft-bodied, gray, white, red, black, or green insects that are found in groups, usually on the new growth of plants. Their feeding causes leaves to die back. They also exude a sticky substance called honeydew, which can drip onto floors and tables, leaving a mess. It sometimes will have a black fungus called sooty mold growing on it. To prevent aphid infestations, don't fertilize your indoor plants heavily. If you find aphids on your

■ *Fungus gnats are small black flies that live in the potting soil of indoor plants.*

windowsill herbs, take the plant into the shower and wash off its leaves. Like whiteflies, the aphids will continue to develop for weeks, so you may have to do this a few times to stop the infestation.

PERENNIALS & VINES

Check any indoor container plants for fungus gnats. Fungus gnats are small black insects that fly around the potting soil of container plants. The larval form of these gnats can feed on plant roots. Usually, established container plants are strong enough to withstand any damage. However, fungus gnats are a nuisance. Consider repotting plants with fresh potting soil.

LAWNS & GROUNDCOVERS

You may notice shallow tunnels on your lawn. These are made by mice and voles scurrying under the snow cover, looking for food. Since the tunnels are shallow, your lawn will usually recover come spring.

ROSES, SHRUBS & TREES

Deer will feed on young branches, especially if we've had a snowy winter so far. Adjust wire cages to cover the branches and consider spraying a deer repellent. It's usually best to rotate repellents, using three to four different types through the season so the deer don't get used to one. Smell-based repellents work better than taste-based ones.

For broad-leaved evergreens, such as rhododendron, mountain laurel, and pieris, reapply an anti-desiccant spray if temperatures reach above 40 degrees Fahrenheit. Sprays that were applied in fall probably have worn off by now. If temperatures don't reach above 40 degrees Fahrenheit, wait until next month to spray.

Check tree guards to make sure mice or voles aren't getting around them. In heavy snow winters, the snowdrifts can pile above the tree guard, allowing these rodents to climb up and girdle the tree above the guard. Pack down the snow to prevent this.

Prune any storm-damaged, broken tree limbs back to a main branch or trunk (see February Care, Trees). Don't bother removing heavy snow loads on most trees. You'll end up causing more damage than good. Let Mother Nature naturally melt it off.

February

After the long, dark month of January, February starts raising our hopes for spring. The days get noticeably longer, especially toward the end of the month, and activity starts to increase in garden preparation and planning. We can start planting in earnest (indoors, that is), getting our hands dirty for the first time this year.

While cold weather persists and the ground outside may still be covered in snow, there are some noticeable changes. Buds of early-blooming shrubs and trees, such as pussy willows and forsythia, are starting to swell. Toward the end of the month, especially in warmer parts of southern New England, you'll start seeing some color as vernal witch hazel, hellebores, and even snowdrops start showing their flowers.

Indoors, flowers overwintering in windowsills and houseplants are starting to awaken with the longer days and are putting on new growth. Fruit tree pruning starts during February and continues into March.

Indoor seed starting is coming into full swing by the end of February, with many annual flowers and vegetables ready to be sown in fresh potting soil. The temptation is high to plant everything this early, but be patient. You'll still have a few months of indoor growing before the ground is ready for outdoor planting.

Regional flower shows start happening in February and continue into March. These are great places to get inspiration for designs using annual and perennial flowers, trees, and shrubs. New varieties are often highlighted at these shows and are for sale in booths. Also, it's a good place to pick up attractive plant supports, tools, and other accessories for your garden. Often there are great examples of trellises and stonework that you might consider creating yourself or hiring out to add more interest to the "bones" of your yard. If you do succumb to the temptation and buy some new flowers, remember that it's too early to plant: bring them home and place them in a bright, cool location, such as a garage, where they will stay protected from frost, but are not enticed to grow too quickly this early in the season.

PLAN

ANNUALS

Check your seed orders for annuals that you'll be planting this May. The sooner you order seeds by mail or purchase seeds at garden centers, the better. Some unusual varieties may sell out later in the spring.

Finish planting plans for beds by sketching the designs out on graph paper. Graph paper is helpful to the get the proper spacing of your plants in the landscape. I often use the calculation of one graph box equals 1 foot. This way, I know how many annuals of each type to start indoors, ensuring I have enough plants to fill in the garden. Always remember to start a few extras in case of poor germination or seedlings dying in spring. I always start about 10 percent more of each type of flower to be safe. You can always find other places to plant the extras or simply give them away to friends or neighbors.

Once you have all the seed-starting equipment together and have evaluated what you need to

purchase, clean the remaining plastic trays and pots. Use a 10 percent bleach solution to disinfect the plastic pots. This will prevent diseases from attacking your young seedlings.

Inventory your seed-starting and container mixes to be sure you have enough for this spring. There is a distinction between a soil mix used for seed starting and a mix used for potting up containers. Seed-starting mixes should be very lightweight. This allows small seeds, such as pansies, an easier opportunity to germinate and grow without rotting. Container soil mixes weigh more. Since you're transplanting actively growing plants into containers, these mixes may even contain compost to help plant growth. Calculate how much of each type of container mix you'll need and plan to purchase both at garden centers.

BULBS

Now is a good time to order summer-flowering bulbs for a late May planting. After inventorying any dahlias, gladiolus, tuberous begonias, and canna lilies you are storing in the basement to see how they are overwintering, decide how many

■ *Woody plants are available for sale as bare-root, container-grown, or balled-and-burlapped specimens. Bare-root plants [left] are the most economical, but they must be planted during the dormant season, before growth begins. Container-grown plants [center] can be planted anytime during the growing season, as long as you can provide ample water. Balled-and-burlapped specimens [right] are the most expensive way to go, but they are usually larger in size and will fill out a garden faster.*

more you'll need to purchase. Include lilies in your order; unless you planted them in fall, order Asiatic, Oriental, and trumpet lilies now.

Once they arrive, store them in a cool, dark location until planting in May. These summer bloomers add a burst of color to the flower garden.

EDIBLES

As with the annual flower beds, finish sketching out your vegetable and herb garden beds, reviewing which seed varieties need to be purchased and getting your seed-starting equipment ready.

If you're interested in planting fruit trees and berry bushes, consider purchasing bare-root plants. These plants are dug from the ground as soon as the ground thaws and are shipped to you at the correct planting time for your area. Usually you'll be planting in April or May. They're called "bareroot" because they don't have any soil on their roots. This makes them easier to ship and less expensive than the container trees you'll find in garden centers. You also will have a greater number of varieties of the various fruits to choose from when you order online. Just be aware that bare-root plants are dormant when they arrive. The roots should be soaked for a few hours in warm water and then planted immediately. They come with a guarantee, but it is more risky than buying a potted tree or shrub that has fully leafed out and is clearly alive.

PERENNIALS & VINES

Plan your perennial flower garden with a goal of achieving color throughout the seasons. Look at photos from last year's garden and see where you have "holes" in your color schedule. Research flowers that will bloom at the right time to fill those gaps and plan on purchasing them this spring or buy them bareroot through the mail. Bare-root plants are less expensive and a good way to go if you need to plant many perennials.

Think about vertical spaces in your garden that need hiding (such as a fence) or could use softening (such as a stone wall). Research perennial vines, such as Virginia creeper, clematis, and wisteria vine, as possible additions to those areas to give you more color and a greener feel. Some of

these vines need strong supports to grow and are long lived. Evaluate your structures to see if they're in good enough shape to hold the larger vines before you decide to purchase and plant.

LAWNS & GROUNDCOVERS

During snow-free times, reset sod that has been dug up by snowplows. Reset any stakes you drove into the ground in December to alert your snowplow driver to where the driveway or sidewalk ends and where your lawn begins.

Continue to research the best groundcovers to grow in your sun (sedum, creeping phlox, thyme) or shade (sweet woodruff, vinca, lily-of-the-valley) conditions. Some groundcovers, such as lily-of-the-valley or ajuga, can become invasive if not grown in the correct location. Think about how they can be contained in an area by growing them where a walkway, house, or edging will stop their spread.

■ *Miniature roses make great Valentine's Day gifts and can be planted outdoors later in spring.*

ROSES

While your planning for adding roses to your landscape continues into February, most roses shouldn't be purchased until closer to May. An exception may be miniature roses. You'll find potted miniature rose bushes showing up in garden centers and at flower shows in February. These small beauties come in a range of flower colors, shapes, and sizes. They make a great Valentine's Day gift, much better than cut-flower rose bouquets (hint, hint). Most of the plants only grow a few feet tall and make nice additions outdoors to a low-growing perennial flower border. They also are great container plants. You can purchase them now and grow them in a sunny window until May, when they can be planted outdoors. Most are very hardy and will flower continuously all summer. However, if they're planted in a flower garden they can easily be

overrun by aggressive perennials such as bee balm and rudbeckia. Plant them where they can flourish without too much competition. In containers, they will need to be protected outdoors in winter. They can also grow as a houseplant, but won't flower in winter.

SHRUBS & TREES

Continue researching the right shrubs and trees for your yard, to be planted in April and May. Consider the light exposure, soil needs, and mature heights and widths of the plants you'll be purchasing. Look for varieties that will give you three or even four seasons of interest. These would be shrubs and trees with spring flowers, summer fruits, fall foliage color, and perhaps interesting bark color in winter. Some good choices for multiseason interest trees and shrubs in New England are blueberries, American cranberry viburnum (*Viburnum trilobum*), and Kousa dogwood (*Cornus kousa*). Some trees with interesting colored or textured bark in winter include paperbark maple (*Acer griseum*) and river birch (*Betula nigra*). When looking at shrubs and trees for multiseason interest, don't forget native New England plants. Gray dogwood (*Cornus racemosa*), serviceberry (*Amelanchier* spp.), and nannyberry viburnum (*Viburnum lentago*) all have attractive flowers, fruit, and colorful fall leaves.

If you're planning on planting only a few shrubs and trees, buying them at a garden center in spring is best. For larger plantings or for unusual varieties, consider bare-root plants ordered through the mail.

PLANT

ANNUALS

Now is the time to plant annual flower seeds indoors in trays. Choose ones that will take up to three months before they're ready to be set out in the garden, such as geranium, lobelia, petunia, vinca, browallia, and verbena, or those that can be transplanted in early spring because they're cold tolerant, such as pansies, violas, and snapdragons. Either sow seeds in rows in trays to be transplanted into individual pots once their true leaves form,

■ *Paperbark maple* (Acer griseum) *has interesting bark, which enhances its winter interest.*

HERE'S HOW

TO SOW SEEDS INDOORS

- Select either large, open trays or individual small pots and fill them with seed-starting soil mix. Moisten the soil mix before planting so it's easier to work and you don't create a mess.

- Mark the names of the varieties you'll be sowing on wood craft sticks using a permanent marker.

- Sow small seeds on top of the soil mix either in rows in a tray or in groups of two or three seeds per small pot. For larger seeds, use a pencil to create a small hole or furrow to drop the seeds in. Check the planting depth on the seed packet. Usually the depth is twice the diameter of the seed.

- Cover small seeds lightly with more soil mix or fill in the furrow. Place the marker near the row or in individual pots.

- Cover the tray or group of pots with clear plastic wrap and place the tray in a warm location (for example, on top of a refrigerator), out of direct sunlight. The plastic covering will help keep the soil evenly moist. Consider purchasing heating mats to place under the trays or pots. The ones to buy are waterproof and will gently warm the soil to enhance and hasten germination. Check the seeds daily to be sure the soil doesn't dry out.

- Consider purchasing a bottom-watering seed-starting system. These systems have water reservoirs placed under the seed-starting tray or pots and a cloth wick that brings moisture into the soil mix from the bottom. Bottom watering is gentler on the germinating seeds and less disruptive than top watering by hand.

- Once the seeds germinate, move the tray or pots under grow lights. Place the lights a few inches above the tray. Using an on/off timer, keep the grow lights on fourteen hours a day. Raise the lights as the seedlings grow to keep them the same distance from the tops of the seedlings. Once the seedlings form their true leaves, transplant those in the tray into individual small pots. For those already growing in small pots, if multiple seeds were sown, thin out all but the largest seedling by snipping the others with a scissors. Keep them growing under grow lights, raised up 6 inches above the seedlings until it is time to harden them off (acclimate them) for outdoor planting.

or sow seeds in small individual pots now for transplanting into larger pots in a month or so. If growing only a few of these flowers, consider purchasing transplants later in spring from garden centers instead.

BULBS

Spring-flowering bulbs that have been chilled in a cold basement or refrigerator can be forced into bloom now. These bulbs of tulips, hyacinths, and daffodils need twelve to fourteen weeks of chilling time at 35 to 45 degrees Fahrenheit in order to fulfill their dormancy requirements. Pot these bulbs up into a shallow container filled with potting soil if they haven't been potted up already. Start watering them and bring the pots into a warm, sunny room. Keep the soil moist as they start growing, and you should have colorful spring-flowering bulbs blooming a month or so before your outdoor bulbs burst into flower.

EDIBLES

We all get itchy fingers this time of year and want to start our tomatoes, peppers, and other favorite vegetables early. However, check the number of weeks required for these vegetables to grow indoors before transplanting. Many only need four to six weeks of indoor growing before they should be transitioned outdoors, around the last frost date. This means that starting them in February is too early and will result in tall, leggy transplants in your home in March and April. Be patient.

However, some vegetables should be started now. Onions and leeks not started in late January should be sown in seed trays now. Celery and parsley can also be added to this list.

If you're desperate for your own fresh greens in February, try sprouting seeds for eating. Purchase untreated vegetable seeds such as beans, peas, alfalfa, and sunflowers online or from a garden or health food store. Soak the seeds overnight in warm water. Rinse the seeds well and place each type in a different pint- or quart-sized glass jar with a lid attached in a bright, warm location out of direct sunlight. Rinse the seeds twice a day; in a week or so you'll have fresh sprouts to add to your salads.

Another option is to grow microgreens indoors under your seed-starting lights. These include lettuce, spinach, mesclun mix, or other greens that are sown in trays and harvested when they're very young. Since they are harvested before they are very old, all you need are grow lights or a sunny window to get them to grow a little past germination. Fill a seed-starting tray 2 to 3 inches deep with seed-starting soil mix. Broadcast seeds on top of the soil and cover lightly with more soil. Water well. Harvest with scissors when they reach the true leaf stage (about one to two weeks after germination) and munch away.

Someone else who is craving greens this time of year is your cat. Consider growing oat, rye, or wheat grass in a container for Felix. Plastic salad greens containers obtained at the grocery store work well. Add a 2- to 3-inch-thick layer of seed-starting soil to the bottom, broadcast the seeds across the top of the soil, and cover with more soil. Keep well watered. Place it in a sunny window. Once they sprout, your kitty will love the fresh grass sprouts, and they will keep her healthy too.

PERENNIALS & VINES

If you're trying to grow many perennials in your garden, consider starting some of them from seed. Now is a good time to sow seed of perennial flowers that need ten weeks or more to grow indoors before transplanting outdoors. Some good perennials to try to grow from seed and then transplant into the garden in May include Shasta daisies, coreopsis, dianthus, gaillardia, and anise hyssop. Be patient; seed of these perennials can take up to two weeks to germinate. Grow them as you would annual flowers.

SHRUBS & TREES

Start to mark which shrubs will be removed or moved in spring. Wait until the snow melts and ground thaws to do any digging.

Based on your research of tree and shrub varieties, contact your local garden center to see if they will by carrying those types or can special order those varieties for you. When contacted early enough they may be happy to add a few plants to their larger order for your needs.

CARE

ANNUALS

Pinch back leggy growth on flowers growing in your sunny window. Use these cuttings to start new plants to transplant into the garden in spring.

Plants such as geranium, coleus, fuchsia, and begonia are all good candidates for taking cuttings. Take a 4- to 6-inch-long cutting, remove the bottom leaves, dip the cut end in a rooting hormone powder (purchased at your local garden center) to stimulate root growth, and stick the cut end in a 6-inch-diameter plastic pot filled with moistened potting soil. You can place three to four cuttings in each pot. Place the pot out of direct sunlight in a warm room and keep moist. Most of these flowers should root in a few weeks. When you can gently tug on the cutting without it coming out of the soil and you see some new

■ *Take stem cuttings of favorite plants, dip the cut end in a rooting hormone powder, and stick them into cell packs filled with moistened potting soil to root.*

growth, transplant each cutting into an individual 2-inch-diameter pot.

Keep any seed-started annual flowers watered and the grow lights raised to sit only a few inches from the tops of the seedlings to encourage stocky growth. Consider replanting any flower seeds that didn't germinate (see Plant, Annuals).

BULBS

Remove spent flower stalks on amaryllis bulbs that bloomed in January and continue to grow the bulbs in a sunny window. For forced tulips, daffodils, and other spring bulbs, either toss the bulbs in the compost or try saving them for spring planting (see January Care, Bulbs).

EDIBLES

Keep your seed-started vegetables growing well under grow lights (see Plant, Annuals).

Finish digging up any overwintered carrots and parsnips that were buried under hay mulch. They will start sprouting as the ground thaws in March, and their flavors will become bitter.

Prune back leggy herb plants growing in a sunny window.

PERENNIALS & VINES

As the snowstorms come and go, the ground may be bare at times. Check the soil around your perennial flowers for any heaving. As the ground freezes and thaws it can push perennial flowers planted last fall out of the soil and expose the roots and crown to drying winds. This often will kill a plant. Shallow-rooted perennials, such as scabiosa and yarrow, are particularly susceptible to frost heaving. If the ground is thawed enough, gently push the perennial back into the ground and cover it with bark mulch as an insulator. Remove the mulch once warmer weather begins in March.

Prune back perennial vines, such as Virginia creeper, Boston ivy, and wisteria, now before they start leafing out in spring. Remove errant branches, and don't be afraid to cut them back strongly to keep them in bounds. Virginia creeper and Boston ivy can have up to one-half of last year's growth removed without damaging the plant. Prune long

HERE'S HOW

TO TUNE UP A LAWN MOWER

- Using the owner's manual, identify and locate all the parts that will need inspection or replacing. Disconnect the spark plug for safety.

- Change the oil and oil filter based on the owner's manual recommendations. I usually change mine annually. Collect the used oil and recycle it at your local hazardous waste center. Inspect the air filter and clean it by tapping out the dirt and dust. If it's very dirty, consider replacing it.

- Inspect the spark plug and clean it. If you've had a hard time getting your mower to start, consider replacing the plug.

- Remove the mower blade and sharpen it. If the mower blade has many large dings in it, consider replacing it.

- Tighten bolts and nuts and lubricate moving parts based on the owner's manual recommendations.

wisteria shoots that grew last summer back to three to five buds on each branch. Also remove any long branches that are growing low on the main trunk. This will encourage better flowering and more manageable growth.

LAWNS & GROUNDCOVERS

Avoid walking on the lawn during thaws because this will compact the surface, pushing needed oxygen from the soil and making it harder for the lawn grass roots to survive.

HERE'S HOW

TO FORCE FLOWERING BRANCHES

By cutting branches of spring-flowering trees and shrubs now, you can bring them indoors and force them into flower weeks before they will do so outdoors. In February, it's best to select early flowering branches, such as forsythia, witch hazel, redbud, pussy willow, and serviceberry. Wait until March to cut and force later spring bloomers, such as lilac, mock orange, flowering quince (*Chaenomeles*), rhododendron, crabapple, cherry, pear, peach, and dogwood. The closer to the actual bloom time you prune the shrub or tree branch for forcing, the faster it will bloom indoors.

- Select a branch with many large, round flower buds on it. Leaf buds tend to be smaller and flatter, and lie closer to the branch. Cut the branch to about 6 to 18 inches long.

- Bring the cut branches indoors. Recut the stems and place them in cold water overnight to take up water and acclimate. The next day place the branches into a vase filled with warm water.

- Place the vase in a room at 60 to 65 degrees Fahrenheit, out of direct sunlight. Once the flower buds start to show color, move them into a sunnier room.

- Some branches, such as forsythia and willow, may root in the water. These can be potted up into containers and eventually planted in your landscape. All other branches can be composted once they're finished flowering.

Now is a good time to tune up your lawn mower before the mowing season begins. Either take it to a lawn mower repair shop now before the rush in spring or do some of the maintenance yourself.

ROSES

Adjust any winter protection, such as rose cones and mulch, on your roses to be sure the crown of the plant is still protected. Wait to prune your rose bushes until the warmer weather in spring.

SHRUBS & TREES

Prune out storm-damaged branches. Adjust any winter protection, such as burlap, around tender evergreens to protect the needles. Consider spraying an anti-desiccant spray in February if you didn't have a chance to in January (see January Problem-Solve, Roses, Shrubs & Trees).

For a touch of spring indoors, consider pruning some spring-flowering branches, such as forsythia, lilac, and crabapple, and forcing them indoors. (See Here's How To Force Flowering Branches, above.)

Start pruning your fruit trees and berry bushes now. Dwarf trees require less pruning than standard or large-sized trees. In general, prune fruit trees to remove dead, diseased, or broken branches, as well as crossing, shading, and rubbing branches. The goal with fruit trees, such as apples, plums, and cherries, is to create evenly spaced branch scaffolds around the tree at different heights. Ideally, the branches will come off the trunk with a wide crotch angle (the angle between the trunk and branch). Narrow crotch angles are weak and more likely to split off the trunk as the branch grows, deforming the tree. Remove vertical shoots or whips, called water sprouts, that grow straight up off main branches. Remove vertical shoots, called suckers, growing straight up from the base of the tree or roots as well. The goal is to create a tree that is open in the center so light can penetrate easily, without branches shading one another. When pruning, cut back to the branch collar. (See Here's How To Prune Large Branches on page 39.)

Apples, Plums & Cherries: These fruits are pruned to a modified leader shape that allows one

■ *Prune your apple tree to have a center leader or modified central leader.*

branch to grow vertically in the center and others to be arranged around it in a scaffold. The tree should have a conical shape. Young trees don't have to be pruned for the first three years. After that, prune to create three to four scaffold branches, 2 to 3 feet off the ground. As the tree grows, create another scaffold of branches 2 to 3 feet higher than the first. The top branches shouldn't shade the bottom branches.

Peaches & Nectarines: Peaches should be pruned to a vase shape, so the interior of the tree is open

■ *Prune your peach tree to have an open center, similar in shape to a vase.*

HERE'S HOW

TO REJUVENATE AN OLD APPLE TREE

Many home gardeners inherit an old apple tree on their property. New England is loaded with old apple trees that came from abandoned orchards or seed spread by animals. Some of these trees are worth saving, and others are not. The first step is to taste the apples on the tree. Even if they are small, if the apples are tasty and have a nice texture, then this tree may be worth saving. The next step is to look at the tree. Is it still growing mostly vertical? Does it have a lot of rotten areas on the main trunk? If it looks like a tree that's still healthy, but overgrown and crowded with branches, then follow these steps to rejuvenate it.

- Remove any dead, diseased, or broken branches. Remove water sprouts and root suckers.

- Remove a few main branches if they are crowding the canopy of the tree. It's better to remove a few large branches to make a sudden impact than it is to remove lots of smaller branches. This will stimulate fewer water sprouts to grow. Cut the large branches back to the trunk or another main branch following the double-cut steps in Here's How To Prune Large Branches (see page 39). Always cut to a branch collar, leaving the swollen area right near the trunk or main branch intact.

- Never cut more than one-third of the overall branches out of the tree in any one year or you may shock the tree into dying. Removing a few main branches and cutting the dead and diseased wood and water sprouts may be all you want to do the first year.

- Remove crossing, shading, and rubbing branches, opening up the canopy so more light can penetrate. Don't use tree paints on the branch cuts; they won't help the wounds heal faster.

HERE'S HOW

TO PRUNE LARGE BRANCHES

Branches larger than 2 inches in diameter need to be pruned carefully or, as they fall, they may rip and tear the bark on the trunk or other branches, creating more damage. Use this double-cut method.

1. Make an upward cut from the bottom of the branch, one-third of the way through the branch, about 1 foot from the trunk or larger branch.

2. Make a second cut a few inches away from the upward cut, farther from the trunk. Cut downward all the way through on this cut, and the branch will drop without ripping the bark.

3. Make your final cut, removing the branch stub that's left. Cut downward, just outside the branch collar. This is the swollen area right next to the trunk or large branch. It has cells that grow quickly to heal over the wound without letting in disease.

like a cup. Remove the central leader when the tree is young. Let three or four scaffold branches grow evenly spaced around the trunk. Prune these branches to grow at a 45-degree angle from the trunk for best fruit production and branch strength.

Pears: Prune pear trees to a strong central leader system. The side branches on pear trees want to grow more upright than apples. Don't try to create a scaffold system on pears, but instead prune to remove shading or crossing branches and to keep the branches evenly spaced around the trunk.

Blueberries: Prune blueberry bushes only if they are at least five years old and need rejuvenation. Most young blueberry bushes will need pruning only to remove dead, diseased, and broken branches. On older bushes remove the weakest and oldest canes to the ground so you have at least five or six main fruiting canes per bush. This should stimulate new growth from the base of the bush. Your blueberry bushes should have a mix of young, middle-aged, and older branches for best production.

Keep potted gift plants received for Valentine's Day, such as flowering azaleas and hydrangeas, well watered indoors. These varieties are not hardy outdoors in New England, so you can either compost them after flowering or, if you want to try to get them to rebloom next year, keep them well watered and growing in a sunny window. In May, move them outdoors to a partly sunny location. Keep them watered and fertilized all summer and then move them back indoors in fall to a sunny window to hopefully flower in winter.

WATER

ANNUALS & EDIBLES

Keep seed-started annual flowers, vegetables, and herbs well watered. Consider using a bottom-watering system to avoid disturbing the tender seedlings when you water from above. (See Plant, Annuals.)

Keep annual flowers and herbs growing in the sunny windows well watered, especially as they start to put on new growth later in this month.

BULBS

Keep amaryllis and forced bulbs that you plan on saving and planting this spring well watered.

PERENNIALS & VINES

Keep seed-started perennial flowers well watered, as you do with the annual flowers, vegetables, and herbs. Be careful not to overwater young seedlings or they can become more susceptible to rot diseases such as damping off (see January Problem-Solve, Annuals).

ROSES

Keep miniature roses growing indoors well watered. Only increase watering as you see signs of new growth. Water until it comes out the drainage holes of the pot.

SHRUBS & TREES

Check any container-grown shrubs and trees kept in a basement or unheated garage. Keep the soil barely moist.

FERTILIZE

ANNUALS & EDIBLES

Fertilize annual flower, vegetable, and herb starts with a dilute solution of an organic plant food. Organic fertilizers are gentler on plants, providing small amounts of nutrients as the plants need them. If seedlings are tall, leggy, and pale, be sure the grow lights are working properly, as this may be a sign of inadequate lighting more than poor fertility.

If you burn wood for heating, collect wood ashes for use in your annual flower, fruit trees, and vegetable gardens. Wood ashes are a good soil amendment. They are high in potassium and will raise the soil pH. If you have high potassium levels or pH already, don't use wood ashes. Based on a soil test, you can apply wood ashes as the ground thaws. In general, don't apply more than 20 pounds per 1,000 square feet of garden. If the ground is still frozen or covered in snow, store your wood ashes in a dry, safe location.

BULBS

Start fertilizing amaryllis bulbs with a water-soluble houseplant food after flowers have faded. Don't bother fertilizing forced bulbs that you plan on saving, such as tulips and daffodils, because these are going into dormancy anyway this time of year.

PERENNIALS & VINES

Lightly fertilize young perennial seedlings with a dilute solution of an organic plant food twice a month.

ROSES

Lightly fertilize miniature roses actively growing indoors with a dilute solution of an organic plant food twice a month, after they show signs of new growth.

PROBLEM-SOLVE

ANNUALS & EDIBLES

Watch your annual flower, vegetable, and herb seedlings for any signs of disease or insect damage. Damping-off fungus can wipe out seedlings quickly so take measures to prevent it (see January Problem-Solve, Annuals).

Check seedlings for aphids or whiteflies and control them according to the suggestions in January Problem-Solve, Edibles.

Adjust grow lighting height so plants are staying short and stocky. If you are keeping your light bulbs 6 inches from the seedlings with the lights turned on fourteen hours a day, and they still are getting leggy, consider moving the seedlings to a cooler room or replacing the light bulbs with new ones. Warm rooms can stimulate fast growth, causing the seedlings to become leggy. Even though grow lights will work for many hours, their intensity will decrease over time and not provide enough light for seedlings to grow properly.

BULBS

Check amaryllis bulbs for mealybugs and scale insects. These insects attach themselves to the undersides of leaves and suck the plant's juices. Their feeding will damage the leaves. They also exude a sticky substance called honeydew that will drop on tables and plant stands, making the surfaces sticky as well. Dab individual mealybugs and soft-shelled scale with a cotton swab dipped in rubbing alcohol to kill them. Flick off individual hard-shelled scale with your fingernail or a knife. For larger infestations consider spraying horticultural oil on the plants. When spraying, it's best to move plants into a heated garage or basement to avoid damaging furniture.

PERENNIALS & VINES

Check seed-started perennial plants for signs of insects and disease according to the Annuals and Edibles section in this month.

Watch for heaving perennials and reset them. (See Care, Perennials & Vines.)

ROSES, SHRUBS & TREES

Reset rabbit and deer protection for your roses. Watch for spots where rabbits may be getting under your fence and repair the fence. Reapply repellent sprays on roses, shrubs, and trees. The materials applied earlier in winter probably have worn off. Animals are getting hungrier as the winter proceeds, especially if we've had a lot of snow. Although they have favorite foods, such as yew and cedar trees, deer will start nibbling on less-common trees and shrubs. If they're hungry enough, deer will eat just about anything. To detect deer damage, look for footprints in the snow as your first clue. If you don't see footprints, look at the damage itself. Deer bite and rip the branches off and leave a jagged edge on the branch end. Rabbits have sharper teeth and cleanly cut the branch ends, leaving a clean, angular cut.

When temperatures are above 40 degrees Fahrenheit, consider spraying dormant oil on your deciduous fruit trees and ornamental trees. Dormant oil is a petroleum product that coats the branches and kills overwintering eggs and insects such as scale. It should not be used on evergreens. Always check the label for instructions on using these pesticides on specific trees and shrubs.

Prune out black knot fungal disease on cherry and plum trees. This black, knobby growth appears on branches. Remove the branch to a spot below the disease and sterilize your pruner with a 10 percent bleach solution after each cut to avoid infecting other branches.

March

The old idiom says, "March comes in like a lion and goes out like a lamb." That certainly can be true in New England. Early March still has biting cold days, snowstorms, and plenty of frozen ground. While this type of weather can persist into late March and April in northern parts of our region, late March in areas of southern New England can be downright balmy. Often the snow will have melted, and warm, sunny, above-freezing days start thawing the soil. The belief that spring is right around the corner is close to everyone's heart. But don't be fooled into gardening outdoors too soon. Growing up in Connecticut, I remember many March and even April snowstorms taking people by surprise and pummeling our yards.

But it is true that the longer days of March signal a time to start increasing your gardening activities. Now is the time to put final touches on garden plans for renovating old beds and making new ones. Pruning shrubs and trees comes into full swing this month, as does seed-starting indoor annual flower, vegetable, and herb plants. You can even start digging in the soil some, but be careful. Digging before the soil is thawed of frost and well drained of water can damage the soil's structure.

Signs of spring will start popping up everywhere, even in northern areas. Early bulbs, such as snowdrops and crocus, are often in bloom, especially when growing against a south-facing wall or building. Vernal witch hazel shrubs and hellebore perennial flowers are blooming strongly now in warmer sections of our region. Migratory birds, such as red-winged blackbirds, start arriving, as if to announce the end of the dark, cold days.

March is a time to be ready to act once Mother Nature gives you an opening. In some years, toward the end of the month you can start sowing peas, spinach, arugula, and radish seed in the garden once the soil has dried out. Other years, it may still be too cold and wet to turn the soil to plant. But be patient—the time will come.

ANNUALS

In many areas as the snow recedes you can test your flower garden plans by going out to measure and diagram where new beds will be and where you'll expand old beds. Now is the time to get specific with your annual flower garden plans. Calculate the number of each type of flower you'll need to start from seed or buy as transplants in the bed. Study online resources and books such as *New England Getting Started Garden Guide* to determine the spacing of each type of annual you want to plant. Then calculate how many plants you'll need to fill that space. Always start or buy extras in case some plants don't make it (also read Plan, Lawns & Groundcovers).

BULBS

Take photos of your gardens as spring-flowering bulbs emerge and flower every week from late March to May. You can chronicle not only where your bulbs are located, but also how they look. Use these photos in fall to determine which bulbs should be replaced, where to plant other bulbs, and where to change the bulb color palette in your garden.

EDIBLES

As seeds that you ordered begin to arrive through the mail, or as you purchase them in garden centers, start calculating how much seed you'll need for the various vegetables based on the garden plan you devised in January and February. You may find out that you have plenty of bean seed, but one packet of lettuce seed won't be enough. This is especially true if you plan on succession planting vegetables in summer and fall. It's better to get all the seed you need now and devise a plan so that you don't come up short in your summer planting.

March is also a good time to test your plans. Make sure fruiting crops such as tomatoes, peppers, squash, cucumbers, beans, and broccoli will be located in a full-sun spot. This means they will receive at least six to eight hours of direct sun a day. Double-check these locations in May once the leaves come out.

If the location you have for edibles only receives four to six hours of direct sun a day, consider planting root crops such as radishes, carrots, beets, and potatoes. They will grow fine under these light conditions.

Finally, if you have a spot that gets only a few hours of direct sun a day, stick with leafy greens such as lettuce, spinach, Swiss chard, kale, and mustard. Although these greens will grow better with more light, they will still yield edible leaves with minimal direct sunlight.

LAWNS & GROUNDCOVERS

As the snow melts and ground thaws, it's important to avoid walking on your lawn, and certainly do not drive tractors or mowers across it until the soil dries out. By walking or driving on your wet lawn now, you'll compact the soil, squeezing out any air spaces in the ground. This will lead to poor grass growth. A good way to tell if your lawn is still too wet to work is if you leave footprints when you walk across it.

As with the annual and perennial flower gardens, if you're planning on planting more groundcovers under trees or in a flower garden, now is a good time to calculate how many plants you'll need and create a budget to determine if it's affordable.

PERENNIALS & VINES

Finalize plans for your new perennial flowers beds and renovations to your older beds based on last year's notes.

ROSES

Bare-root roses ordered through the mail may start showing up on your doorstep even as early as the end of March. It's still too early to plant roses unless they're protected. Roses should be planted in April and May. You can store these bare-root roses in a cool, dark room, making sure the roots stay moist. Place the roots in slightly moistened peat moss in a plastic bag until the weather and ground are ready for planting.

SHRUBS & TREES

Contact local garden centers for specialty plants you might have ordered to see when they may

HERE'S HOW

TO CALCULATE THE NUMBER OF PLANTS YOU NEED

A simple way to calculate the number of plants needed is to measure the square footage of the bed. Determine the spacing for the type of groundcover or annual you'll be growing. Use the plant spacing multiplier once you know the spacing of your plants. Design the planting in a triangular pattern, and leave the right amount of room for spacing near the bed edge.

Multiply the square footage of your bed by the multiplier to determine how many plants you'll need. For example, if you're planting vinca in a 60-square-foot bed at 8-inch spacing, then you'll need 60 feet × 2.25 inches = 135 plants. Always add 10 percent more plants for irregularly shaped areas where it will be hard to accurately determine the square footage.

■ *You can plant annual flowers in rows or stagger them to fit more plants in the bed.*

PLANT SPACING MULTIPLIER

CENTER-TO-CENTER SPACING (INCHES)	PLANTS PER SQUARE FOOT
6	4
8	2.25
9	1.77
10	1.44
12	1
15	.64
18	.44
24	.25

arrive. While you're there, ask to see their catalog to determine what other plants they might have that will be of interest.

PLANT

ANNUALS

Indoors, continue to sow annual flower seeds that need eight to ten weeks before transplanting into the garden following the instructions in February Plant, Annuals. These include alyssum, salvia, dusty miller, and moss roses. Gardeners in southern areas can start these earlier in the month, and gardens in northern locations can start them toward the end of March.

Replant cuttings from geraniums and fuchsias that you took last month into individual pots as you see signs of new growth (February Care, Annuals).

BULBS

Check overwintering bulbs of dahlias, canna lilies, and tuberous begonias for signs of new shoots forming. Often these bulbs are on their own internal timer and will start sending out new growth in response to the day length, not necessarily the temperature. Keep the soil and air temperatures below 60 degrees Fahrenheit so they don't sprout too much before planting in a few months.

You can get a jump on the summer bulb gardening season by potting up these sprouting bulbs as they grow. This will allow you to have flowers sooner in summer. This is a particularly good idea for gardeners in northern areas that often don't get a good canna lily and dahlia flower show due to early fall frosts killing these late bloomers.

Once new growth appears, divide the dahlia tubers and canna lily clumps, making sure each root division has at least one healthy bud, or eye, on it. Take these divisions and plant them so the bud or eye is facing upward, about 1 inch deep in individual containers filled with a well-drained potting soil mix.

HERE'S HOW

TO BUILD A COLD FRAME

1. Cut the parts. This project, as dimensioned, is designed to be made entirely from a single 4 × 8 sheet of plywood. Start by cutting the plywood lengthwise to make a 36"-wide piece. Remove material in 4"-wide strips and use the strips to make the lid frame parts and any other trim you may want to add. Cut the parts to size with a circular saw or jigsaw and cutting guide. Mark the cutting lines first.

2. Assemble the front, back, and side panels into a square box. Glue the joints and clamp them together with pipe or bar clamps. Adjust until the corners are square. Reinforce the joints with 2" or 2½" deck screws driven through countersunk pilot holes. Drive screws every 4 to 6" along each joint.

3. Make the lid frame. Cut the 4"-wide strips of ¾" plywood reserved from step 1 into frame parts (two at 31" and two at 38"). Assemble the frame parts into a square 38 × 39"

frame. There are many ways to join the parts to create a flat frame. Because the Plexiglas cover will give the lid some rigidity, simply gluing the joints and reinforcing with an L-bracket at each inside corner should be more than adequate structurally.

4. Paint the box and the frame with exterior paint, preferably in an enamel finish. A darker color will hold more solar heat. Lay thick beds of exterior adhesive/caulk onto the tops of the frame and then seat the Plexiglas cover into the adhesive. Clean up squeeze-out right away. Once the adhesive has set, attach the lid with butt hinges and attach the handles to the sides.

5. Move the cold frame to the site. Clear and level the ground where it will set, if possible. Some gardeners like to excavate the site slightly.

Tuberous begonias have a hollow side to their bulb that needs to be planted facing upward at the soil surface. Place tuberous begonias in trays filled with moistened potting soil. Try not to let water sit in this depression or the tuber may rot.

EDIBLES

You can start sowing seeds of vegetables and herbs such as parsley, broccoli, cabbage, cauliflower, celery, and lettuce indoors early in March in southern areas and later in the month in northern areas. Wait until early April to start peppers and tomatoes (read more details under April Plant, Edibles). Tomatoes grow very fast and are ready to transplant four to six weeks after sowing. Unless you are growing them in a greenhouse or large cold frame, they will be ready to plant too early for our area.

Once the ground has dried, sow peas, spinach, radishes, and arugula in southern areas toward the end of this month. Be sure the soil is ready to plant before sowing seeds. Soil that is still too wet will compact easily if turned too soon. To check, grab a small handful of soil and squeeze it. If water dribbles out of your fist, the soil is still too wet to sow.

Consider building or buying a cold frame to extend the garden season and allow you to plant greens earlier than normal (see September Care, Edibles).

For planting these very early crops outdoors, build raised beds and amend the soil with compost a week or so before planting. The raised beds will dry out faster and warm up quicker, allowing for faster germination (read more at April Plant, Edibles).

Soak pea seeds overnight in warm water the night before planting to stimulate germination. The sooner peas germinate, the less likely they are to rot during periods of cold, wet weather. Inoculate pea seeds with rhizobia bacteria found in garden centers or online. Rhizobia bacteria help legumes "fix" atmospheric nitrogen into a usable fertilizer.

LAWNS & GROUNDCOVERS

Start researching the proper type of grass seed you'll need for your new yard or for renovating a lawn area. Most home garden grass seeds are a mix of northern hardy grasses such as Kentucky bluegrass, perennial ryegrass, and fescue. For sunny locations, choose a grass mix with more Kentucky bluegrass. For shadier spots, choose one with more tall and creeping fescues.

Whatever grass mix you select, check to see if it has any white clover in it. Clover used to be a regular ingredient in lawn grass seed because its roots fix atmospheric nitrogen that helps feed the grasses. Unfortunately, it got a reputation as a weed over the last fifty years and has been omitted from many lawn mixes. That attitude is changing, but many mixes still don't contain clover. If your mix doesn't have clover in it, consider buying it separately and mixing in 5 to 10 percent clover by weight.

PERENNIALS & VINES

Repot seed-started perennials from February that are growing under lights into larger pots once the height of the plant is three times the diameter of the pot. This will ensure that the root system continues to grow strongly and the plant isn't stunted when it's time to plant in the ground in April or May.

ROSES

To get a jump on the rose season, consider potting up some of the bare-root roses you've received in containers filled with moistened potting soil. Place these roses in a brightly lit garage or room where they will stay cold, but not freezing. The roots will start growing. Once it's warm enough in April or May, place the containers outdoors and the shoots will grow as well.

SHRUBS & TREES

Prepare holes for shrubs and trees that you'll transplant early next month if we have a dry early spring. Otherwise, wait until the soil has warmed and dried out before starting to transplant shrubs and trees.

CARE

ANNUALS

Move seed-started, cold-weather-tolerant annuals such as snapdragons, violas, and pansies outdoors to start hardening them off for planting in the ground or containers. (See Here's How To Harden Off Seedlings.)

In warmer sections of New England you'll be able to plant these frost-tolerant flowers into the ground late this month; in northern areas wait until April when the threat of a deep freeze has passed. While these annuals can take a frost, frozen soil and temperatures in the low 20s Fahrenheit can kill the plants through dehydration.

Check other seed-started annual flowers growing under lights. Transplant young seedlings from trays into individual pots once their true leaves form.

Transplant rooted cuttings of annuals, such as geraniums and fuchsia, into larger pots as they grow.

BULBS

Move bulbs potted up for winter forcing out of a cold basement or room and into a warm location to start growing. (See February Plant, Bulbs for more details.)

Compost forced bulbs that have finished flowering, or cut back the flowers and keep the foliage growing until spring. (See January Care, Bulbs.)

Remove mulch from early spring-flowering bulbs, such as snowdrops and crocus, as they start to emerge. Sometimes if you mulched perennials and roses where these bulbs are also planted, they will struggle to grow through the mulch. If a cold snap is predicted, recover these bulbs with a floating row cover to protect them.

EDIBLES

Keep indoor seedlings started this month and last growing strongly under lights. Transplant broccoli, cabbage, cauliflower, and parsley plants, once their true leaves form, into individual containers. Thin out those seedlings started in small pots, four-packs, or six-packs to the healthiest seedling. Keep the lights 4 to 6 inches way from the tops of the seedlings.

Cut onion seedlings back by one-third to encourage strong root growth and keep the plants from flopping over.

Prune blueberries if haven't already. (See February Care, Shrubs & Trees.)

Now is also a good time to prune grapes. Grapes have become a popular small-space edible for fresh eating, juicing, and winemaking. The most efficient way to grow grapes is on a wire trellis strung between two sturdy posts. This system allows you to keep the grapes in bounds without sacrificing production. Grapes need to be aggressively pruned, removing up to 70 percent of the canes each winter.

HERE'S HOW

TO HARDEN OFF SEEDLINGS

Whether you're buying annual flowers, vegetables, or herb seedlings at the garden center or starting them indoors yourself, before planting them outdoors they need to get used to the air temperatures and weather conditions. This process is called hardening off. If you gradually let your transplants get used to the outdoor weather, they will be less likely to suffer from transplant shock and poor growth early in the season. Here are the steps to hardening off seedlings.

1. Water your seedlings well before moving them outdoors.

2. On the first day, move your seedlings to a location with morning sun, protected from the wind. Keep them outdoors only for an hour or so, then move them back indoors under lights or a sunny window.

3. The next day, place them outdoors again, keeping them out for a little longer period before bringing them back inside.

4. Continue this process, leaving the plants out a little longer each day. Consider moving them to a spot where they will get exposed to some wind and more sun.

5. By day seven, your seedlings can be left outdoors overnight. They are now ready to plant in containers or the ground.

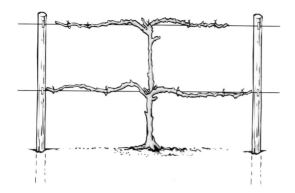

String the metal wire about 5 feet high between the posts. For newly planted grapes, select the healthiest cane and prune off all the rest. Attach that cane, with plant ties, to a stake placed in the ground near the plant. The first two years you need to train this cane to grow vertically to the height of the wire trellis.

By the third winter, the cane should have reached the wire's height. Top the cane now to force it to grow branches (arms) in either direction along the wire. Remove all the rest of the shoots coming off the bottom of the main trunk.

The next winter, select one of the healthiest of those arms on either side of the trunk, attach it to the wire, and remove all the other branches. Cut the selected branches back to eight to twelve buds. Select one additional branch on each side of the trunk and cut each back to two buds. Prune off all other growth. Continue with this pruning method each winter.

LAWNS & GROUNDCOVERS

It's too early to sow lawn grass seeds, but once the lawn dries out, usually toward the end of this month and into April, start cleaning up your yard. Rake out the lawn, removing thatch that has built up from last year. Thatch is a dead grass layer that is prevalent in thick, lush lawns. If it's more than ½-inch thick, this layer can stop the flow of water and air to grass roots. Using an iron or dethatching rake, remove the dead grass layer and compost it.

Once the ground thaws, flush out any road salts that have accumulated along driveways

HERE'S HOW

TO PRUNE GRAPES ON AN ARBOR

1. Construct a sturdy arbor to hold the weight of the grapevines. It may be a two-, four-, or six-post arbor, depending on whether it's attached to the house or another structure. The top can be secured with 2-inch by 4-inch wooden boards that hold the arbor together and topped with 1-inch by 2-inch wood slats to create the latticework for the vines to grow on. You may also need corner braces to secure the whole structure.

2. Grow the grapes, one per post, selecting the strongest cane and pruning off the rest. Allow it to grow to the top of the post the first year, securing it to the post as it grows.

3. The first winter, top the cane and allow it to grow side branches along the top of the arbor. If you let the vines just continue to grow, they will produce dense shade but little fruit.

4. Prune the grapes each winter by removing those canes that fruited the previous year, cutting back one-year-old canes to five to six buds, and leaving some renewal canes pruned back to two to three buds. The goal is to have canes on the trellis spaced 2 to 3 feet apart.

5. Each winter, remove any weak, thin canes. You want to leave enough fruiting canes on the trellis to fill it back in each summer, but not so many that it becomes a tangled mess.

or walkways by watering the area heavily with a hose. These salts can kill lawn grass roots if left unchecked.

Remove dead leaves from overwintering evergreen groundcovers such as ivy and pachysandra. Gently rake the dead leaves out of these groundcovers, opening up areas for new growth to fill in.

■ *Once the snow melts and the ground dries out, rake and remove thatch or dead grass buildup on your lawn.*

PERENNIALS & VINES

Once the snow leaves and the ground thaws, it's time to get back into the perennial flower garden. Remove any dead growth and old flowers that you didn't get to last fall. Remove old seedpods of black-eyed Susans and coneflowers you left in the garden for birds to enjoy. Be careful working in the flower garden if you have spring-flowering bulbs planted. Try to avoid stepping on any emerging shoots.

Cut back ornamental grasses to the ground. You may need hedge trimmers or even loppers to trim thick grass clumps.

Check woody perennials such as candytuft, basket-of-gold, and lavender. Remove broken or dead branches with hand pruners. Clean out dead leaves, making room for new growth later this spring.

Cut back trumpet vines now, as they bloom on new wood each year. (See May Plan, Perennials, Vines & Roses.) Prune clematis varieties such as sweet autumn clematis and 'Jackmanii'. They also bloom on new wood. Prune this group of clematis back to a few feet off the ground, just above a set of healthy buds. Remove thin, twiggy growth.

ROSES

Wait until the weather consistently warms to remove mulch and winter protection on roses. A sudden dip in temperatures can damage newly exposed canes. Check under the mulch or inside the rose cones for signs of bud swelling. Most likely that will occur in April in our climate, but a warm March may stimulate faster growth, especially in southern parts of New England. If you do remove some mulch or the rose protection, carefully watch the temperatures. If temperatures in the 20s Fahrenheit threaten, recover the bushes with mulch. Prune roses next month (see April Care, Roses) when it's more obvious what growth is alive or dead.

SHRUBS

Start to assess winter damage on your shrubs. Prune damaged branches back to a main branch or the trunk, making a clean cut.

For shrubs near roads or walkways that had salt applied to them, once the ground thaws, wash out the soil with water to flush out the salts. Road salts that accumulate in the soil can harm plant roots.

Now is the time to begin pruning summer- and fall-blooming shrubs, such as butterfly bush. Spring-flowering shrubs, such as forsythia, lilac, rhododendron, and weigela, should be pruned after flowering (see May Care, Shrubs).

TREES

Continue to prune fruit trees (see page 37 covering February Care, Shrubs & Trees). Finish pruning all deciduous trees before their buds start to open.

Remove tree wraps later in the month and check all trees for damage from mice, voles, and rabbits from the past winter. Any young tree that has had the bark chewed or girdled completely around the trunk will eventually die. Such chewing damage cuts off the flow of water and nutrients from the roots to the shoots. It's best to replace this tree. Partially girdled trees may still survive as long as they are otherwise healthy.

Assess storm damage to trees. Prune out major limbs that were broken (see February Care, Shrubs & Trees).

HERE'S HOW

TO PRUNE SUMMER-BLOOMING SHRUBS

Summer-blooming shrubs bloom on new growth, so pruning in spring will stimulate more growth and, consequently, more flowers. Some common summer-blooming shrubs include summersweet (*Clethra*), butterfly bush (*Buddleja*), rose of Sharon, bluebeard (*Caryopteris*), potentilla, smokebush (*Cotinus*), and smooth and panicle hydrangeas.

1. Remove dead, broken, and diseased branches back to the base of the trunk.

2. Remove individual branches that are crowding or crossing other branches back to a main branch or the base of the plant. It's better to remove whole branches to open up the shrub than to remove small branches around the shrub's edge.

3. Remove twiggy growth. The goal is to open up the shrub, leaving large-sized branches that can support more flowers.

4. Cut back main branches to balance the size of the shrub and ensure they are strong enough to support the flowers.

Prune ornamental trees such as crabapples, flowering plums, and flowering pears. These trees don't need as much pruning as fruit trees, but they will benefit from some touching up. Save pruned branches that have flower buds and force them into flower indoors (see February Care, Shrubs & Trees to learn how).

WATER

ANNUALS & EDIBLES

Water annual flowers, vegetables, and herbs growing in seed-starting trays and pots. Consider bottom watering as a way to not disturb the young seedlings (also see February Plant, Annuals).

Keep annual flowers grown indoors from cuttings moist, but not overwatered. Too much water can cause the cuttings to rot.

Begin watering overwintered annuals in pots, such as geraniums, more frequently. Water thoroughly, allowing the water to drain out the bottom. Let the top few inches of the soil dry out between waterings.

BULBS

Keep amaryllis bulbs well watered, keeping the soil moist. Add water until it runs out the drainage holes in the bottom of the pot.

Water any dahlias and canna lilies that you potted up last month. Keep the soil moist, but not soggy wet to avoid rotting the tubers.

LAWNS & GROUNDCOVERS

Wash road salts from the lawn areas close to paved streets and sidewalks to remove them from the root zone.

HERE'S HOW

TO PRUNE A CRABAPPLE TREE

Crabapples are common New England street and home trees. There have many different shapes, depending on the variety. Most are small- to medium-sized trees that fit well in smaller yards. The white, pink, or red flowers put on quite a show when in full bloom in May.

1. Prune any dead, diseased, or broken branches back to a main branch or trunk.

2. Remove water sprouts (vertical shoots growing off main branches or trunk) and root suckers (vertical shoots coming from the base of the tree).

3. Remove crossing branches or branches growing too close to each other and shading one another. Always select the thinnest diameter of the two branches to remove.

4. Cut back errant branches or those growing straight up to keep the tree balanced.

5. Remove small, twiggy growth from the center of the tree. These branches will not flower and eventually just crowd the tree. A tree with crowded branches is more likely to get diseased.

PERENNIALS & VINES

Keep seed-started perennial flowers well watered. If they are drying out quickly, it may mean your seedlings need to be repotted into larger-sized pots.

ROSES

Water miniature roses and potted up bare-root roses until the water comes out the pot drainage holes.

SHRUBS & TREES

If we've had a dry, late winter with little snow, the soil (especially sandy soil) may be dry come March. Water shrubs and trees planted last fall to ensure they survive the dry spell. Water deeply, letting the water sink at least 6 to 12 inches into the soil.

FERTILIZE

ANNUALS & EDIBLES

Using a diluted organic fertilizer, keep annual flowers, vegetables, and herbs started indoors fed weekly.

Any vegetable seed already sown outdoors in warmer locations won't need fertilizer until it's more actively growing.

BULBS

Keep amaryllis bulbs fed with a diluted organic fertilizer when you water.

Fertilize spring-flowering bulbs that are just emerging from the ground with a granular bulb plant food such as 9-9-6. Fertilizing early helps the bulbs grow stronger and flower better. Don't fertilize bulbs in bloom. You'll just be wasting the fertilizer.

LAWNS & GROUNDCOVERS

Spread compost around groundcovers that are starting to put on new growth toward the end of this month. A light, annual sprinkling is all that's needed to help them grow.

Wait to fertilize lawns until they green up.

PERENNIALS & VINES

As perennial flowers begin to wake up, sprinkle a layer of compost around those plants.

PROBLEM-SOLVE

ANNUALS, BULBS & EDIBLES

Keep watch for insects on your seed-started or indoor annual plants. Whiteflies, aphids, and mealybugs can devastate tender seedlings. (January Problem-Solve, Annuals has more details.)

Dig out perennial weeds, such as dandelions and horsetail, in vegetable and annual flower beds now so they don't take over this spring.

LAWNS & GROUNDCOVERS

Rake out dead grass or thatch (also see Care, Lawns) to stop the spread of snow mold disease. This fungal disease thrives on dead grass and wet conditions. By raking the lawn early you can stop it from spreading and killing the grass.

Push down elevated tunnels caused by moles in the lawn. Spray castor oil on the lawn to repel them.

PERENNIALS, VINES & ROSES

Watch for and control insects on perennial seedlings and miniature roses growing indoors (also see January Problem-Solve, Annuals).

Reset any perennials that have heaved from the soil during the winter weather.

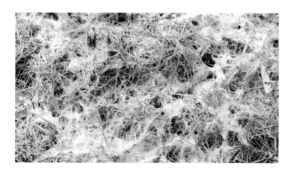

■ *Snow mold is a lawn fungal disease that occurs right after the snow melts, killing patches of grass.*

■ *Korean viburnum* (Viburnum carlesii) *is resistant to the viburnum leaf beetle.*

SHRUBS & TREES

Spray dormant oil on deciduous trees as long as the buds haven't started to show signs of color and open (February Problem-Solve, Trees).

Assess arrowwood (*Viburnum dentatum*), European cranberry (*V. opulus*), American cranberry (*V. trilobum*), and other susceptible viburnum species that had viburnum leaf beetle damage last year. This beetle defoliates viburnum bushes in spring. To control this pest, grow resistant species such as doublefile viburnum (*V. plicatum*) and Korean spice viburnum (*V. carlesii*). Look for the small, raised, brown bumps (egg cases) on the branch tips and prune those branch tips off to reduce the infestation for the coming year.

If you live along the southern coast of New England up to southern Maine and saw brown moths flitting around your outdoor lights during warm days of November and December, chances are your trees are infested with winter moth. This relatively new insect likes the moderate temperatures along the New England coast. The caterpillars hatch in March and April to feed on the leaf buds of many hardwood trees, including oak, maple, apple, and ash, and even shrubs such as blueberry. The defoliation of the trees weakens them. Spray Bt on emerging leaves to kill this caterpillar.

April

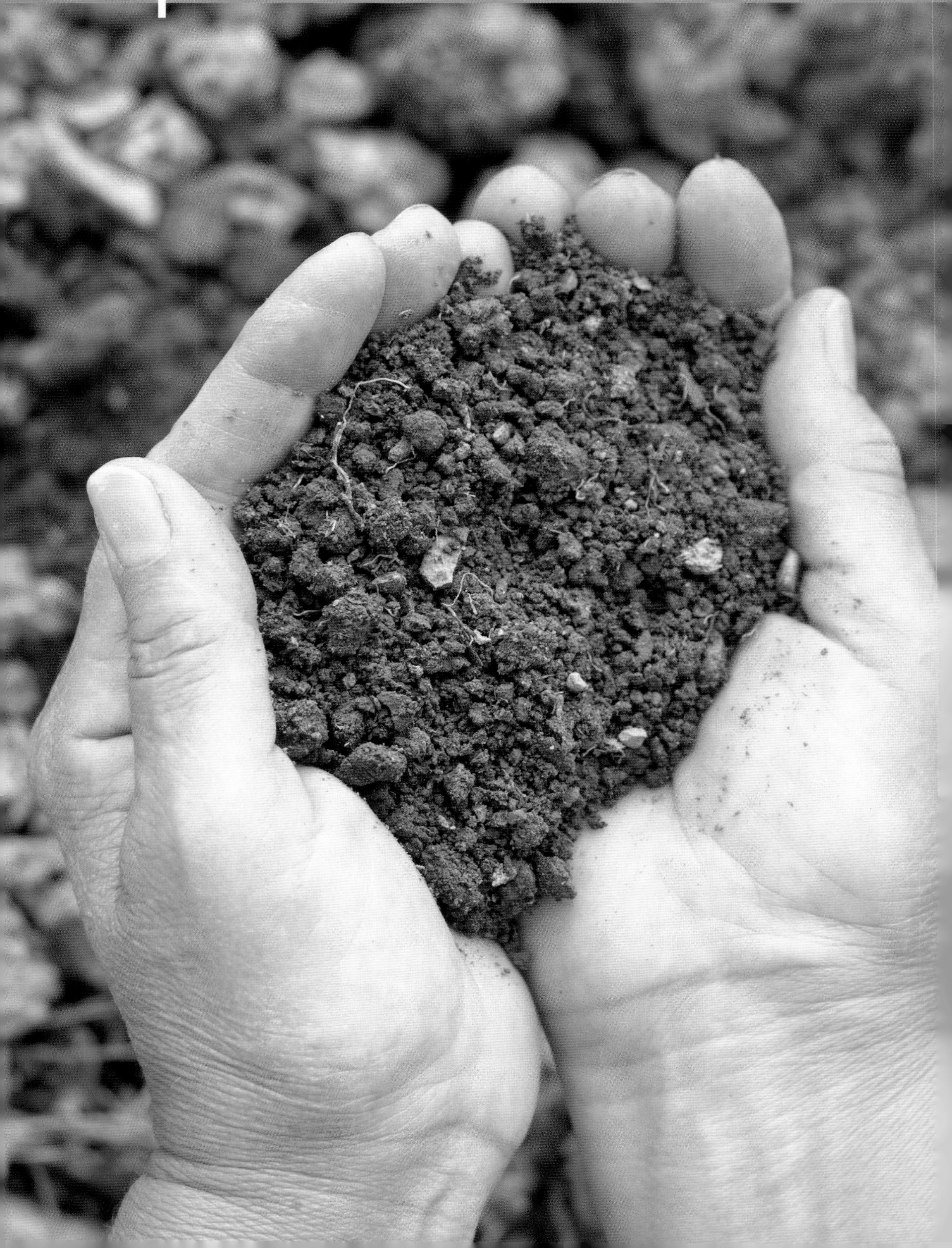

The gardening fever is burning hot come April. The weather has started to consistently warm and, hopefully, the ground has dried out enough to start working in the garden and yard in earnest. In northern areas of New England we can still expect freezing air temperatures, snow piles on the north side of buildings, and wet, cold soil. But in northern valleys and certainly in southern New England, it's really feeling like spring.

The last frost date along coastal areas of Connecticut and in eastern Massachusetts is the end of this month. Microclimate areas on the south side of buildings and walls are heating up fast, and life is emerging from the soil. Spring bulbs are really blooming now. and early-blooming shrubs and trees are showing color. Ahhh, spring!

But you don't want to get too far ahead of yourself. This is especially true with working the soil. Turning or tilling wet soil can squeeze oxygen from the soil and create smaller spaces between soil particles. This results in a soil with large clods that is hard to work. Ideally, soil should be made of small, crumbly soil aggregates. A simple test to determine if your soil is too wet to work is to dig out a handful of soil from your garden bed and roll it into a ball. If the soil either doesn't form a ball or crumbles easily when it's poked, then your soil is probably dry enough to work. If the ball is wet and stays intact, so much so that you can shape it, then wait a few more days to plant.

April is a good time to see what survived the winter. New growth should be starting to pop on roses, perennial flowers, shrubs, and trees, but don't make any snap judgments yet on what's alive. Some shrubs, such as summersweet (*Clethra*), and perennials, such as hardy hibiscus, are slow to leaf out in spring. It may be May before you see any signs of life. Record when flowers and leaves appear in a print or online calendar or journal so you roughly know when to expect them each spring.

PLAN

ANNUALS & EDIBLES

Get plant markers ready as you start planting your annual flowers, vegetables, and herbs this month. Marking the plant and variety name will enable you to remember the name of those varieties that shine in your garden when friends come to visit.

Determine the planting-out dates for your annual flowers, vegetables, and herbs based on their air and soil temperature preferences. See Plant, Annuals in this chapter for more details.

BULBS

As the spring-flowering bulbs bloom, note your favorite varieties in your online or print journal. Record those bulbs that didn't bloom or come up. Mark bulbs with plant markers to remember which ones to keep or replace.

■ *Use metal plant labels to help you keep track of where your perennials, annuals, vegetables, and bulbs are planted, or their variety name.*

LAWNS & GROUNDCOVERS

Wait until the lawn grass soil dries out before starting to mow this month and next (see March Care, Lawns). Get your mower ready for the season with a proper tune-up, if you haven't already (more on this in February Care, Lawns).

PERENNIALS & VINES

Notice which early spring perennial flowers are blooming, such as primroses, creeping phlox, and hellebores later this month. As these early bloomers show their colors, mark down which you like and don't like. Also, if any of these flowers should be moved into a better location due to overgrowing their location or flowering poorly, do so after they finish flowering.

ROSES

Get containers ready for planting your miniature roses outdoors after all danger of frost has passed by cleaning out old soil and purchasing potting soil.

SHRUBS & TREES

Watch for early-blooming shrubs and trees, such as flowering quince (*Chaenomeles*), Cornelian cherry (*Cornus mas*), and pussy willows, blooming this month. Look at varieties at public gardens or in your neighborhood to get ideas for your yard.

PLANT

ANNUALS

Prepare annual flowerbeds for planting by mixing in a layer of compost. On beds that have been productive in the past, add a layer 1 to 2 inches thick as a maintenance dose. On beds with poor soil where plants haven't grown well in the past, add a layer 3 to 4 inches thick. Consider building raised beds to plant annual flowers in (see Plant, Edibles).

Plant cool-season annuals in all but the coldest northern regions by the end of this month. These annuals include pansies, violas, snapdragons, and dusty miller. Harden off annual flowers grown indoors or purchased at the garden centers (see March Care, Annuals for tips on how to do this).

Start seeds indoors of warm-season annuals that will enjoy the heat of May. These flowers include zinnia, celosia, cosmos, marigold, and calendula. Sow these seeds four to six weeks before your last frost date. In southern areas sow seeds in early April; in northern sections sow seeds in late April. Plant outdoors after the last frost date for your area (see the frost maps on page 17).

BULBS

Pot up any sprouting tuberous begonias, dahlias, and canna lily bulbs that you've been storing all winter into containers. (See March Plant, Bulbs for more details.) It's still too early to place these outdoors, but keep them growing in a bright, cool room. They will be planted outdoors toward the end of May or even early June in northern sections.

EDIBLES

Start working your beds as they dry out to plant cool-season vegetables. Follow the guidelines under Plant, Annuals for adding compost to the beds.

Consider building raised beds to plant edibles in all but sandy soil. Raised beds warm up faster and dry out quicker in spring. They allow you to work the soil without stepping on it so the soil is not compacted. You can also concentrate your watering, fertilizing, and weeding in a smaller space that's easier to manage.

Start hardening off cool-season vegetable transplants such as broccoli, cabbage, and onions for planting later this month. (See March Plant, Edibles also.)

Plant seeds of other cool-season vegetables, such as peas, spinach, lettuce, mache, radishes, beets, carrots, Swiss chard, parsnips, and turnips, this month once the soil has dried out. See May Plant, Annuals to learn how to plant seeds.

Plant seed potatoes (young tubers) purchased at the garden center or online now in trenches dug 4 inches deep. Space tubers 1 foot apart. Don't plant in areas where other potato family crops grew in the past three years to avoid transmitting diseases to your plants. (See January Plan, Edibles for further details.)

■ *Plant seed potatoes in trenches spaced about 1 foot apart. Cover them with soil and hill more soil over the plants as they grow.*

Start seeds of warm-season vegetables, such as peppers and eggplant (if you didn't start them in late March), and tomatoes, indoors under grow lights in early April. Start basil in mid- to late April. (You will plant these warm-season crops in the garden in mid-May in southern areas, and at the end of May or early June in northern areas.)

Plant bare-root fruit trees and berry bushes as they arrive in the mail or are bought at the local garden centers (see Plant, Roses).

LAWNS & GROUNDCOVERS

Continue replacing sod damaged by snowplows as the ground dries out.

HERE'S HOW

TO BUILD A RAISED BED

There are two types of raised beds you can build. A freestanding raised bed is simply soil piled up and then leveled on top into a bed form. A permanent raised bed has some type of structure holding the soil in place. Freestanding raised beds allow you to reshape the bed each spring into different configurations. However, they require rebuilding each year because they will flatten out over the summer. Permanent raised beds don't need to be rebuilt each spring, but their shape is static. Decide which raised bed is right for you, and follow these steps to building one.

1. *For a permanent raised bed, use rot-resistant woods such as cedar and hemlock, or stone, brick, or composite boards to build the bed 6 to 10 inches tall. Don't use chemically treated wood in your raised-bed garden.*

2. *For permanent wooden raised beds, use 2-inch-thick wood that won't warp over time. Secure a support piece of wood or metal in each corner to keep the angles square.*

3. *Position the bed frames. Make sure the beds are no wider than 4 feet. This way you'll be able to reach into the center without stepping on the bed. The beds can be as long as you please to fit the space.*

   Leave room to walk around the beds. If you use a wheelbarrow or garden cart in your garden, make the pathways wide enough to accommodate these tools.

4. *In permanent and freestanding beds, take soil from the pathways or bring in compost and topsoil to fill the beds.*

   If you're filling the bed with compost and topsoil, use 40 percent compost to 60 percent topsoil. Rake out the soil on top of the bed so it's flat.

HERE'S HOW

TO SEED A LAWN

Whether you are reseeding a dead patch in your yard or growing a new lawn, follow these steps for proper lawn grass seeding.

1. In small areas, rake out dead grass areas, removing weeds and debris. To renovate larger lawn areas, till the area thoroughly and then rake it out.

2. Till or rake the soil so it's loose to 6 inches deep.

3. Fill in low spots with soil.

4. Amend the soil with compost and fertilizer, based on a soil test. In many areas of New England phosphate fertilizers are now banned on lawns because of the risk of phosphate runoff into waterways. Check with your local garden center about the best fertilizer for your area.

5. Mix in amendments and rake the ground flat, removing rocks and debris.

6. Let the site settle for a few days.

7. Sow seed by hand or with a lawn spreader. Follow the seeding rate on the bag.

8. Lightly rake the soil to cover the seed with a ¼-inch layer of soil.

9. Roll the lawn or bare spots with an empty lawn roller to create good seed-to-soil contact for better germination.

10. Mulch the area with straw. Hay tends to have weed seeds in it and shouldn't be used. Some garden centers now carry cellulose-based mulches for covering newly seeded lawns. Apply a mulch layer only 1 to 2 inches thick, so the soil is still slightly visible.

11. Water frequently to keep the soil evenly moist if it doesn't rain.

12. Mow once more than half of the lawn grass reaches 3 inches tall. Don't fertilize until fall (see September Fertilize, Lawns & Groundcovers).

Notice where the lawn is thin and rake out those areas to remove dead grass and weeds. Reseed those areas with a grass variety similar to what is in your lawn, such as Kentucky bluegrass and tall fescue. Topdress the area with a layer of topsoil 1 to 2 inches thick. Sow seeds by sprinkling them evenly by hand for small areas, or use a seed spreader for larger areas. Cover with straw and keep well watered.

For smaller lawns, consider laying sod instead of seeding. Look for sod at your local garden centers. Try to find grass varieties similar to your existing lawn if you are using the sod to patch areas. Prepare the soil as you would for seeding a lawn. If you aren't laying sod the same day, store the rolls in a cool, shaded place and keep them well watered. Lay the sod pieces starting at an edge, such as a sidewalk or driveway. Butt pieces close together and cut pieces with a knife to fit if need be. Stagger the pieces for a better visual effect. Roll the sod with a lawn roller to flatten it and provide good root contact with the soil. Keep well watered. Don't mow until new growth appears and the sod is well settled.

HERE'S HOW

TO PLANT BARE-ROOT PLANTS

Bare-root roses, perennial flowers, shrubs, and trees are arriving through the mail or can be purchased locally this time of year for immediate planting. If you can't plant that day, place the plants in a dark, cool area and keep the roots moist. Try to plant as soon as possible.

1. Once the plants arrive, open the package and inspect them. You should see signs of swollen leaf buds and healthy roots. Mushy, brown, and rotting roots and dead branches are signs you may need to get a refund.

2. Remove the plants from their packaging and soak the roots for a few hours in warm water.

3. Dig a hole wide and deep enough to accommodate the root system. You should be able to spread out the roots in a fan shape so that the tips of the roots won't touch the sides of the hole. For grafted roses, dig the hole deep enough so the graft union (the bulge near the base of the trunk) is 2 inches below the soil line. For trees and shrubs (including fruit trees), the graft union should be a few inches above the soil line. For roses, shrubs, and trees without graft unions, and for perennials, dig the hole deep enough so the crown is level with the soil line.

4. Backfill the hole with soil and add water as you backfill to eliminate air pockets.

5. Mulch with a 2-inch-thick layer of bark, crushed stone, or wood chips, keeping the mulch away from the trunk.

■ *Stone mulch is attractive and helps keep the soil cool and moist.*

■ *Bark is a good mulch for perennial flowers, shrubs, and trees. Choose bark types and colors that will look attractive in your yard.*

HERE'S HOW

TO MULCH A BED

1. Before adding any mulch, spread a pre-emergent herbicide. There are organic and conventional choices for pre-emergents. Pre-emergents work by preventing weed seeds from sprouting. You'll save yourself a lot of time and backaches if you use it. (However, if you have an area where you like to let plants go to seed and you leave the seeds to resprout, don't use pre-emergent.)

2. Next, add the mulch by creating little piles around your landscape beds. You can buy mulch two ways: in bags or in bulk. Most home improvement stores sell bagged mulch, and they'll probably have several different brands of the same type of mulch. Some home improvement stores and garden centers sell bulk mulch. To buy bulk mulch, you usually need a truck so that you can bring home a big load. If you're buying more than 3 cubic yards of mulch, you will want to consider delivery. A pitchfork and wheelbarrow are handy for moving bulk mulch.

3. Use a hard rake or a four-tine claw to rake the mulch around the bed. Start raking from either the back or one side of the bed so that you can leave "fluffy" mulch behind you. You will want to put mulch across the entire bed, at least 3 inches deep.

4. After spreading the mulch in the landscape bed, pull the mulch slightly away from plant stems and leaves. Mulch is usually warm and moist—the perfect environment for bacteria and fungi to live and thrive. These microorganisms can rot your plant stems, so leave a little breathing room between the mulch and plants.

HERE'S HOW

TO PLANT A CONTAINER TREE OR SHRUB

1 *Locate your tree, shrub, or rose in the appropriate spot for that variety based on its sun and shade tolerance, soil needs, and ultimate size. Avoid planting near power or underground lines.*

Dig a hole three times as wide as the rootball and just as deep.

Loosen the soil around the circumference of the hole another 1 foot wide with a well-made metal fork or spade (poorly made ones can bend). This will encourage the roots to penetrate the native soil.

2-3 *Remove the plant from its pot. Roll the pot on its side and loosen the roots with your hands, removing some of the potting soil. This will encourage the roots to grow into the native soil faster. Check for crossing roots or any that wind in a circle. Prune these so the roots are heading away from the trunk.*

4 *Place the plant in the hole so the crown (where the roots meet the trunk) is at the soil line. If it's a grafted tree or shrub, make sure the graft union is above the soil line. Roses should have their graft union below the soil line. (See Here's How To Plant a Bare-Root Plant.)*

5 *Backfill with native soil. Don't add any soil amendments unless your soil is very poor quality. Add water as you backfill soil to remove any air pockets in the hole.*

Mulch with a layer 2 to 3 inches thick of bark mulch, crushed stone, or wood chips, keeping the mulch away from the trunk.

PERENNIALS & VINES

Harden off perennial flowers growing indoors (See March Care, Annuals). Begin planting perennial flowers and vines in southern areas in late April after danger of a frost has passed. (Wait until May in northern areas to start planting.)

Bare-root plants arriving through the mail should be potted up if it's too cold to plant in your area. Keep these containers well watered and in a sunny location until after the last frost date for your area (see the maps on page 17).

ROSES

Plant bare-root roses at the end of the month in southern areas and in May in northern areas.

Transplant miniature roses growing indoors into more decorative or larger containers for

moving outdoors after all danger of frost has passed. Watch the weather: if frost threatens, protect these tender roses by moving the container indoors or into a protected location. (Wait until May to plant leafed-out roses into the ground.)

SHRUBS & TREES

As bare-root trees arrive in the mail or are purchased locally, plant them now after danger of a freeze has passed, following the tips in Here's How To Plant Bare-Root Plants.

Container shrubs and those that have been balled and burlapped can be planted now in southern areas as they come available in garden centers. In northern areas it's best to wait until May, once the last frost dates have passed. Many of these plants have been grown in warmer climates and may be leafed out when they arrive in your nursery. A late spring frost can damage the leaves and set back the newly transplanted shrub or tree.

CARE

ANNUALS

For annuals still growing under lights indoors, keep the seedlings watered well. Transplant those seedlings in trays into individual pots after the

■ *Edge along walkways and beds with a sharp, flat spade to give your garden a formal look and to help keep lawn grass and weeds from encroaching.*

HERE'S HOW

TO PLANT A BALLED-AND-BURLAPPED TREE OR SHRUB

1 *Dig the hole as described in Here's How To Plant a Container Tree or Shrub.*

2 *Remove the twine and wire cage (if it has one). Peel back the burlap or wrap and remove it.*

3 *If you have a large tree, place the tree in the hole first, then remove the burlap cover. This way you won't have to move the rootball around as much, which helps to keep the root ball intact.*

4 *Once in the hole, backfill with native soil, adding water as you backfill to eliminate air pockets. Only use soil amendments if you have very poor soil.*

5 *Keep well watered and mulch with a layer 2 to 3 inches thick of bark mulch, crushed stone, or wood chips, keeping the mulch away from the trunk.*

true leaves form. For those seedlings in small pots, once the height of the transplant is three times the diameter of the pot, transplant it into a larger pot. Keep the grow lights 4 to 6 inches above the seedling tops for the best light intensity.

Although the cold-hardy annuals such as pansies and violas are frost tolerant, that doesn't mean cold weather will help them grow. If temperatures are predicted to dip into the 20s Fahrenheit, cover your annual flowers in the ground and containers with a floating row cover. This cheesecloth-like material will let air, light, and water through, but it provides enough protection to reduce damage from cold weather. For plantings in rows use wire hoops to create a tunnel and then drape the row cover over the hoops. The air layer between the top of the plants and the row cover will help insulate the plants.

Check for germinating seedlings of annual flowers that self-sow readily, such as cleome, calendula, and California poppies. Remove those that are growing in the wrong places or are germinating too thickly. Thin those seedlings so they are spaced the right amount for that variety.

Edge your annual beds (see Care, Perennials & Vines).

Pot up overwintered geraniums beginning to sprout in the basement and grow them in a sunny window.

BULBS

Deadhead early flowering bulbs such as early daffodils and tulips. The plant will put more energy into producing a bigger bulb instead of seeds, and it will look nicer in your yard. (Wait to cut back the foliage until after it yellows. The foliage provides energy to the bulb for next year's flowering.)

For small bulbs, such as crocus and scilla that are naturalizing in the yard, let them set seed this month and next. This will help them spread.

Compost the last of your forced bulbs from this winter, or pop them in the ground now. While most bulbs won't flower next year, some gardeners can't stand throwing them out.

Pot the last of the dahlias, canna lilies, and tuberous begonias you stored in the basement. For those growing in pots, move them out on warm days, but remember, planting in the ground isn't happening until later in May.

EDIBLES

Keep peppers, eggplant, and tomatoes growing under lights healthy with regular watering, fertilizing every two weeks, and lights hanging 4 to 6 inches from their tops. To keep tomatoes stocky, gently brush the tops with your hand daily. The motion strengthens the stems and makes for a better transplant.

Continue to harden off transplants, such as broccoli and cabbage, if you haven't planted them already (see March Care, Annuals for more details).

Divide rhubarb plants now as they emerge from the soil. Rhubarb likes full sun and well-amended soil. Dig the plants. With a sharp knife divide the rootball into two to four sections, each 1 foot in diameter, depending on its size. Replant in soil amended with composted manure. Pot up the other sections to give away to friends and neighbors.

Asparagus should be starting to grow now. Harvest 6-to-8-inch-long spears from plants three or more years old by snapping them off at the soil line.

Remove mulch from strawberries. Rake out the dead leaves and use the mulch in the paths. Weed the strawberry patch to remove dandelions and other perennial weeds.

Turn under cover crops sowed in fall (see September Plant, Edibles). These will need two to four weeks to decompose before you plant your crops.

LAWNS & GROUNDCOVERS

Reseed bare spots, sow a new lawn, or renovate one once the soil dries out this month (see Plant, Lawns).

Continue to remove thatch (see March Care, Lawns & Groundcovers for more detail).

TO POWER AERATE

1. Water the entire yard lightly for a few hours before you aerate it to ensure that the soil is moist—but don't overwater or the machine will become bogged down with mud.

2. Set the depth gauge on the coring machine to maximum. Run the machine back and forth across the lawn in one direction. Then run it again, perpendicular to the original direction.

3. Allow the cores pulled up by the aerator to dry for a day, then gently rake across them to break them up and help them decompose faster.

Aerate existing lawns with a commercial aerator, available for rent at a rent-all store. For a small lawn, use a metal fork. Aeration helps break up compacted soil and creates holes through which air, water, and fertilizer can better penetrate to the grass roots. A commercial aerator will create plugs of sod that drop on the soil surface. They eventually dissolve into the lawn. An iron fork won't create the sod plugs, but the tines create holes in the sod. Push the iron fork 6 to 8 inches deep into the soil every foot or so.

In southern areas, especially during warm springs, you may be mowing lawns now. Wait until the grass is 3 inches tall and the soil dried out to run the mower. See May Care, Lawns & Groundcovers for more on how to mow a lawn.

Continue to remove dead leaves and weeds from existing groundcover patches. Once a groundcover patch starts growing strong in May it will fill in those bare spots where the weeds were.

PERENNIALS & VINES

Weed out any self-sown seedlings of foxgloves, black-eyed Susans, oat grass, and other perennials that pop up. Self-sown perennials can become weeds in your perennial garden unless they're controlled.

Remove weeds between perennial plants, but refer to your map or photo of the garden to properly identify the perennials coming up to make sure you aren't pulling up one of your flowers instead!

Edge your perennial and annual flower beds with a sharp spade. Dig 6 to 8 inches deep at an angle to create a steep cut. This will help prevent invasions of weeds and grass from the lawn.

Continue to prune vines that bloom on new wood, such as trumpet vine and honeysuckle, before they leaf out to shape them and control growth. Remove thin, dead, or broken branches. For trumpet vines, cut back side shoots to three buds. Cut back honeysuckle vines to the desired height. Prune overgrown honeysuckle vines to 2 feet tall.

Begin dividing perennials now, and move divisions into new locations with similar light and soil conditions.

ROSES

In southern parts of New England, if the leaf buds are swelling and starting to grow, remove all the overwintering mulch and use it around the plant. In northern areas, check under the mulch. If the buds are still dormant, wait until May to remove the mulch.

Once you remove the mulch, prune your roses. Prune hybrid tea and floribunda roses, removing thin canes from the base of the plant and leaving three to five main canes. Prune to a healthy, outward-facing bud. Make the cut at a 45-degree angle right above the healthy bud. Cut back these main canes by one-third. If your roses have died

■ *Prune roses once the buds start to swell so you can see where the dead and live growth is on the stem.*

back severely in winter, be patient. They may still grow from the crown.

Prune landscape, old-fashioned, and species roses to remove dead, diseased, or broken branches. Open up the plant by pruning out spindly shoots and shape the shrub by cutting back errant branches growing in a direction that you don't want. Rugosa roses and other species roses can be cut back to 2 to 3 feet tall to rejuvenate an overgrown plant, if needed.

Climbing roses that were removed from their trellis, covered in burlap, laid down, and buried in mulch can be propped back up again the end of this month. Prune back dead, diseased, or broken branches and side shoots coming off the main trunk to 1 foot long. Attach the canes to their trellis.

SHRUBS & TREES

Remove burlap wraps and other winter protection.

Spray dormant oil to kill overwintering insects on deciduous shrubs if you haven't already. (See February Problem-Solve, Roses, Shrubs & Trees.)

Assess animal damage on trunks and branches. (See March Care, Trees for more details.)

Edge around the mulch ring of your trees and shrubs (see Care, Perennials).

Remove the old bark mulch and add a layer of new mulch 2 to 4 inches thick. Don't just keep applying new mulch on top of the old. You'll create a pile or "volcano" of mulch against the trunk that will lead to the trunk rotting.

Finish pruning before the buds open.

WATER

ANNUALS & PERENNIALS

Keep young seedlings growing indoors and cuttings rooted from annual flowers, such as geraniums under grow lights, well watered. Bottom water seedlings (see February Plant, Annuals

HERE'S HOW

TO DIVIDE PERENNIALS

The rule of thumb is to divide spring-blooming perennials, such as bleeding hearts and peonies, in late summer or fall, and summer- or fall-blooming perennials, such as phlox and aster, in spring.

1. *As soon as growth appears in spring, dig up the clump. In fall, cut back the foliage to the ground first before digging up.*

2. *With a sharp spade, iron fork, or knife, cut the perennial plants into sections 1 foot in diameter with a strong root system. Some spreading perennials, such as bee balm, won't have a solid clump. To divide this type, slice into the main plant in the ground and remove a chunk of it, backfilling the hole with fresh soil.*

3. *Replant each division in the appropriate locations (sun or shade) in well-drained, compost-amended soil. Plant at the same depth as it was in its original hole. Keep well watered.*

   Give away extra divisions to friends, family, or local plant sales.

for more details). Water cuttings in individual pots until the water runs out of the bottom drainage holes.

Keep plants being hardened off well watered. Transplants in small pots can dry out quickly on a warm, sunny April day. Check them regularly, especially during windy days, to make sure they stay moist. Seedlings are tender and often will die if the pots dry out.

BULBS

Usually New England springs are wet enough with periodic rains that watering established bulbs isn't necessary. However, if we have a drought, and you can dig into the soil 6 or 8 inches and the soil is still dry, then deeply water to a depth of 8 inches so these bulbs will continue to grow unhindered.

Keep dahlia, canna lily, and tuberous begonia bulbs growing in pots watered so the soil stays evenly moist until transplanting at the end of May.

Keep the soil of amaryllis bulbs growing indoors in pots well-watered.

EDIBLES

If the spring is dry and the soil is dry to a few inches deep, water newly sown vegetable seeds and transplants. Larger seeds, such as peas, will be able to withstand short dry periods in spring better than smaller seeds, such as lettuce, spinach, and carrots. Keep these smaller seeds watered daily if it stays dry, and consider covering them with a floating row cover to conserve moisture and keep the soil evenly moist.

Keep young indoor seedlings that are growing under lights evenly watered and vegetables and herbs that are being hardened off moist (see Water, Annuals).

Perennial vegetables, such as asparagus and rhubarb, have deep root systems and usually don't need additional water in spring unless we have a drought. Periodically check the soil to a depth of 8 inches to see if it's still moist.

Mulching with straw or bark helps conserve soil moisture as well.

If newly planted bare-root fruit trees and berry bushes were watered properly at planting, they shouldn't need more water until they leaf out.

LAWNS & GROUNDCOVERS

Keep newly seeded or patched lawns evenly watered so the top few inches of soil stays moist. This is critical for even and complete lawn grass germination.

ROSES

Keep potted roses, such as miniature roses, well watered as you move them outdoors during warm days. Recently planted bare-root roses should be fine until they start to leaf out.

SHRUBS & TREES

Water newly planted evergreen trees well to keep the soil moist and help the new roots penetrate the existing soil. Newly planted deciduous trees should be fine if watered and mulched when planted. Once they leaf out, start watering. Check the soil during dry springs to be sure it's moist to 8 inches deep. This is particularly important on sandy soils that dry out quickly.

FERTILIZE

ANNUALS

Continue fertilizing indoor annuals growing under lights every two weeks with a diluted organic product.

Fertilize rooted cuttings taken from other annual flowers when you start to see new growth emerging from the stems.

BULBS

Fertilize spring-flowering bulbs as they emerge from the soil. Once the flowers begin to form, don't fertilize: it will not help the bulb grow larger. Don't fertilize bulbs planted and fertilized last fall. Add a diluted fertilizer to indoor amaryllis bulbs every two weeks.

EDIBLES

Continue fertilizing indoor vegetable and herb plants with diluted organic product.

Fertilize established rhubarb beds with a layer of compost 1 to 2 inches thick, applied once the rhubarb starts growing.

Fertilize established asparagus beds with 1 pound per 100 square feet of a granular 5-5-5 organic fertilizer now.

LAWNS & GROUNDCOVERS

In most areas it's too early to fertilize the lawn. Wait until it's actively growing in May to apply fertilizer, or wait until September.

Once you've cleaned out the beds of evergreen groundcovers such as vinca and pachysandra, and before they start growing, apply an organic granular fertilizer such as 5-5-5 to those patches that are thin to help them fill in. A light, ¼-inch-deep topdressing of compost on the whole bed will also help keep the plants healthy.

PERENNIALS & VINES

Continue fertilizing indoor perennial flowers growing under lights every two weeks with a diluted organic product.

As perennials emerge from the soil, topdress around the plants with a layer of compost 1 to 2 inches deep.

As perennial vines, such as wisteria and Virginia creeper, start to leaf out, topdress these vines with a 2-inch-thick layer of compost spread around the drip line. Many perennial vines are very aggressive, so there's little need for additional fertilization unless the vine is growing poorly.

ROSES

Fertilize potted roses with a commercial rose food at the dosage recommended for container plants.

As ground roses start to wake up and the buds swell, fertilize landscape and old-fashioned roses with a 2-inch-thick layer of compost.

HERE'S HOW

TO FERTILIZE TREES AND SHRUBS

- Trees and shrubs are fertilized in spring once the soil warms enough to stimulate root growth, but before the leaves emerge.

- Evaluate your tree or shrub. If the leaves are normal size and branches are growing at least 6 to 8 inches a year, then all you'll need is to add a layer of compost 1 to 2 inches thick around the drip line of the shrub or tree for fertilization. The drip line is that area on the outer edge of your plant where water naturally drips in a circle around the plant. It roughly coincides with the most active young roots that will benefit most from fertilization.

- If your tree or shrub needs additional fertilizer, determine the best type for that plant. Some trees and shrubs, such as hydrangea and rhododendron, need an acidifying fertilizer. Perform a soil test to get recommendations for your types.

- The best fertilizers for trees and shrubs are slow release. These allow nitrogen and other nutrients to be released over time as the plant needs them. Organic fertilizers are naturally slow release, but other types of slow-release fertilizers are also available. A granular form is usually best. Avoid using tree spikes. These concentrate fertilizer in small areas and may actually "burn" the roots (scorching due to overfertilization) in that area while not properly feeding the other roots.

For hybrid tea, floribunda, and grandiflora roses, in addition to the compost add granular rose food at amounts suggested on the rose fertilizer packages. Fertilize monthly beginning now and continuing into summer.

SHRUBS & TREES

Fertilize established shrubs and trees now, before new growth starts. Follow the guidelines in Here's How To Fertilize Trees & Shrubs. Don't fertilize newly planted trees or shrubs or those planted last fall.

PROBLEM-SOLVE

ANNUALS & EDIBLES

Continue to watch indoor growing seedlings for damping-off disease and insects such as aphids, whiteflies, and mealybugs. Control these as recommended in January Problem-Solve, Annuals.

Protect outdoor young transplants, such as broccoli and cabbage, from cutworms. These caterpillars emerge from the soil at night to cut off the seedlings at the stem level. Wrap a 2- to 4-inch-wide strip of newspaper around the stem to form a collar, placing it about 1 inch deep into the soil to protect the transplants.

Protect emerging seedlings and transplants from animals and rodents such as rabbits with fencing and repellents (also see June Problem-Solve, Perennials & Vines).

Protect young seedlings from slugs and snails (refer to May Problem-Solve, Annuals & Edibles).

BULBS

Protect opened bulb flowers from a frost. If your bulbs have only foliage and no flower stalks yet they can withstand a frost. However, once the flower buds form, cover them during chilly nights.

LAWNS & GROUNDCOVERS

Spread corn gluten organic crabgrass killer as crabgrass seed starts to germinate. This product kills the germinating seeds and is a 10 percent nitrogen fertilizer. Spread it on the lawn when your forsythia bushes start to bloom. That's when crabgrass traditionally starts to germinate. Don't spread lawn grass seed in this area for one month, as the corn gluten kills all germinating seeds too.

Rake out lawns to remove dead grass and prevent snow mold fungus from killing patches of your lawn. Reduce your fall fertilization to lessen this problem.

PERENNIALS AND VINES

As soon as your lilies start emerging from the ground, look for the bright red lily leaf beetles. (May Problem-Solve, Bulbs has more details.)

SHRUBS & TREES

On evergreens, such as mugo pine, at the end of April in southern areas start looking for damage from European sawflies. These caterpillar-like insects will feed on young growth of evergreens, deforming the shrub. Handpick small infestations.

Destroy the webby tents and egg masses of eastern tent caterpillars as you notice them on apple, birch, cherry, and other trees. These eggs will hatch with warmer weather, and the caterpillars will feed on the emerging leaves. Destroy the nest with a stick or prune off the branch containing the nest to remove it. Spray Bt to kill hatched caterpillars.

During early springs in southern New England, if apples start leafing out early, control for apple scab disease (see May Problem-Solve, Shrubs & Trees for control tips).

May

Spring is finally here! May means it's truly garden time throughout all of New England. The workload increases quickly as flowers, trees, and shrubs start growing and blooming, and everything from vegetables to trees needs planting. It's easy to get overwhelmed by the list of chores.

In warmer parts of the country, the opportunity to plant is spread out over many weeks. But in New England, especially the northern areas, you need to plant annual edible crops in May for them to have enough time to grow, bloom, and fruit before fall.

This rush to plant can be impeded by the weather. While May is consistently warmer than April, the weather remains variable. May weather can range from cool and wet to hot and dry. It's not uncommon to have 40 degrees Fahrenheit and drenching rains followed by 90-degree Fahrenheit heat waves. You have to watch weather conditions to find opportunities to plant and to be alert for any late spring frosts. Flowers of fruit trees and berries, such as strawberries, are particularly susceptible to frosts that will kill blossoms and decrease your crop.

But May is also the time to enjoy your work. Spring bulbs are finishing up their flowering in most locations. The bulb flowers are being replaced by blooms of early spring perennials, such as peonies, iris, and bleeding hearts. Early crops of greens, radishes, and peas sown in April are starting to grow, and you might even be eating fresh greens from cold frames or other protected areas of your garden.

The lawn needs mowing, beds need weeding and edging, soil needing turning, and containers need planting. Yes, there's a lot to do. The best plan is to go slowly. Remember to stretch before working. A fifteen-minute yoga routine will go a long way toward stretching those winter muscles so you'll have less pain after a hard day in the dirt. Wear a protective hat and sunscreen, and don't overdo it the first few warm days. Vary your work routine so you use different muscles, never overtaxing one muscle group. This is just spring, so you want to be feeling good for the long haul.

ANNUALS & EDIBLES

It's shopping time! Visit your local garden centers as annual flower, vegetable, and herb transplants arrive. Look early to get the best selection. Look for substitute varieties if the ones you desire aren't available. Always try to find plants with similar shapes and sizes to fit into your location. Use the Here's How To Calculate the Number of Plants You Need in March, Plan, Lawns & Groundcovers to know how many annual flowers to buy. Remember to include any annual flowers, vegetables, and herbs you're starting indoors or ones you'll sow directly as seed in your calculations for how much to buy.

As leaves emerge on deciduous trees in the middle and end of May, double-check the light levels in your beds to be sure you're planting sun- and shade-loving flowers in the right locations.

BULBS

As in April, continue to assess the bulbs that flowered well and those that did not. Mark areas in your garden where you'll be planting replacement bulbs in fall with wooden or metal markers. Create a rough sketch (no one will see but you) to remind you of the types of bulbs to plant to complement the spring-blooming perennial flowers, shrubs, and trees.

For those bulbs that came up but didn't flower, wait until their leaves yellow to dig up, divide, and replant them (see Care, Bulbs). This often will rejuvenate bulbs and help them flower again.

Since you'll need to let bulb foliage yellow before cutting back, flower gardens that are interplanted with bulbs may look messy in May. However, there are ways to camouflage the yellowing leaves. Plant bulbs near fast-growing perennials such as hosta and daylilies and let their foliage hide the bulb's foliage. You can also plant early blooming annuals, such as pansies, primulas, and snapdragons, in those beds to draw the eye away from the bulb foliage.

Check the survival rate of any summer-flowering bulbs, such a dahlias, gladiolus, and canna lilies, that you overwintered in your basement. How many do you have, and where would you like to plant them? Don't plant yet—wait until later in May in southern areas and early June in northern areas.

PERENNIALS, VINES & ROSES

By the end of this month, all your perennial flowers, roses, and vines should be growing. Mark down any that didn't survive the winter and start looking for replacement plants at local garden centers. You can also consider dividing some of your existing perennial flowers and moving them into the empty spots.

Don't pass judgment too quickly on late-emerging plants such as trumpet vine (*Campsis radicans*) and butterfly bush (*Buddleja*). In northern areas, especially during a cool, wet May, I've seen these plants not start growing until early June. Select an errant branch on the trumpet to prune to see if it's green inside. Watch for new growth from the base of butterfly bushes if the tops died back in winter.

Watch for new growth above the graft union on roses. If the stem above the graft is dead, but new growth is emerging from the roots, remember that the root variety is *different* than the shoot variety on grafted roses, so you can either wait and see what the rose looks like or replace it. Roses grown on their own rootstock will always be the same variety.

For gardeners along the coast, salt spray and salt water are hazards for many perennials. Select

■ *Black Lace elderberry features finely cut, purple leaves with attractive white flowers and black berries. It's a good substitute for Japanese maples in colder or coastal regions.*

flowers that can tolerate salt spray, especially if you're planting in an exposed area. Even if you aren't right on the coast, storms can blow salt spray inland for *miles*. For salt-tolerant perennial flowers try yarrow, foxglove, seathrift, coral bells, phlox, sea holly, fleabane, lavatera, sedum, reed feather grass, and fountain grass. For vines, grow Virginia creeper, climbing honeysuckle, and climbing hydrangea.

SHRUBS & TREES

Check fall-planted trees and shrubs for signs of life. Some trees and shrubs, such as birch, beech, honeysuckle, and aspen, leaf out early. On these trees and shrubs it will be easy to see the amount of winter damage and survival rate. Trees and shrubs that leaf out late, such as black locust, hickory, white oak, ash, and buttonbush (*Cephalanthus*), should be given time to leaf out before deciding what survived winter. For those that are dead, check your guarantees at local garden centers for replacement plants.

Coastal gardeners looking for shrubs and trees that are salt-spray tolerant can try these:

Shrubs: Beach plum, blueberry, common lilac, elderberry, forsythia, honeysuckle, Japanese lilac, juniper, mock orange, potentilla, rugosa rose, serviceberry, spirea, viburnum

Trees: Apple, Austrian pine, black locust, blue spruce, chamaecyparis, crabapple, hawthorn, horse chestnut, linden, mugo pine, Norway maple, tamarack

PLANT

ANNUALS

Continue to harden off annual flowers grown indoors under lights for planting in May. (See March Care, Annuals.)

Pot up flowers, grown yourself or purchased, into containers using the "Thriller, Filler, and Spiller" technique. This technique allows you to maximize the amount of color in your container by growing plants that rise above and fall below the pot.

Plant annuals into the ground based on your last frost date for your area. In southern regions early to mid-May is the last expected frost, while

■ *Choose evergreen shrubs that fit the space you have and won't grow out of control as they get older.*

■ *Evergreen trees can have a variety of needle colors depending on the type. Chamaecyparis with blue-green needles make attractive additions to a tree and shrub border.*

northern mountains should wait until Memorial Day. Unless you're growing cold-tolerant annuals, such as pansies and snapdragons, it's best to err on the side of caution and wait to plant until you're sure frost isn't expected.

Space annuals based on what's indicated on the plant tag, and plant at the same depth there were in the container. Gently squeeze the container to remove the rootball without damaging it. For peat moss, cow pot, and other biodegradable containers,

HERE'S HOW

TO PLANT A THRILLER, FILLER, AND SPILLER CONTAINER

- Thriller plants are those planted in the center of the pot. These plants are upright growing and have attractive foliage or flowers. Some good examples are canna lilies, yucca plants, and fountain grass. It's best to start with your thriller plant and then build the other plants around it.

- The filler plants are mounding plants that will "fill" in around the thriller plant. Not only does this add color to the container, it can also hide an unattractive stem of the thriller plant. Look for plants that complement or contrast well with the thriller plant for leaf texture and flower color. Some good examples of filler plants include coleus, begonias, and 'Profusion' zinnias.

- The spiller plants are the cascading varieties that will "spill" over the pot edge, extending your attention all the way to the ground. These plants are tucked in next to the fillers. Some good annuals to grow include bacopa, scaevola, calibrachoa, and petunias.

gently break some of the bottom and sides of the pot and plant the annual, pot and all, in the soil. This will help the roots reach the native soil as the biodegradable pot decomposes. If you don't break up the pot, it may inhibit early root growth. Be sure the top of the pot is *below* the soil line so water isn't wicked away from the rootball.

Some flowers can be grown as transplants or sown directly into the ground. Transplants will flower sooner, but using seeds is less expensive, especially if you're planting many flowers. Sow seeds of annual flowers such as nasturtiums, zinnias, cosmos, sunflowers, and cleome after all danger of frost has passed (see Here's How To Sow Seeds Outdoors). You can sow in rows or broadcast over the bed. Rows are good for seeds such as sunflowers, zinnias, and nasturtiums. Broadcasting is good for seeds such as cleome, California poppies, and cosmos.

BULBS

Wait to plant tender summer bulbs, such as gladiolus, dahlias, and canna lilies, until the *end* of May or June in all areas. There's no rush getting these in the ground because they need warm soil temperatures to grow their best. The exception would be if you're growing these flowers in containers. Then pot them up earlier and protect them from cold nights.

For those bulbs you started indoors, transplant them out into the garden at the same depth they were growing in their container.

Plant canna lilies 4 to 6 inches deep and 1 to 2 feet apart. Dahlias should be planted 4 inches deep and 2 feet apart. Tuberous begonias should be planted only 1 inch deep and 1 foot apart.

Start planting gladiolus corms after your last frost date. Plant corms 4 inches deep and 1 foot apart in rows if you are growing them for cutting. Otherwise space them among other annual and perennial flowers. To ensure cutting flowers are available all summer, plant in stages, every two weeks from May to the end of June.

For any spring-flowering bulbs you forced indoors this winter and are trying to grow out in the garden, plant them outdoors now. (Later, cut back the leaves once they yellow; the bulbs go dormant in summer.)

HERE'S HOW

TO SOW SEEDS OUTDOORS

1. Create a bed amended with compost.

2. Decide if you will broadcast the seeds randomly over the bed or sow seeds in rows. For rows, make a 1-to-2-inch furrow in the bed with a garden trowel and sow seeds in the furrow. Larger seeds, such as sunflowers, should be planted deeper than smaller seeds, such as cleome. Space the seeds according to the seed package directions. Cover with garden soil.

3. For broadcasting, sprinkle seeds on top of the bed. Cover with soil to the proper depth for those seeds (see the seed packet).

4. Tamp down the soil and water.

5. Once the seeds emerge, you'll probably have to thin them to their final spacing in both methods.

6. Label the row or bed with the flower and variety so you know what to look for when seedlings emerge from the soil in a few weeks.

■ **Bulbs**, *such as daffodils, go dormant after flowering. Now is a good time to dig and move daffodils that aren't flowering.*

■ *Plant gladiolus* **corms** *once the soil warms.*

■ *Iris* **rhizomes** *are visible on the soil surface. Divide irises this summer after flowering if your irises aren't blooming well or have a dead area in the center of the plant.*

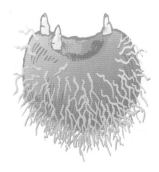

■ *Caladium* **tubers** *can be planted once the soil has warmed. These are great shade-loving foliage plants.*

EDIBLES

May is time to plant the vegetable garden. When to plant is best dictated by the average frost date in your area. This can run from early to the end of May, depending on your location. Cool, wet weather may mean planting a little later, while hot, sunny, dry days may mean planting earlier. You certainly can push the season by planting earlier and protecting seedlings with floating row covers, cold frames, and other devices.

Harden off seedlings grown indoors following the steps described in March Care, Annuals.

Check this list to help you decide when to plant which vegetables (plants or seeds). In southern areas some of these veggies, such peas and radishes, may already have been planted in April (see April Plant, Edibles). Because May's weather is so variable, you may plant cold-hardy vegetables and herbs later in the month than indicated, but rarely will you plant the frost-tender vegetables earlier than noted.

Plant your vegetable and herb seeds following the Plant, Annuals instructions. Plant transplants following the description for annual flowers.

For warm-season vegetables, such as melons, tomatoes, and peppers, lay black or red plastic down over the planting bed one week before planting. This will heat up the soil. To plant, poke holes in the plastic at the proper spacing and place your transplants in those holes.

Plant asparagus crowns now. Purchase them from the local garden center or through the mail. Dig a trench 6 to 10 inches deep and wide enough to space the asparagus crowns 12 inches apart. With average yields, about ten plants per person is right for asparagus lovers. In the bottom of the trench, make a small mound of soil and drape the spiderlike asparagus crowns over the mound. Fill the trench with native soil (not amended), covering the crowns so they're 3 inches deep. Water well. After six weeks, backfill the remaining native soil into the trench to the soil line (make a note in your garden notebook to follow up).

Plant raspberry and blackberry plants now. Clear an area in full sun, removing weeds, sod, and other plants. Amend the soil well with layer 2 to 4 inches thick of compost and till it under. Plant bare-root plants (ordered through the mail) following the

■ *Space bean seeds the proper distance apart in rows so that they grow strong and you don't have to thin them.*

guidelines in April Plant, Roses. Or plant container berry plants purchased locally and follow the guidelines for planting container shrubs in April Plant, Roses. Keep plants well watered.

Two Weeks before Last Frost (Frost Tolerant): Beet, broccoli, cabbage, carrot, cauliflower, celery, kale, kohlrabi, leek, lettuce, onion, parsley, parsnip, peas, potato, radish, rutabaga, Swiss chard, turnip

At Last Frost Date: Bush bean, edamame, pole bean, sweet corn

One to Two Weeks after Last Frost (Frost Sensitive): Basil, cucumber, eggplant, melon, pepper, pumpkin, summer squash, sweet potato, tomato, watermelon, winter squash

LAWNS & GROUNDCOVERS

Aerate lawns if you haven't already in April (see April Care, Lawns).

Sow a new lawn or patch bare spots in an existing lawn now, or install sod (see April Plant, Lawns).

Plant groundcovers after your last frost date.

PERENNIALS & VINES

Harden off any perennial flowers growing indoors under grow lights (March Care, Annuals).

Plant perennial flowers now. Dig a hole slightly larger than the rootball. Loosen the soil around the hole. Amend the planting hole with compost and plant at the same depth as the transplants are growing in their pots. Label the plant and variety.

Sow perennial flower seeds such as black-eyed Susans, coneflowers, and dianthus. Prepare the soil as you would for annual flowers. Broadcast seeds over the area and cover with garden soil to the proper depth for that seed. Thin to the spacing indicated on the seeds packet. Water well.

Dig and divide summer- and fall-blooming perennials such as hosta, aster, and tall phlox now (see April Care, Perennials).

Plant perennial vines, such as clematis, Virginia creeper, and climbing honeysuckle, following the

guidelines on how to plant a shrub (April Plant, Shrubs & Trees). Understanding how vines attach themselves will help you decide where to plant and what structure to use to support them. Clinging vines, such as Boston ivy and Virginia creeper, have suction cups that attach to walls, boards, and solid fences. Sprawling vines, such as climbing roses and trumpet vines, need to be tied to a trellis or support. Twining vines, such as grapes and clematis, have tendrils that attach to whatever they grab. They need a sturdy fence or a structure with thin boards to wrap themselves around and hold on to.

ROSES

It's rose planting time. Wait until after your last frost date to plant container roses (April Plant, Roses). Finish planting bare-root roses as well (April Plant, Roses).

Plant potted miniature roses growing indoors into new containers outdoors or into the garden.

SHRUBS & TREES

Bare-root and container shrubs and trees, and those that have been balled and burlapped, can be planted now, following the guidelines in April Plant, Shrubs & Trees.

In very poor soils such as heavy clay, consider raising the soil level by building a mound of soil. This will help the soil dry out faster and avoid the shrub or tree developing root rot.

Amend the soil for acid-loving shrubs such as rhododendrons, blueberries, and hydrangeas, based

■ *Plant bare-root roses by digging a good-sized hole and making a cone of soil at the bottom. Lay the roots over the cone of soil and back fill it with native soil. Keep it well watered.*

TO PLANT GROUNDCOVERS

1. *Amend the soil with compost and turn it under.*

   Select flats of groundcovers from your local garden center, following the guidelines on Here's How To Calculate the Number of Plants You Need (March Plan, Lawns & Groundcovers).

2. *It's best to stagger the groundcover plantings so they fill in faster. Space plants based on the recommendations on the plant labels.*

   If planting small plants or plugs, dig the hole just large enough for the roots and tuck them in well. If planting larger plants in containers, plant as you would a perennial flower (May Plant, Perennials).

   If growing a groundcover on a steep slope, create a flat spot in the slope to plant and mound up soil on the slope side to hold the plant and water.

3. *Water well and keep the bed well weeded until the plants establish.*

on a soil test. Follow the guidelines on the fertilizer bag for the right amount of lime or sulfur to add to raise or lower the pH.

Create a moat around the drip line of a shrub or tree to hold water. This will keep any water you add in the area where the roots are growing.

CARE

ANNUALS

When direct-seeded annuals begin to germinate, thin plants to their proper spacing as indicated in the seed packet. Thin once the true leaves (second set) form. Remove the weakest-looking seedlings.

Pinch back annual flower transplants that are leggy or have errant branches. Pinch them to just above a side branch to encourage bushier growth.

Stake tall-growing annuals, such as larkspur and tall cosmos, before the plants get larger. By placing a stake early in the season, you'll cause less root damage and will be able to attach the stems of these tall annuals to the stake with plant ties as they grow.

Thin out self-sown seedlings of cleome, nicotiana, and calendula in areas that you don't want them. Thin any seedlings intentionally left behind to their proper spacing and move other seedlings to other parts of the garden.

BULBS

Continue removing dead flowers on late-blooming bulbs such as hyacinth, but let the foliage naturally yellow before removing.

Mow around naturalized bulbs in the lawn, trying not to mow the leaves until they start to yellow. This may make your lawn look shaggy for a while, but it's essential for the bulbs to replenish their energy for next year's flowering.

Stake gladiolus corms as they grow if you desire perfectly straight flower stalks for cutting.

EDIBLES

Continue to harden off the remaining vegetable and herb seedlings you've been growing indoors under grow lights (March Care, Annuals).

Harvest asparagus spears on established beds when the spears are at least the diameter of a pencil and 8 inches tall. Cut the spears just below the soil line.

Harvest rhubarb leaves on established plants, removing the lower leaves first, discarding the leaf, and using the leaf petiole (or stalk) for cooking. Remove any rhubarb flower stalks that form: they take energy away from the leaf formation.

Thin out seeded cool-weather crops of lettuce, carrot, beet, radish, Swiss chard, and kale seedlings as they germinate and true leaves form. Use these thinnings in salads.

LAWNS & GROUNDCOVERS

Lawns in our whole area will need mowing by May. Mow lawns to 3 inches tall for the best growth. Mowing high allows the grass to develop a strong root system that results in a lush lawn. A thick lawn is your best deterrent for weeds and will be less likely to suffer during dry periods.

Use a mulching mower or traditional mower with a mulching blade. Mulching blades chop the grass clippings into small pieces so they decompose into the lawn faster. It's better to leave the clippings than to pick them up because these clippings can add up to one-third of the nitrogen needs of your lawn. The exception would be if you allow your lawn to grow too tall due to rainy weather. Ideally, you should never let your lawn grow to more than 4 to 5 inches tall so you won't take off more than one-third of the total height of grass blade at any one mowing. This prevents the grass from getting scalped and not growing strongly. However, if you must mow when it's high and have piles of dead grass on your lawn, then it's best to rake and remove the dead grass so it doesn't smother your lawn.

Spread corn gluten organic herbicide when the forsythia is in full bloom to kill crabgrass seed as it germinates. (See April Problem-Solve, Lawns.)

PERENNIALS & VINES

Place cages around shrubby herbaceous perennials that will flop with age, such as peonies and baptisia, as they start growing. Use grow-through rings that allow the stems and leaves to grow though the cage, hiding the ring with the foliage and flowers. Another option is to make a chicken-wire cage and wrap it around the plant. Place these cages around plants now, before they get too big.

Thin out self-sown seedlings of black-eyed Susans, California poppies, dianthus, and coneflowers in areas where you don't want these plants. Thin to the proper spacing for these plants. Transplant the thinnings into other areas as needed.

Deadhead early-blooming perennials, such as iris and bleeding hearts. Some early-blooming perennials, such as dianthus, will rebloom once deadheaded.

Pinch back the tops of tall, later-blooming perennials, such as bee balm and phlox, to encourage more branching and flowering. This is also a good technique to delay flowering and reduce their height.

After your last frost date, move overwintered tropical vines in containers, such as mandevilla, back outdoors gradually, getting them used to the light and wind.

ROSES

If you haven't removed the winter mulch or protection already, do so now. Use the bark or wood chips as a mulch around your rose bushes.

Finish pruning your roses as described in April Care, Roses.

Remove or transplant rose suckers (new plants growing from the roots) that are growing in areas you don't want. Species roses and old-fashioned roses make good hedges because of their vigorous suckers. However, in the garden, these suckers can take over. To transplant, use a sharp spade to dig around the sucker and sever it from the mother plant. Dig up a small rootball with the plant and move it to a new location. Keep the transplant well watered and prune its top to force it to branch into a shrub.

SHRUBS

Once spring-flowering shrubs, such as rhododendrons, lilacs, spirea, and forsythia, finish blooming, prune to shape the plant. You have about a six-week window to prune these spring bloomers before they set their flowers for next year. In general, don't prune after July 1.

Prune overgrown shrubs back by one-third to stimulate new growth. For lilacs, do a three-year rotational pruning (see June Care, Shrubs).

Prune summer-blooming shrubs that bloom on new wood, such as panicle hydrangea, bigleaf hydrangea, summersweet (*Clethra*), and butterfly bushes (*Buddleja*). This will stimulate more new wood and, consequently, more flowering. Prune crowded, diseased, or broken branches back to the ground or a main branch.

Move overwintered shrubs growing in containers, such as blueberries, back outdoors with the warm weather. As with hardening off seedlings, slowly acclimate the plants to the weather by bringing them out for a few hours the first day. Gradually increase the time outdoors in the sun and wind for one week, then leave them outdoors for the summer.

TREES

Mulch around trees with an organic product such as shredded bark, bark chips, or wood chips. Organic mulch conserves soil moisture, adds organic matter to the soil as it decomposes, and prevents weed growth. Avoid piling new mulch on old and

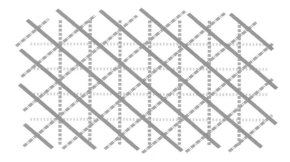

■ *Mow lawns in alternating patterns so that the grass is cut evenly.*

■ *Mow lawns frequently, never removing more than one-third of the grass height during any mowing.*

creating volcano mulch, and don't pile the mulch near a tree trunk. (See April Care, Shrubs & Trees).

WATER

ANNUALS & EDIBLES

Keep newly planted seedlings and seeds moist. Apply water as soon as the top few inches of soil dry out. This can happen daily during periods of windy, sunny weather.

Once seedlings germinate, begin to water more deeply, to a soil depth of 4 to 6 inches. This will encourage the root systems to go deeper into the soil, and the plants will be less susceptible to drying out in summer.

Water containerized annual flowers, vegetables, and herbs when the potting mix is dry, until the water drains out of the drainage holes. If you forget and the container dries out completely, the soil will shrink, creating a space along the pot edge. Any watering you do from the top will just run out of the container along the edge of the pot without soaking the rootball. To avoid this, place the container into a larger container or tub with water in the bottom and let the water slowly soak back into the soil from the bottom.

Keep newly planted berries, such as raspberries, blackberries, strawberries, and blueberries, evenly moist. Some, such as blueberries, have shallow root systems and may need more frequent watering to keep the roots growing strong.

Keep asparagus and rhubarb well watered during dry periods (see April Water, Edibles).

LAWNS & GROUNDCOVERS

Keep newly seeded lawns and bare patches well watered with at least 1 inch of water a week.

Keep newly planted groundcovers well watered. Keep the soil evenly moist and water to a depth of 4 to 6 inches to encourage the roots to grow deeply into the native soil.

PERENNIALS & VINES

Water newly planted perennial flowers and vines well. Keep the soil evenly moist and water 4 to 6 inches deep to encourage deep root growth. Established plants should be fine as long as we get spring rains. If growing on sandy soil or during dry periods, supplement the rains by watering individual plants with a hose or watering can.

ROSES

Keep newly planted bare-root and container roses well watered. It's best to water infrequently and deeply to 1 foot.

Water container roses, keeping the soil evenly moist. Soak the rootballs until the water runs out of the drainage holes.

SHRUBS & TREES

Water shrubs and trees planted last fall and this spring regularly to encourage strong root growth. Water more frequently on sandy soils than on

clay soils. Trees and shrubs that are mulched with bark mulch will need less watering because the mulch conserves the soil moisture. Once the soil is dry to 6 inches deep, apply enough water so moisture soaks about 8 to 10 inches deep into the native soil. This will encourage the roots to get established in the native soil faster.

For established trees and shrubs, only water during dry periods. Again, use the "water deep" philosophy to apply water once a week.

FERTILIZE

ANNUALS & EDIBLES

Fertilize annual flowers, vegetables, and herbs at planting with compost or a small handful of an organic fertilizer mixed into the bed. Check for nitrogen deficiency on your young transplants. One week after transplanting, if the leaves are yellow, consider watering with a mixture of fish emulsion to give them a quick boost of nitrogen to green up.

Purple leaves on transplants of broccoli and cabbage, among others, are common in May because of the cool soils. It's a sign of phosphorous deficiency caused by plants being unable to take up the available phosphorous in the cool soils. This will naturally go away once the soil warms.

Fertilize strawberries with a complete organic granular product such as 5-5-5 before they flower.

BULBS

Spread a small handful of an organic granular fertilizer when planting summer bulbs such as dahlias, gladiolus, canna lilies, and tuberous begonias. Organic fertilizers are slow release and will gradually feed the roots of a plant as it wakes up and starts growing.

LAWNS & GROUNDCOVERS

Don't fertilize newly sown lawns now—wait until fall. In fact, if you're planning on fertilizing your established lawn only once, it's better to do it in fall than spring. (See September Fertilize, Lawns.) Fertilizer applied in spring goes mostly to encourage grass shoot growth. That's the quick green-up we often see after fertilizing. When

■ *Cage peonies or other flowers as they start growing to support the mature plants and flowers once they bloom.*

applied in fall, the fertilizer helps the roots grow stronger instead of encouraging shoot growth only. This makes for a stronger lawn grass that will green up faster and fill in quicker in spring.

PERENNIALS, ROSES & VINES
Fertilize as described in April Fertilize, Perennials, if you haven't already.

PROBLEM-SOLVE

ANNUALS & EDIBLES
Keep newly planted annual flowers, vegetables, and herbs well weeded. Weeding frequently in spring is a good way to kill newly germinating weed seedlings before they take over. If you're using a hoe, cultivate shallowly and be careful not to harm the tender roots of your new transplants.

Protect tender seedlings from cutworms (see April Problem-Solve, Annuals).

Keep rabbits and woodchucks away from newly germinating or planted flowers and vegetables with fences and repellents. (See June Problem-Solve, Perennials.)

Check for leaf miners on spinach and Swiss chard. Cover plants with floating row covers to prevent damage (see Problem-Solve, Perennials).

Prevent birds from pulling tender seedlings by covering the bed with a floating row cover until the seedlings are a few weeks old and large enough that birds won't bother them.

Check young impatiens plants for downy mildew. A virulent strain of mildew has lately been devastating impatiens plants throughout the East Coast. Some nurseries have stopped selling garden impatiens for this reason. Downy mildew causes leaves to turn yellow and drop, leaving just the impatiens stems. Often the undersides of the leaves will have a white, powdery growth. Once in your yard, it can remain for a number of years to reinfect plants each spring. The best solution is to grow garden impatiens in containers and grow resistant varieties such as 'Sunpatiens' and New Guinea impatiens in the ground.

Protect plants from slugs and snails.

To combat flea beetles, cover your radish, eggplant, and broccoli transplants with a floating row cover or dust with diatomaceous earth to prevent these small black-shelled insects from creating shotgun-like holes in the leaves.

Handpick the bright red asparagus adult beetles as you see them around asparagus. Drop them in soapy water to kill them and prevent them from laying eggs.

Protect grapes from black rot and other diseases (see August Problem-Solve, Edibles).

BULBS
The red lily leaf beetle is a relatively new pest affecting Asiatic and Oriental lilies. This bright red adult beetle emerges in spring as lily shoots grow. They feed and lay eggs on the leaves. The eggs hatch into sluglike black larvae that continue to attack the plants. Their feeding can defoliate lilies, weakening the plant. Handpick adult beetles in spring to prevent egg laying. Spray the larvae with Neem oil or spinosad organic insecticide to control them.

LAWNS & GROUNDCOVERS
During cool, wet periods in spring, mushrooms often pop up in your lawn. Mushrooms are harmless and just a sign that organic matter, such as buried stumps or branches, is starting to decay. Mow the mushrooms down if you don't like their look.

PERENNIALS & VINES
Finish weeding beds as perennials start actively growing. On unmulched beds, cultivate the soil shallowly to kill young germinating seedlings before they get established (see June Care, Annuals).

Watch for leaf miners on a wide variety of perennial flowers such as columbine, aster, delphinium, and chrysanthemum. These small insects create snakelike tunnels in the leaves. Leaf miners also attack vegetables, shrubs, and trees. For small infestations, just pick individual leaves and discard them. For more severe infestations, cover

■ *Use toilet paper rolls as cutworm collars to prevent this caterpillar from killing young transplants. The collars will eventually decompose and by then the caterpillars will be gone.*

plants with a floating row cover as soon as they start growing. After a few weeks, the plant will be large enough to withstand any future damage.

Aphids and mites are easy to dislodge from the new growth of perennial flowers, such as lupines, with sprays of water from the hose. They tend not to climb back up the stem once knocked down. You can also spray insecticidal soap to kill them.

Check bearded iris plants for iris borer. This caterpillar tunnels between the leaf layers, eventually making it to the rhizome. Their tunneling causes water-soaked streaking on the leaves and rotting in the rhizome. The best control is to examine the leaves regularly in spring and squish tunneling larvae with your fingers. For iris that are dying back early, dig up the plant and examine the rhizomes for telltale holes and softness caused by the rot disease. Discard these rhizomes.

Botrytis blight is a common fungal disease on roses, peonies, and many other perennial flowers. It thrives during periods of cool, cloudy, humid weather. The fungus attacks developing flower buds and causes them to shrivel and die before opening. To control botrytis blight, remove and discard infected flowers. Make a note to clean up the foliage and old flowers in fall. Space plants farther apart to encourage airflow. This will allow the leaves and buds to dry out more quickly, lessening the chance of infection. Spray an organic fungicide on developing flower buds to prevent the disease.

Watch for scale on hydrangeas and other perennial vines (Problem-Solve, Shrubs & Trees).

HERE'S HOW

TO CONTROL SLUGS AND SNAILS

Slugs and snails *love* cool, dark, moist conditions. They thrive in our New England weather, and if we have a rainy spring, they can be devastating to newly emerging seedlings and transplants. They feed at night and hide near plants during the day.

- Create an environment they don't like. Space plants farther apart and cultivate between them frequently. Spread crushed seashells, eggshells, or raw sheep's wool around plants. Slugs and snails don't like crossing these scratchy materials. Don't use mulch where they can hide during the day.

- Spread granular organic bait containing iron phosphate around seedlings. The bait lures slugs and snails to eat it, which kills them. This bait is safe for pets, wildlife, and kids.

- Use beer traps to lure the slugs and snails. Place a saucer of beer in the soil near their favorite plants. Sink the saucer so it's at soil level and fill the saucer so the beer is a few inches below the rim. The slugs and snails will stretch to drink the beer, fall in, and drown. Remove the slugs each morning and refill the saucer.

- On raised beds and containers, run a strip of copper flashing around the top edge. As the slugs and snails crawl up to get into the container or bed, they have to cross the flashing and will get a chemical shock that discourages them. Be sure to remove the slugs and snails from inside the bed and container first.

ROSES

Check rose leaves during periods of wet weather for blackspot disease. This fungal disease starts as yellow halos surrounding black spots on the leaves. If it's severe, the leaves yellow and drop and the rose bush can defoliate by summer. To control this disease, plant resistant rose varieties such as 'Simplicity', 'Knock Out®', 'Tropicana', and 'Angel Face'. Clean up the leaves and plant debris well in fall. Spray plants early in the season with *Bacillus subtilis* organic fungicide. This naturally occurring bacteria kill fungal growth.

Watch for rose rust disease. This appears in spring as rust-colored lesions on the leaves. If it's severe, it causes the leaves to drop. It spreads during periods of cool, wet weather. Plant disease-resistant rose varieties such as 'Living Easy' and 'Pink Meidiland®'.

Check rose leaves for rose slugs. These small, caterpillar-like insects are translucent. They feed on the undersides of leaves, skeletonizing the leaves. Small infestations are mostly cosmetic, but severe infestations can weaken the bush. At first sign of rose slug damage, spray Neem oil or horticultural oil to control them.

SHRUBS & TREES

Control tent caterpillars and mugo pine sawflies (see April Problem-Solve, Shrubs & Trees).

During periods of wet weather, watch for branch dieback on junipers caused by *Phomopsis* fungal blight. Prune out dead branches to live growth and sterilize your pruners between cuts so as not to reinfect the bush.

Although you might find leaf miners on lilacs and on birch, cherry, and other trees, it's rare that you'll need to spray to control this pest.

Scale insects infest a broad range of trees and shrubs, such as lilac, euonymous, hemlock, yew, azalea, pine, hydrangea, spirea, and boxwood. Scale insects have either soft shells, as with mealybugs, or hard shells, as with oystershell scale. Scale insects are often found in groups on small branches or along leaf veins. Their feeding can weaken a branch and eventually cause it to die. Soft-shelled scales and mealybugs also exude a sticky substance called honeydew when feeding. A fungal disease called sooty mold will often grow on the honeydew, creating a black, moldy growth. Encourage the natural predators of scale insects, such as ladybugs, in your yard. Soft-shelled scale can be easily removed from branches with sprays of insecticidal soap and horticultural oil. Completely cover the insects with these sprays to kill them. Hard-shelled scale is best controlled with dormant oil sprays in winter and horticultural oil sprays during the growing season. These oils will coat and suffocate the scale insects. Be sure to follow label directions about using oil sprays on various plants.

As soon as apple leaves and flower buds start to swell, they are susceptible to a number of diseases. The most common is apple scab. Apple scab causes characteristic black splotches on the leaves and eventually the fruit. If severe, the leaves can yellow and drop. Apple scab also attacks crabapples.

The best control of apple scab and other apple diseases is to grow disease-resistant varieties; 'Liberty', 'William's Pride', and 'Jonafree' are some of the apple varieties grown in New England that resist these diseases. Otherwise, you'll spray based on the weather to keep apple scab at bay. This fungal disease thrives during cool, wet weather. Check your local Extension office for timing of sprays for apple scab and what products to use.

Fireblight is widespread in New England, affecting apples, crabapples, pears, mountain ash, cotoneaster, and hawthorn. This bacterial disease causes the branch ends to turn black, making them look like they have been burned. It also causes the blossoms to die. Like apple scab, fireblight likes cool, wet weather to spread. Usually you'll see signs of this disease two to four weeks after bloom. Grow disease-resistant varieties such as 'Kieffer' pear, 'Empire' apple, and 'Adams' crabapple. Also avoid nitrogen overfertilization, which promotes young, succulent growth that is more prone to getting the disease. Prune off infected limbs 12 inches below the sunken canker, sterilizing the pruners with a solution of 1 part bleach to 9 parts water between cuts.

HERE'S HOW

TO CREATE A SUNNY PERENNIAL GARDEN

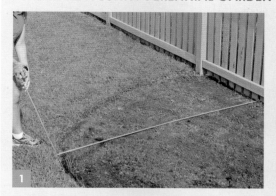

3 Use a four-tine claw or hard rake to mix the soil into the planting bed. In new housing developments, topsoil is scraped off and sold. Adding compost or garden soil replenishes nutrients and helps plants grow.

4 Set the plants out where you want to plant them. Stagger the plants so that they aren't arranged in straight lines. You can also create groupings with one of each type of plant and repeat the groupings in several places throughout the flower bed. If you know you'll have time to plant on the same day that you set out the plants, take all of the plants out of their containers before you set them in the planting bed—you'll save yourself a lot of time.

1 Measure the area where you're planning to plant the garden. Take length and width measurements and multiply them to get the square footage of the planting bed. You'll use these when calculating the amounts of soil, mulch, and plants to purchase for the garden bed.

2 Add 2 inches of soil or compost to the bed. To determine the total cubic feet needed, multiply the area of the bed (length × width) by 2 and divide by 12. (For 3 inches of mulch, multiply the entire area of the bed by 3 and divide by 12.)

5 Dig the planting holes just as deep as the rootballs of the plants. If you're planting larger perennials (plants in gallon-sized containers), use a spade or shovel for quick work. Really pay attention to the depth of your planting hole. Perennials can't handle being planted too deep. The top of the rootball of a plant should be level with, or just slightly higher than, the ground around it.

June

June is officially the start of summer. Long days and warm temperatures make the garden explode in color and growth. You really can feel that summer is coming into its own.

Work in the garden is shifting too. Most of your annual flowers and vegetables are planted for now. Many gardeners have planted shrubs, trees, perennial flowers, vines, and groundcovers, although in New England you can plant all summer and the plants will grow fine with proper care. There may still be some warm-season stragglers, such as sweet potatoes and melons, left to plant in the cooler regions, but the attention is now mostly turning to maintenance.

Weeding is the number-one chore in June. As warm temperatures and moist soil help your seeds and transplants grow, it also helps the weeds explode. June is a critical time to stay on top of your weeding or you'll be swimming in unwanted vegetation come July. One key is not to turn the soil frequently or cultivate deeply. This just brings weed seeds to the surface to germinate. Another key is mulching. After a good weeding, mulch to prevent more weeds from growing.

June is all about getting your young plants off to a good start. This includes replacing frost-damaged or disease-damaged seedlings. You still have plenty of time to reseed the squash or replace that petunia that a disease or animal devoured. Even if a plant is only partially damaged, it's best to remove it and start again. A healthy younger plant will outgrow the old, damaged one. Keeping young plants well watered and fertilized helps them grow well.

Watch for signs of pest damage. Because of the vulnerable nature of young seedlings and transplants, catching a pest infestation early is the key to plant survival. Often it's just a matter of handpicking insects or removing some diseased leaves.

It's not all work in the June garden. Harvesting early crops of lettuce, peas, and radishes boosts the flavor and vitality of our early summer meals. And picking flowers of early bloomers, such as iris and peonies, for bouquets helps bring the garden indoors—where their beauty enhances our lives.

JUNE

PLAN

ANNUALS & EDIBLES

Look for spots in your annual flower, vegetable, and herb gardens for additional plants. Some openings may occur due to plants dying or just not filling in well. Consider planting extra flowers, vegetables, and herbs that won't fit in your garden into containers. This is especially recommended for heat-loving plants such as eggplant, okra, basil, lantana, and pineapple sage. These types of plants love the heat, and if you keep the pots well

watered, they will reward you will plenty of food and flowers.

Plan on replacing any fruit trees and berries that didn't survive the winter. Try to understand why these young plants died. It could be due to the wrong hardiness zone or too much water or little water. Make adjustments before replanting.

BULBS

As bulbs fade, be sure to mark the ones you'll be replacing next fall with golf tees or plant markers

HERE'S HOW

TO PLANT TRANSPLANTS

1 To plant tomatoes and other vegetable transplants, dig a good-sized hole and loosen up the soil in the bottom and sides of the hole.

2 Squeeze the plastic container and gently lift out the transplant, making sure you don't crush the stem.

3 Place the transplant the same depth as it was in the pot. Tomatoes can be planted a little deeper and will root along their stem, making the plant stronger.

4 Press the same soil you dug out of the hole firmly around the transplant's roots and water it well.

and the locations of the ones you'll save. This will help you dig in the right locations later this summer.

LAWNS & GROUNDCOVERS

Plan on renovating areas that didn't fill in well from a spring planting with new grass seed. If kept well watered, the grass seed should still grow strong even with the early summer heat.

PERENNIALS & VINES

Continue to look for perennials that died over winter and replace these with hardier plants.

ROSES

Watch roses for signs of new growth. You should be able to tell which plants survived and which are dead. Try to discern why they died and select replacement rose varieties that are hardier and more adaptable to your soil and weather conditions. Some top reasons for rose death include cold temperatures and winds, animal damage, and wet soils.

SHRUBS & TREES

Replace shrubs and trees that have died over winter with hardier, more adaptable selections such as lilac, forsythia, spirea, maple, and oak.

Repair damage to established trees from storms. For severely damaged trees, consider cutting them down or removing the plant.

By June you'll have a good idea of the amount of shade cast by your trees. Consider removing some trees or limb some trees up to allow more light to enter your property and expand the palette of flowers and vegetables you can grow.

PLANT

ANNUALS

Finish planting annuals and replacing those that didn't fare well from earlier plantings in April or May. Gardeners in northern and mountainous areas should be planting warm-season annual flowers, such as moss roses, lantana, and geraniums, now that the soil has warmed. There's no need to plant these seedlings into cool soil in May because they need the warmth to flourish. See May Plant, Annuals for more specifics.

BULBS

Plant tender summer-flowering bulbs, such as canna lilies, dahlias, and tuberous begonias, in the ground, especially in northern areas (also see May Plant, Bulbs). Those planted in containers in May should be off and running, but the cooler soils mean waiting until June for in-ground planting is a better bet.

Continue planting gladiolus corms every few weeks to the end of June to have a continuous harvest of flower stalks in summer.

EDIBLES

Continue to sow and transplant warm-season vegetables and herbs, such as eggplants, tomatoes, peppers, squash, melons, and sweet potatoes. They are less likely to suffer from transplant shock due to cold weather if they're planted during the warm days of early June.

Remove spent crops of spinach and radishes planted in April and May and replace those crops with summer vegetables by succession planting. Succession planting means planting a new crop, of the same or a different plant, right after you harvest. Succession planting is a good way to maximize space in the garden and keep favorite crops, such as lettuce and beans, coming at a regular pace all summer. Whenever there is an empty bed or area in your garden, plant some of these quicker-maturing crops. Depending on the variety, you can plant lettuce, mesclun mix, kale, and other greens every two weeks throughout the summer. Making small plantings of bush beans every two weeks until the end of July will ensure that you have a manageable harvest of fresh beans into fall.

Another way to use space wisely in the garden is to intercrop. Intercropping is planting quick-maturing, small-sized vegetables in between slower-growing, larger vegetables. Some vegetables, such as squash and tomatoes, are spaced 2 to 3 feet between plants. In June this space can be used to sow mesclun greens, radishes, and lettuce. By the time the larger plants fill in, you will have harvested the quicker-maturing, smaller plants.

Another way to interplant is to add attractive edibles such as Swiss chard, hot peppers, and colorful lettuces between shrubs and flowers to

■ *To keep insects off your prized vegetables, consider laying insect netting over the plants. This also acts as a shading device during hot days, helping to cool vegetables, such as lettuce, so they can grow well.*

create an edible landscape. This is a good way to use extra plants and diversify your yard with edibles and ornamentals in various locations.

For gardeners with little space, consider planting vegetables in containers. There are many dwarf varieties, such as 'Terenzo' tomato and 'Little Leaf' cucumber, that fit well in large containers. Add lettuce, bush beans, carrots, and other vegetables around the main plant. Use the Thriller, Filler, and Spiller technique (May Plant, Annuals has more details), substituting vegetables and herbs for flowers.

LAWNS & GROUNDCOVERS

There's still time to seed a lawn (May Plant, Lawns & Groundcovers has more on this) or lay sod, especially in northern areas where the temperatures are still cool.

Continue to plant groundcovers, such as vinca, pachysandra, and sweet woodruff, under trees and on banks.

PERENNIALS & VINES

Continue to plant perennials right into summer. Garden centers still have a good selection of perennials in June, so shop for replacement plants or ones to add to a new bed (May Plant, Perennials).

Check the sturdiness of trellises before planting perennial vines such as wisteria and hardy kiwi.

ROSES

Finish planting container roses (April Plant, Roses).

Plant miniature roses in outdoor containers to dress up a patio or deck. Most miniature rose varieties flower on and off all summer.

SHRUBS & TREES

Continue planting container shrubs and trees and plants that have been balled and burlapped into summer (April Plant, Shrubs). New England summers are cool enough, and usually rainy enough, that these plants will survive. It's still best to plant in spring and fall, but summer planting works too if you keep the plants well watered.

Keep plants protected from the wind as you transport them home in a truck, and keep the root ball moist if you aren't able to plant the shrub or tree immediately.

CARE

ANNUALS

Deadhead spent flowers from annuals to keep the garden looking good and encourage more flower formation. To deadhead, pinch the flowers just below the dead blossom. Some newer varieties of annuals are self-cleaning, meaning they drop their own dead flowers and don't need deadheading.

Pinch back long branches of sprawling annual flowers such as scaevola, petunia, and calibrachoa. This will encourage more branching and flowering and keep the plant in bounds while still allowing it to cascade.

Weed annual flower beds now to stay on top of the germinating weeds. Generally you'll have two types of weeds in your garden: annual and perennial. Annual weeds, such as galinsoga and chickweed, have seeds that lie dormant in the soil. When those seeds have enough light and moisture, they germinate. Kill those weeds as they get started by shallowly cultivating the soil around plants with a sharp-bladed hoe. Perennial weeds, such a dandelions, quackgrass, and plantain, need to be dug out individually. If you just cut them off at the soil line, they will regrow from their roots.

After a thorough weeding, mulch with 1 to 2 inches of an organic material such as bark mulch, wood chips, or straw. Organic materials not only

■ *Prevent dandelions from invading your garden by digging out the roots when they are young and cutting flowers down before they go to seed.*

■ *Plantain weeds in the yard are a sign of compacted soil. Dig out this weed, loosen the soil, and add compost before planting flowers or lawn grass seed.*

prevent more weed growth, they also preserve soil moisture and add organic matter to the soil as they decompose. Another option is to mulch with crushed stone. Although it does not add organic matter, stone gives the garden a clean look.

BULBS

Mulch newly planted tender bulbs such as dahlias and canna lilies as described in Care, Annuals.

Stake tall bulbs, such as gladiolus and dahlias, with wooden or metal stakes. Attach the gladiolus flower stalk to the stake with plant ties. This will keep the stalk straight, making for a better cut flower. For dahlias, make a wire cage, supported by stakes, around the plant to keep tall varieties from flopping over.

Cut back yellowing foliage from spring-flowering bulbs to clean up the garden.

Dig up bulbs that didn't flower this spring and reset them in new holes amended with compost. Mark the area so you know where to look for these bulbs next spring.

Move amaryllis bulbs growing in pots outdoors if you haven't already.

EDIBLES

Support your tomato, eggplant, and pepper plants. For eggplants and peppers, use a small stake, attaching plant ties to the main stem or small tomato cages.

■ *Deadhead spent flowers, such as these cosmos, after blooming to encourage more flower buds to form.*

Grow vining edibles, such as cucumbers, melons, and summer squash, up a trellis. Cucumbers grow best on a 45-degree-angle trellis. On a vertical fence you may have to support the developing fruits of squash and melons with old nylon stockings or cloth.

Thin carrot seedlings a second time three weeks after your initial thinning, spacing plants 3 to 4 inches apart. Thin beets to about 4 inches apart. Use these thinnings in salads.

Harvest radishes, scallions, spinach, mesclun mix, and peas as they mature. For cut-and-come-again

Stake tall-growing bulbs so that they won't blow over during a summer storm.

Place bamboo stakes around the plant and wrap twine around the stakes.

varieties of looseleaf lettuce, such as 'Salad Bowl', either remove outer leaves, letting the inner leaves form more lettuce, or cut the whole head to within a few inches of the ground and let it regrow.

After harvesting asparagus spears for six to eight weeks, let the rest of the spears grow into ferns. This will help rejuvenate the asparagus crown for next year's crop.

Mulch cool-season vegetables, such as broccoli and cabbage, with untreated grass clippings, hay, or

straw. Hay is usually more plentiful and cheaper than straw, but it does contain weed seeds.

Mulch warm-season vegetables in plastic mulch when you plant (May Plant, Edibles). If you don't use plastic, wait until later in June to mulch with hay or straw so the soil has time to warm up.

Weed and mulch raspberry plantings and blueberries. Brambles especially like a 3- to 4-inch-thick layer of wood chips or bark mulch to eliminate weed competition and preserve soil moisture.

Harvest strawberries as they ripen. Remove rotting berries so they don't infect younger berries.

LAWNS & GROUNDCOVERS
Keep mowing your lawn at 3 inches tall to thwart weeds from growing and keep a thick, lush grass. Leave the clippings to add fertilizer to the lawn (see May Care, Lawns).

Mulch groundcover beds with a 2-inch-thick layer of bark mulch. Weed again so the groundcovers can fill in bare spots in the bed. For extra-weedy beds, consider digging up the whole groundcover bed, removing the weeds, and resetting the plants. Amend the soil before replanting with a layer of compost 1 to 2 inches thick and keep the plants well watered.

PERENNIALS & VINES
Stake tall perennials, such as delphiniums, once the flower stalk starts to form. (See May Care, Perennials for more details.)

Deadhead spring-blooming perennials, such as peonies and iris, to tidy up the garden. Cut back other spring bloomers, such as catmint and perennial geraniums, after flowering. This will stimulate the plant to send out a second flush of flowers.

Pinch aster and chrysanthemum plants back to 4 inches tall to encourage more branching and denser flowers in fall.

For perennial flowers that have flopped over in the past, such as Russian sage, 'Autumn Joy' sedum, and balloon flowers (*Platycodon*), pinch back the growth tips now to stimulate shorter, stockier growth. This may delay flowering as well.

Cut back to the ground any early spring bloomers, such as bleeding hearts, that are yellowing and dying back. Plant annuals to fill in the space they leave behind.

Mulch around perennials if you haven't already (see Care, Annuals).

Prune early-blooming climbers, such as climbing hydrangea, after the flowers fade.

Edge to dress up flower beds and prevent lawn grasses and weeds from invading your beds (more in April Care, Perennials).

ROSES

June is rose month in New England. Shrub, species, climbers, and hybrid roses all come into their own this month with a bevy of flowers. Species and old-fashioned roses only bloom once this time of year; don't deadhead spent flowers on these. The flowers will form rose hips, which will be colorful come fall. Rose hips also can be used to make tea and jams.

For everblooming hybrid roses and shrub roses, deadhead spent blooms to encourage more growth. Cut the stem back to just above a five-leaflet leaf. This will encourage better branching and flowering later in summer.

Remove any spindly growth from climbing, old-fashioned, and shrub roses by pruning out those branches to the ground. Also remove any errant branches.

SHRUBS

Prune spring-flowering shrubs, such as forsythia, spirea, lilac, rhododendron, bigleaf hydrangea, oakleaf hydrangea, and weigela, after flowering and before July 1. After that they begin to form flower buds for next year, and any pruning will

---

HERE'S HOW

TO SUPPORT TOMATOES

All but dwarf varieties of tomatoes benefit from being supported. Keeping your tomato plants off the ground results in fruits with less insect and disease damage. There are many ways to support tomatoes.

Stakes: Drive a sturdy wooden or metal stake next to the tomato. As the plant grows, loosely attach one or two main stems to the stake with plant ties. Pinch off any suckers (branches that form between the trunk and side branch) to keep the tomato plant a manageable size. This will reduce the overall yield, but it keeps the plant small.

Cage: Place a tomato cage around newly planted, indeterminate tomato plants. These varieties include most heirloom varieties that will grow into large plants. Purchase or make a metal cage that is at least 5 feet tall and sturdy enough to support the mature plant. I even place a metal stake through some of the rings of the cage and into the ground to help support it.

Trellis: Create a wooden, PVC, or metal trellis. A common version is to create two teepees connected with a horizontal pole 5 to 6 feet long, placed about 6 feet off the ground. Plant tomatoes under in a row under the horizontal pole and run sturdy string from the pole down to the base of the plant stem, attaching it to the tomato transplants as they grow.

eliminate those buds. The exception is if you are going to renovate an overgrown shrub. This can be done anytime in summer.

Replenish mulch rings around shrubs as needed, being sure to keep the mulch away from the trunk (May Care, Trees).

Prune hedges starting in June. Hemlock, yew, cedar, and privet make excellent hedge plants. These respond well to shearing, creating a thick mass of green. The key is to prune properly and often. Prune evergreens so the bottom of the hedge is wider than the top. This will allow sunlight to reach the bottom and keep those branches alive. If the hedge is completely vertical, light can't reach the bottom and the lower branches die and won't regrow. Using a manual or electric hedge trimmer, shear the new growth. Don't cut into the old,

woody growth or you'll create a hole that may take years to fill. Shear the hedge again in a few weeks or as needed.

TREES

Edge and weed under trees. Replenish mulch rings as needed, being sure to keep the mulch away from the trunk (see May Care, Trees). A mulch ring not only reduces weed composition and maintains soil moisture, it also provides a barrier between the lawn and the trunk to reduce damage from the string trimmers used to edge lawns.

WATER

ANNUALS & PERENNIALS

Keep new transplants watered well if Mother Nature doesn't provide it regularly. Water when

HERE'S HOW

TO RENOVATE AN OVERGROWN SHRUB

Some shrubs, such as lilacs and rhododendrons, can get *huge*. They often outgrow their space, crowding out other shrubs and encroaching on walkways. Also, the flowers form mostly on the top of the shrub, so it's hard to appreciate them. These shrubs need drastic pruning or renovation.

Many spring-flowering shrubs, such as forsythia, spirea, and lilac, can be cut to the ground or a few feet above the ground and will then grow back. The process takes a number of years, and the shrub won't flower during that time, but that's the easiest way to correct an overgrown plant. A better solution, for lilacs in particular, is to reduce the height over time by using a three-year rotational pruning technique. In this technique, you prune back one-third of the plant each year until you've reduced the height to an acceptable level.

1. In year one, select one-third of the oldest branches coming from the ground and prune them out at ground level.

2. In year two, take one-third more branches to remove in early summer. Remove any new growth forming from the roots so you have only three or four new shoots. Top these shoots to encourage branch formation.

3. In the third year, remove the remaining third of the tall branches. By now the first-year shoots should be large enough to start flowering. Remove all but three or four new shoots coming from the roots and top these.

the soil is dry to a few inches deep. Wilting plants don't necessarily mean the plant needs water; always check the soil first. If a plant is overwatered its roots will rot and the plant will droop. The solution is *not* more water, but rather cultivating around the plant to help the soil dry out.

Water in the morning to prevent having wet leaves going into the evening. Wet leaves plus a cool evening is an open invitation for fungal diseases to get started.

Check flowers in containers every few days for water. Check reservoirs of self-watering containers and fill as needed.

BULBS

Keep newly planted summer bulbs moist, adding about 1 inch of water a week. Sandy soils will require more frequent watering than clay soils, so check regularly for dry soil before watering.

EDIBLES

Keep young germinating seedlings well watered; check the soil daily. Raised beds dry out faster than flat beds, so check these more frequently. Older transplants and those with mulch around them will require less watering.

Use soaker hoses or drip irrigation systems with a timer to reduce the maintenance of these beds.

LAWNS & GROUNDCOVERS

New and established lawns will require 1 inch of water a week. The best way to know how much water you're applying to your lawn is to measure it.

Keep newly planted groundcovers well watered. Established groundcovers only need extra water during hot, dry periods.

ROSES

Water roses as you would shrubs. Water in the morning so the leaves don't stay wet into the evening. Fungal diseases, such as blackspot, thrive on wet leaves.

Keep container roses well watered, checking daily. Container roses that dry out will have yellow leaves that drop early and poor flowering.

HERE'S HOW

TO MEASURE YOUR SPRINKLER OUTPUT

If you're using overhead sprinklers to water your lawn, here's a way to measure how much you are applying so you know how long to run the sprinklers to reach 1 inch of water.

1. Place six to eight empty tuna or cat food cans randomly around your sprinkler.

2. Run your sprinkler until the water level in most of the cans is 1 inch deep.

3. Time how long you ran your sprinkler: that's how much time it takes to apply 1 inch of water to your lawn.

SHRUBS & TREES

Newly planted trees and shrubs should be checked every few days. Another way to understand adding an inch of water a week is that it's equivalent to adding 1 gallon of water per square foot. If you have a 2-foot by 2-foot planting hole, then you should be applying 4 gallons of water per week. Apply one-half of the water every three to four days. This should be enough water to moisten the soil 1 foot deep. On sandy soils you may have to apply more water and on clay soil less. Don't overwater: many shrub and tree roots don't survive well in waterlogged soils.

Winds can dry out shrubs even faster than warm temperatures. Protect newly planted shrubs from drying winds with a burlap screen until the roots can get established.

Established shrubs and trees that are well mulched shouldn't need supplemental water unless there is an extended drought.

FERTILIZE

ANNUALS & EDIBLES

Apply a soluble organic liquid fertilizer high in nitrogen, such as fish emulsion, to young transplants that have yellowing leaves.

■ *To prevent black spot fungal disease on roses, grow resistant varieties, space plants further apart; don't wet the foliage after noon; and try organic sprays, such as baking soda and* Bacillus subtilis, *to prevent the disease from spreading.*

Sidedress heavy-feeding vegetables, such as broccoli, tomato, and squash, with a complete granular organic fertilizer, such as 5-5-5, to encourage more production.

For container plants, regular watering is necessary to keep the container soil moist, but it will leach out nutrients from the soil. Apply a slow-release granular fertilizer that will release nutrients every time you water. Otherwise, mix in a soluble liquid fertilizer in your watering can and apply every two weeks.

Fertilize blueberries with an acidifying fertilizer, such as ammonium sulfate or cottonseed meal, once leaves emerge.

BULBS

Mix an organic granular fertilizer in the planting hole for summer bulbs such as canna lilies, dahlias, and tuberous begonias. Fertilize container-planted bulbs as you would annuals and edibles.

LAWNS & GROUNDCOVERS

If you fertilize your lawn only once a year, do so in September (see September Fertilize, Lawns). If you plan on fertilizing now as well, apply a fertilizer with a 3-1-2 ratio of nitrogen, phosphorus, and potassium. In some areas, applying phosphorous fertilizer is banned due to runoff causing pollution in waterways. Look for no-phosphorous lawn fertilizers at your local garden center.

PERENNIALS & VINES

Perennials and vines topdressed with compost last month should be growing fine. Fertilize only nutrient-deficient plants, based on a soil test.

ROSES

Shrub, species, and old-fashioned roses grow well with just a topdressing of compost. However, hybrid roses enjoy supplemental fertilizer throughout the growing season.

Fertilizer these roses at bloom time and again in July with ½ cup of an organic 5-5-5 fertilizer sprinkled around the drip line of the bush.

Some gardeners have heard of adding coffee grounds, banana peels, and Epsom salts to the soil to increase rose vigor. While these homemade fertilizers may have an impact, they are *not* substitutes for compost and proper fertilization.

HERE'S HOW

TO TIME SIDEDRESSING

VEGETABLE	WHEN TO SIDEDRESS
Beans, peas	No sidedressing needed
Broccoli, cabbage, cauliflower	3 to 5 weeks after transplanting
Cucumbers	When plant vines begin to run
Squash	At first flowering
Tomatoes, peppers, eggplant	3 to 4 weeks after transplanting
Lettuce, Swiss chard, greens	3 to 4 weeks after sowing/transplanting

Fertilize containerized roses more frequently, as described in Fertilize, Annuals.

SHRUBS & TREES

Only fertilize shrubs and trees that show signs of nutrient deficiency. Take a soil test to determine the proper fertilizer to apply.

Fertilize containerized shrubs and trees more frequently, as described in Fertilize, Annuals.

PROBLEM-SOLVE

ANNUALS

Watch annual flowers for signs of insect attacks on the leaves and flowers. The first line of defense should always be handpicking infected leaves or insects. Only resort to sprays, even organic ones, after you've exhausted other means of control. Pick and destroy leaves with leaf miner damage. Apply a vigorous spray of water to dislodge aphids on flowers, stems, and leaves. Handpick and destroy caterpillars feeding on flower leaves. Spray insecticidal soap to control thrips on flowers.

Protect containers of annual flowers from marauding chipmunks and squirrels with repellent sprays. These rodents love to dig around looking for food, and in the process damaging your flowers. Spray early before they get curious to thwart their digging (Problem-Solve, Perennials).

Continue to pull out perennial weeds such as dandelions, ground ivy, and quackgrass. Pull these weeds after a rain. This will make it easier to get more of the root system. Don't compost weeds such as quackgrass because the root pieces will survive and reinfect your garden when you apply the compost.

Watch for downy mildew on impatiens (see May Problem-Solve, Annuals).

BULBS

Continue to watch for the red lily leaf beetle adults and larvae and handpick to control them (read more in May Problem-Solve, Bulbs).

EDIBLES

Now is the time to monitor your vegetables for insect, animal, and disease attacks. If you can stop them early in the season, you're more likely to have a bountiful harvest. See the introduction for more on organic pest-control strategies. Here are some of the worst edible pests to watch for this month.

Cabbageworms: Monitor cabbage family vegetables, such as broccoli, cabbage, cauliflower, kale, and kohlrabi, for signs of the cabbageworm and cabbage looper caterpillars. Look for a small, white butterfly with a black spot on its wings. This butterfly is laying small, individual eggs on the undersides of the leaves. The eggs hatch to form small green caterpillars that feed on the leaves. You'll often see dark green droppings in the leaf crotches as a sign of cabbageworm feeding. If the cabbageworm caterpillar goes undetected it can damage young plants so they are less productive. Find and crush the eggs on the leaf undersides, cover the whole crop with a floating row cover so the adults can't lay eggs, or spray the organic pesticide at the first sign of damage.

Colorado potato beetle: Watch potato, eggplant, and tomatillo plants for signs of the Colorado potato beetle. This large, brown-and-yellow-striped beetle lays masses of orange eggs on the leaf undersides. These eggs hatch into orange- or red-colored, soft-shelled larvae that feed on the leaves. To control, handpick adult beetles and kill them. Crush the egg masses when you see them. Spray *Bacillus thuringiensis tenebrionis* to kill the larvae.

Cucumber beetle: Watch cucumbers, melons, and squashes for signs of cucumber beetle activity. These black-and-yellow-striped or -spotted small beetles start feeding on newly emerged seedlings and transplants. Their feeding can cause seedlings to die or be stunted. As plants get older, the beetles' feeding can transmit a bacterial wilt disease. To control cucumber beetles, handpick adults when you see them. Place a yellow sticky trap near the young plants. Cucumber beetles are attracted to the color yellow. When they land on the yellow card they get stuck and die. Cover young plants with a floating row cover, but check daily under the row cover to look for beetles that have snuck inside. Spray young plants with a light layer of kaolin clay. This organic product creates a dusty environment that the beetles don't like.

Protect plants and containers from slugs and snails (May Problem-Solve, Annuals & Edibles).

Continue to weed vegetable beds and lay mulch to stop weed growth (May Problem-Solve, Annuals & Edibles).

Place holographic reflective tape, aluminum pie pans, or old CDs in the strawberry and blueberry patches to scare birds away.

LAWNS & GROUNDCOVERS

Damage to lawns mostly occurs though animal digging and the feeding of insects on the grass roots.

Control grubs in the soil (Problem-Solve, Edibles).

Moles are often found tunneling in lawns. Moles are carnivores, so they aren't interested in your bulbs and plant roots. They mostly eat earthworms and other soil critters. However, their tunneling causes uneven spots in the lawn. Mole tunnels tend to have a pile of soil at the entrance or exit. Voles are small rodents that do feed on plant roots. They often use mole tunnels to cause damage. To repel moles and voles, spray castor oil. These creatures hate the smell and will get very active for a few days, then leave. Use castor oil recommended for animal control, not the type you get in grocery stores.

Clean up spotted or dying groundcover leaves, especially during wet weather, to eliminate any potential diseases. Keep the groundcover patch well weeded to reduce the incidence of disease.

PERENNIALS & VINES

Watch perennial flowers and vines for signs of disease and remove diseased stalks, flowers, and leaves.

Prune clematis stems that have blackened and wilted to remove disease. Disinfect the pruners between cuts to avoid spreading disease.

Protect plants from slugs and snails. (May Problem-Solve, Annuals & Edibles has more)

TO CONTROL JAPANESE BEETLES

This shiny, metallic green beetle with coppery brown wings feeds on a broad range of edibles, flowers, shrubs, and trees. They are particularly fond of grapes, cherries, raspberries, and roses. The adults usually emerge from the soil in late June or July in New England and feed most of the summer. Their feeding can defoliate plants, reducing yield and weakening them for future years. Here's how to control this pest.

- The young stage of the beetle is a C-shaped white grub in the soil. This grub feeds on lawn grass roots and can cause damage. It lives in the upper layers of the soil in June and August, so applying sprays to kill the grub now will reduce the number of adults that emerge later and protect your lawn grass. Spray beneficial nematodes on lawn areas around where the beetles like to feed. Spray in the evening and water it in well. These microscopic wireworms will parasitize the grubs.

- To kill the adults, handpick them in the morning when they're sluggish and drop them into a pail of soapy water.

- Cover prized plants with floating row covers.

- Spray Neem oil and insecticidal soap to control small infestations.

- Place Japanese beetle traps 200 feet away from your plantings, preferably upwind and only a few feet off the ground, so the beetles find the traps before they find your plants.

ROSES

Watch for rose chafer beetles feeding on rose and peony flowers and leaves. Handpick these brown beetles or cover plants with a floating row cover.

Continue to control blackspot and rust diseases (see May Problem-Solve, Roses) and Japanese beetles (see Problem-Solve, Edibles).

Watch for signs of powdery mildew on roses and other perennials. This fungal disease thrives during periods of warm, dry days and cool, humid nights. Leaves have white, cottony growth on their surface before they yellow and die. Grow resistant varieties, spacing plants farther apart so they dry out quicker, cleaning up dropped leaves, and spraying *Bacillus subtilis* or baking soda spray on the leaves at first sign of an infection.

SHRUBS & TREES

Continue to control scale insects on euonymous, lilac, and other shrubs. (Read more in May Problem-Solve, Shrubs & Trees.)

Continue to monitor and spray for apple scab and fireblight on fruit trees and crabapples (see May Problem-Solve, Shrubs & Trees).

Properly identify diseases that aren't a strong concern if the tree is healthy. Anthracnose disease causes leaves of sycamore, oak, walnut, and hickory to brown and drop. Rake to remove these leaves. Tar spot disease causes black spots on maple leaves. Although unsightly, the disease rarely causes permanent damage to the tree.

HERE'S HOW

TO PROTECT PLANTS FROM DEER, WOODCHUCKS, AND RABBITS

The best ways to thwart these animals are good fences or repellent sprays. Deer love a wide number of edibles, flowers, and shrubs. Hosta is often called "deer lettuce" because they enjoy it so much. Woodchucks and bunnies munch on many types of edibles and flowers. They only sure protection for your plants is a good fence.

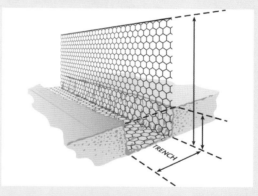

• Fence in the garden area with a 7-foot-tall deer fence around the perimeter of the garden. For a less-intrusive and less-expensive fencing option, try an electric fence.

• For woodchucks, construct a 3 to 4-foot-tall wire fence around the garden. Bend the bottom foot of the fence at a 90-degree angle away from the garden and bury that section under a few inches of soil. Don't attach the top of the fence to stakes. As the woodchuck tries to dig under the fence it encounters the bent section. If it tries to climb the fence, it will bend back and keep it out of the garden.

■ *Keep rabbits and woodchucks out of your garden by bending the bottom foot or so of your wire fence at a right angle away from the garden. Bury this portion underground. When an animal comes to the fence, their natural instinct is to dig their way under it, but they will encounter this wire apron instead.*

• Use a similar fence for rabbits, but don't worry about them climbing the fence.

• For repellent sprays, rotate three or four different sprays on plants throughout the growing season. Alternate sprays containing products such as garlic, hot pepper, rotten eggs, and blood so they won't get used to any one scent.

July

We're into the heart of summer. By July, your annual and perennial gardens should be growing strong. While many flowering trees and shrubs have finished their blooming for the season, some shrubs, such as hydrangeas and roses, keep the flower show going right into fall.

Vegetables and flowers in northern parts of New England that may have been up to two weeks behind in their growth and flowering have by now caught up to their southern counterparts due to longer days. The focus in annual flower and vegetable gardens continues to be on keeping up with weeding and watering. The weather is consistently warm, but watch out for the summer thunderstorms and occasional droughts that can occur throughout our region.

Pests start really being noticed this month, especially the nemesis of many gardeners: the adult Japanese beetle. It's important to stay on top of insects, diseases, and animal damage so your plants continue to thrive.

July is also when harvesting starts to come into full swing. Warm-season vegetables such as tomatoes, beans, peppers, cucumbers, and squash are ready to pick. Keep up with the harvest and your plants will continue producing. Annual flowers can be cut for indoor bouquets and to keep them in bounds.

Perennial flowers are in full bloom as we transition from a spring garden with blossoms of peonies, iris, and bleeding hearts to a summer flower palette of bee balm, tall phlox, delphiniums, and daisies.

July is also the time to start planning for your fall annual and vegetable gardens. Hard as it is to believe, you do need to think now about what you want in the garden come September and October, so you can extend the growing season.

July is vacation month for many gardeners, so make plans to have friends or neighbors look in on your containers and plants and water them as needed. While on vacation, take a look around at gardens in other areas. July is a good time to get inspired by gardens near and far and make changes to your own garden.

PLAN

ANNUALS

Take a look at your annual flower beds and pull out plants that are struggling or have been so damaged by pests and diseases that they may not survive. Look for replacement plants at garden centers.

Look for new plants to change out your flower containers if the flowers in them are looking ratty and need replacing.

EDIBLES

Start thinking about your fall garden. Now is the time to plan what crops can be removed soon to make room to plant cool-season crops for a fall harvest. Some of these, such as cauliflower and broccoli, will need to be started indoors from seed if you can't usually find transplants locally at a garden center.

LAWNS & GROUNDCOVERS

Midsummer can turn hot and dry in New England, depending on the year. Often lawns on sandy soils and in the hotter southern parts of New England will go dormant, turning brown, if they're not watered regularly. If you've been mowing high and leaving grass clippings on the lawn, you stand a better chance of your lawn staying green all summer.

Notice if your groundcovers are moving into areas you don't want them. You may have to pull some out so they don't become a weed.

PERENNIALS & VINES

How is your perennial flower garden growing? Which flowers are thriving and which are struggling? Make notes about which ones will need to be replaced, moved, or just cut back to keep to your original plan. However, remember that a garden design is a living, changing thing, and plants will tell you if they're happy in their location.

Notice if some of your vines are growing too rampantly for the space and make notes about pruning them at the appropriate time.

ROSES

While old-fashioned and species roses are probably finished blooming for the season, hybrid tea, floribunda, climbing, and shrub roses will continue all season long in spurts. If the weather turns hot and dry, their flowering may slow until it cools. Make note of which varieties are thriving and which may need moving or replacing.

SHRUBS

Look at shrub plantings in islands and around the house. Which ones are growing out of control and need pruning? Make note of which shrubs are being crowded out and need to be moved.

TREES

Assess the functionality of your lawn and shade trees. Do lawn trees need some lower limbs removed for easier mowing underneath them?

■ *Plant your fall and winter gardens now, selecting vegetables that will thrive during the cool days of fall, such as spinach, peas, broccoli, lettuce, and kale.*

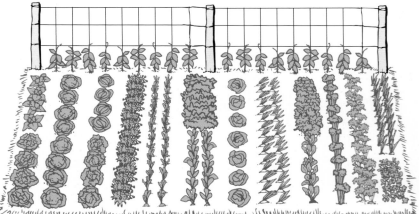

Are locations where you gather shady enough? Do you need to think about planting shade trees or building a shade structure to make your outdoor room more livable?

PLANT

ANNUALS

Early in July many garden centers are cleaning out their stock of annual flowers. Now is a good time to get some replacement plants and some cool-season plants for a fall container or bed. Transplants that have been sitting in a garden center all spring may be leggy, rootbound, and not in the greatest shape. That's okay, because with a little attention you can bring them back to health. Before planting, cut back the plants to a side branch or strong buds. Remove them from their pots, tease the roots apart if they are winding in a circle, and repot them. Fertilize with fish emulsion to give them a quick boost of nitrogen. Pamper them for a few days in a partly shady location before planting in a bed or container.

EDIBLES

Continue to succession plant. Remove spinach, lettuce, radishes, peas, and other plants that are mostly finished producing. Replace these with plantings of bush beans, heat-tolerant lettuce such as 'Summertime', kale, beets, and carrots for a fall harvest. The key to succession planting is to remove plants after their main harvest is finished but to *not* wait until they die completely. This will give you more opportunities to plant for fall.

There's still time early in the month to replant summer squash, zucchini, and cucumbers that died due to weather or pest attacks.

LAWNS & GROUNDCOVERS

July is not an ideal time to sow grass seed in southern New England because of our tendency for hot, dry weather. Even if you keep the soil well watered, the soil temperature may be too warm for proper seed germination. It's best to wait until September to renovate lawns. However, in northern and mountainous areas, the soil temperatures stay cooler all summer, so planted grass seed is more likely to be a success.

■ *Dig and divide bearded iris rhizomes now. Discard soft rhizomes with holes in them. Make sure each division has a healthy rhizome with at least one fan of leaves attached.*

Replace groundcovers that have died due to weather or pest attacks. Look for similar varieties so you don't have a hodgepodge of groundcover types growing in a bed.

PERENNIALS & VINES

Cut back bearded iris plants that need dividing after the leaves have yellowed. Dig and divide the plants (see May Problem-Solve, Perennials). Remove rhizomes with holes in them and those that are soft; discard them. Take healthy rhizomes with one 6-inch-tall fan of leaves and plant them in compost-amended soil in full sun. Plant deep enough so the top of the rhizome is still showing on the soil surface, with the fan of leaves facing upward. Keep well watered.

ROSES

Continue to look for container roses in garden centers to add to your collection (April Plant, Roses). Roses in garden centers should be in bloom, so it's easier to see the true color of the flowers and match them with other perennial flowers and roses in your landscape.

SHRUBS & TREES

Continue to plant container shrubs and trees and those that have been balled and burlapped (read more in April Plant, Shrubs). The July heat means you'll need to pay special attention to watering these new plants well.

CARE

ANNUALS

Continue to deadhead spent blooms on those annual flowers that don't self-clean. Pinch back the flowers to just behind the blooms. For cascading annuals, such as petunias and scaevola, you can combine deadheading with pinching back the stems so the plant stays more in bounds and sends out more branches.

Pinch back flowers on foliage annuals, such as coleus, so more attention is on the colorful leaves and not the flower stalks.

Stake tall, floppy annuals, such as cosmos, so the plants will be more upright and attractive when blooming. Secure the main stem to a stake with twine.

Cut flowers for indoor bouquets.

BULBS

Stake and tie tall dahlias before they grow large. Use wooden or metal stakes and wrap twine around the stems. Another option is to wrap chicken wire around the base of the dahlia to keep the whole plant upright. Next year, consider planting dahlias next to shrubs or woody perennials that will help support them as they grow.

For larger but fewer dahlia flowers, consider pinching off some of the side buds below the main flower bud. This will send more energy into producing a larger main flower. The opposite also works. For more but smaller-sized flowers, pinch off the main flower bud and let more side buds develop.

Stake gladiolus bulb flower stalks as needed if you're growing your glads for cut flowers (see June Care, Bulbs).

EDIBLES

It's harvest time in the vegetable garden and berry patch. Continue to harvest strawberries. Check beds every few days for more ripe berries. Hot summer weather will cause them to ripen fast.

Continue to harvest greens, such as lettuce, Swiss chard, and kale, as needed. Remove whole heads

■ *Harvest tomatoes when they're fully colored for that variety. Gently tug the fruit off the plant.*

HERE'S HOW

TO MAKE A FRESH FLOWER BOUQUET LAST

Fresh-cut flowers need water, food, and an antibacterial agent to help them last longer in a vase. Use these tips to preserve your fresh-cut flowers.

1. Cut the flowers in the morning while the air temperatures are still cool.

2. Bring the flowers indoors and recut the stem ends under water to prevent air bubbles from getting into the stem and blocking the flow of water up the stem.

3. Select the right-sized vase for the number of stems.

4. Add a solution of warm water and commercial cut flower food to the vase. There are also many home recipes to make cut flowers last longer. Some involve using aspirin, soda, and even pennies in the water. One popular recipe is to combine 2 tablespoons lemon juice, 1 tablespoon sugar, and ¼ teaspoon bleach in a quart of warm water. The sugar feeds the stems while the lemon juice and bleach lower the pH and keep bacteria at bay.

5. Change the water every few days to make the bouquet last more than one week.

■ *Prune whole branches of basil plants, not just the leaves. This will encourage new branches and large leaves to form.*

■ *To harvest mesclun greens and loose leaf lettuce, cut the plants just above the soil line with scissors or pruners. This will encourage the plant to grow back for a second harvest.*

■ *Harvest herbs for drying in the morning when the oil content is high. Snip the branches, group them, and hang the herbs in a well-ventilated indoor location out of direct sunlight.*

of romaine and head lettuce to open up room for succession planting for fall. Continue to harvest the outer leaves of greens. Once the flavor of lettuce starts to turn bitter or the plant starts to bolt, pull them and plant more crops.

Hill potatoes to create mounds of soil around the plants. This will provide more space for the tubers to form and is especially important in clay soils.

Hill sweet corn plants with soil to prevent the stalks from lodging over during a summer storm.

Pinch out suckers of tomatoes if you're trying to get an early crop and keep the plant size manageable.

Harvest root crops, such as carrots and beets, once they are large enough to eat. Use the tops in salads.

Harvest garlic when the bottom leaves start to yellow. Place the plants in an airy, well-ventilated place until the tops dry. Then cut off the tops just above the bulb and store for winter.

Harvest broccoli heads before the flower clusters open to yellow flowers. Once they open the flavor of broccoli becomes bitter. Cut the heads with a sharp knife and smaller side heads will form that you can harvest all summer.

Keep harvesting vegetables. For plants such as beans, summer squash, peppers, and eggplant, the more you harvest, the more the plant will produce. If you let the fruits form mature seeds inside them, the plant will stop flowering and producing fruit (because its job is done). So even if the fruits are overgrown, as with those monster zucchini, harvest them even if you won't use them so the plant keeps growing and making more zucchini.

Harvest herbs, such as basil, parsley, and oregano, as needed for eating fresh or preserving. When harvesting basil and creeping herbs, such as thyme and oregano, remove entire branches. This will encourage more branching and bigger leaves.

Dry herbs, such as lavender, by cutting whole stems, wrapping them with twine, and hanging them upside down and out of direct light in a well-ventilated, warm spot, such as a barn or garage.

After harvesting brambles, prune raspberry and blackberry canes that have finished bearing fruit to the ground. These canes will naturally die back in summer, but now is a good time to see which canes had fruit and which are the new canes that will produce fruit this fall or next summer, depending on your variety.

LAWNS & GROUNDCOVERS

Keep lawns properly mowed (see May Care, Lawns).

Apply enough water to lawns to prevent them from going brown and dormant. If water restrictions are in place due to a drought, you may have to let the lawn go brown. It will bounce back and green up with cooler, wetter weather. In fall, try overseeding your lawn with white clover to help it stay green even during droughts (read September Plant, Lawns). Clover has deeper roots than lawn grass and is better able to withstand drought.

Keep groundcovers in bounds by thinning or cutting back plants that are invading lawn, flowerbeds, or other areas. You can transplant some groundcovers, such as ajuga, and move them to a new location as you thin your main patch.

PERENNIALS & VINES

Continue deadheading spent flowers of earlier bloomers, such as catmint, hardy geraniums, and

HERE'S HOW

TO PREVENT DOG URINE FROM DAMAGING LAWNS

Whether it's your dog, a neighbor's, or just one wandering the neighborhood, frequent dog urination and defecation can cause brown spots and dead areas on your lawn that you constantly have to mend. Here are some tips to prevent doggy damage.

- Dog pee damage is more prevalent with dogs that squat to pee. The urine gets more concentrated in the location.

- The damage is caused from the high nitrogen and salts in the pee.

- Giving your dog supplements to change its urine pH won't work to prevent damage and may harm your dog.

- The best prevention is to designate an area just for peeing, with gravel or mulch. Fence out neighbor dogs that seem to wander over to your yard and use it as a bathroom.

- To repair brown spots, rake up the dead area, water well, and overseed in fall with grass variety similar to what's growing in the lawn. Keep well watered until the seed germinates.

delphiniums, to encourage new growth and a second flush of flowers.

Cut back flower scapes of daylilies after they finish flowering. Daylily flower buds and open flowers are edible, so try having some for a snack too.

Cut back errant stems on aggressively growing vines such as wisteria, trumpet vine, and climbing honeysuckle. Prune back to a side branch. This is mostly a cosmetic pruning to keep the vines looking good.

ROSES

Deadhead spent blossoms on roses (June Care, Roses).

Prune climbing roses after their flush of flowering is finished to remove errant branches and bring the whole plant back in bounds with its trellis. Adjust plant ties that are holding the branches to the trellis and tie up new canes to the trellis.

SHRUBS

Continue to prune evergreen hedges of yews, cedar, and hemlock (see June Care, Shrubs). On individual shrubs, clip back errant shoots to a side branch. Stop pruning in northern areas by the end of July.

Unless you're pruning to form a hedge, try to trim shrubs to accent their natural shape. Remove individual branches of shrubs, such as junipers, spirea, and pieris, back to a main trunk or side branch. Allow the shrub to grow in its natural form as long as it doesn't intrude on walkways, windows, and other shrubs.

■ *To get fewer but larger blooms on your chrysanthemum flowers, snip off a few flower buds now as they form.*

TREES

Clean up any limbs damaged by summer thunderstorms and high winds. Remove broken branches back to a main trunk or side branch. For large jobs, consider hiring a professional arborist. Talk to neighbors and friends about companies they have used.

WATER

ANNUALS, PERENNIALS & EDIBLES

Keep your annual and perennial flowers and vegetables well watered, especially those in containers. Follow the 1 inch of water per week rule for established plants. Plants growing in sandy soil and new plants will need more water (June Water, Annuals).

LAWNS & GROUNDCOVERS

If you allow your lawn to go dormant and brown in summer, leave it that way until rains come to green it up. Avoid watering it heavily once it's gone dormant, unless you can keep it well watered the rest of the summer. It's harmful to the lawn to come in and out of dormancy in summer.

ROSES, SHRUBS & TREES

Roses, shrubs, and trees need 1 inch of water a week, which translates to 5 gallons of water. It takes two to three minutes of watering from a hose to produce 5 gallons of water. Create a moat around the base of plants to apply the water where the roots are growing. Target newly planted shrubs and trees first.

For newly planted trees use watering sleeves, also called "gators." These plastic sleeves wrap around the trunk of your tree. They have pockets that hold water and slowly drip it out onto the rootball of the tree.

FERTILIZE

ANNUALS & BULBS

Only fertilize annual flowers in July that you have cut back due to errant growth, pest problems, or dieback. Select a fertilizer high in nitrogen, such as fish emulsion, to stimulate new growth.

—

HERE'S HOW

TO WATER WISELY

During drought conditions you may be under watering restrictions. You'll be faced with deciding which plants to water and which to neglect. Here's a list to help you decide.

1. Determine which plants are most important and focus your watering on those. If you're growing vegetables to save money, these plants would be a good place to start. Lawns, in contrast, can go dormant and brown and will recover with rainy weather.

2. Focus on young plants or newly transplanted plants that have smaller root systems that aren't yet established.

3. Refresh mulch on all your plantings to conserve soil moisture.

4. Water in the morning so the plant can absorb most of the moisture, losing less to evaporation.

5. Avoid overhead watering, which wastes water on walkways and paths and through evaporation. Use drip irrigation or soaker hoses on a timer so you're adding just the right amount of water. Create a moat around the base of a plant and fill it with water by hand. The idea is to concentrate the water where the roots can get it without wasting water.

6. Use self-watering containers that have a reservoir to hold water. The water naturally migrates to the dry soil, keeping the medium moist.

7. Remove weeds from the base of plants to eliminate competition for water.

Avoid adding high-nitrogen fertilizers to late-flowering annuals, such as cosmos and zinnias, and bulbs, such as dahlias, because it may delay flowering even further. In northern areas, this may mean you'll get a frost that kills the plants before you get to enjoy the flowers.

Fertilize tuberous begonias and other summer bulbs growing in containers. These are heavy-feeding plants and require flowering plant food every few weeks in summer to grow strong and flower. Also, keep these containers well watered to avoid fertilizer burn.

EDIBLES
Follow the instructions for sidedressing fertilizer for vegetables described in June Fertilize, Edibles.

Leafy greens—such as kale, Swiss chard, and lettuce—and herbs—such as basil—will benefit from application of additional balanced fertilizer, such as 5-5-5, in July.

Vegetables planted for a fall harvest, such as broccoli, cauliflower, cabbage, kale, carrots, and greens, need to be fertilized at planting with an organic granular fertilizer such as 5-5-5.

Fertilize renovated beds of strawberries after production has finished (see August Care, Edibles).

LAWNS & GROUNDCOVERS
Don't fertilize lawns in midsummer.

■ *Another way to fertilize tomatoes is to add compost to the plants when they are young. Compost slowly releases nutrients into the soil.*

Fertilize newly planted groundcovers with a balanced organic granular fertilizer, such as 5-5-5, only if they need a boost to get established.

PERENNIALS & VINES

Avoid fertilizing perennials now with a high-nitrogen product. Perennials grown in high-nitrogen soils or close to a lawn where a high-nitrogen fertilizer has been used will grow lush and tall, but will be delayed in flowering.

Vines rarely need additional fertilizer once they're established.

ROSES

Fertilize hybrid roses monthly with a rose plant food. Fertilize container roses every few weeks. Container roses need more fertilizer because they have less soil to absorb fertilizer. Also, the fertilizer leaches out of the container with rain and frequent watering.

SHRUBS & TREES

Don't fertilize shrubs and trees again until next spring.

PROBLEM-SOLVE

ANNUALS

Control diseases on your annual flowers by picking off and destroying infected leaves. Clean up plant debris around the plants. During wet, humid summers, powdery mildew, botrytis blight, and a number of other diseases can attack leaves and flowers. See Problem-Solve, Perennials for more on controlling these diseases.

Check annuals for aphids, whiteflies, thrips, and plant bug infestations. Check on the new growth and underside of the leaves. Damage can include stippling and yellowing of the leaves and flowers. Spray insecticidal soap to kill these common soft-bodied insects.

BULBS

Continue to monitor iris plants for borers (read more details in May Problem-Solve, Perennials) and lilies for lily leaf beetles (May Problem-Solve, Bulbs).

Check for thrips on gladiolus and dahlia flowers. The damage signs are yellowing, streaking, and spots on flowers and leaves. If you suspect you have thrips, take a flower and tap it over a white sheet of paper. These very small insects should fall off and be more visible. To control them, encourage beneficial insects, such as ladybugs, and hang yellow sticky traps around infected plants. Spray Neem oil or insecticidal soap.

Control diseases, such as powdery mildew, leaf spots, and botrytis blight, on canna lilies, dahlias, and tuberous begonias by cleaning up dead and diseased foliage, keeping weeds away, thinning plants to increase air circulation, and spraying an organic fungicide such as *Bacillus subtilis*.

EDIBLES

Continue to watch for and control common vegetable insects, such as cabbageworms, Colorado potato beetles, cucumber beetles, and Japanese beetles (see June Problem-Solve, Edibles).

Design your garden to attract beneficial insects, creating an ecological balance so you can use fewer sprays (see page 13 in the introduction).

Watch out for squash bugs. These gray insects are found on the undersides of melon, pumpkin, and squash leaves. A few squash bugs aren't usually a problem, but the population will build quickly and

HERE'S HOW

TO CONTROL BLIGHT ON TOMATOES

Early and late blight are probably the most well-known blight diseases, but *Septoria* leaf blight and bacterial speck can also infect plants. Depending on the summer, these blights can be devastating or mild. During cool, wet springs and early summers these blights thrive. They cause spots and yellowing of leaves, often starting on the bottoms of the plants and working upward. Some, such as late blight, cause gray, water-soaked spots on the leaves, killing it quickly. This disease needs to be controlled immediately by removing and destroying infected plants. If you do not, it can spread to all tomato and potato plants. Here are tips to control tomato leaf diseases.

1. Properly identify the diseases, using resources such as the Master Gardener organizations (see page 178 in the appendix) and your local garden center.

2. Follow proper sanitation rules. Remove and destroy brown-spotted leaves early in the season.

3. Mulch under tomato plants with black or red plastic to reduce the amount of disease spores splashing from the soil to the leaves during rain.

4. Spray preventive fungicides to thwart the disease. Copper and *Bacillus subtilis* have proven effective if used early in infestations.

5. Clean up tomato and potato patches well in fall to reduce the amount of disease spores in the soil. Late blight disease only survives on live tissue in the soil, so remove as many potato tubers as possible and any self-sown tomato seedlings in spring.

6. Next year grow blight-resistant tomato varieties, such as 'Defiant', 'Matt's Wild Cherry', 'Mountain Magic', and 'Iron Lady'.

■ *Adult Colorado potato beetles eat the leaves of potatoes and eggplants. They lay clusters of orange-colored eggs underneath leaves. The eggs hatch into red larvae that cause most of the damage. Plant resistant varieties; handpick and squish the adults, eggs, and larvae; and use the organic spray* Bacillus thuringiensis *variation san diego to kill the larvae.*

eventually cause leaf and flower damage. If you find squash bugs, collect and kill them a pail of soapy water. Look for the cluster of copper-colored eggs on the underside of the leaves and squish these as well. If you're diligent, this should be enough to stop an infestation.

Squash vine borers attack zucchini, summer squash, pumpkins, and winter squash vines. An adult fly lays eggs on the stem near the base of the plant. The eggs hatch, and the caterpillars tunnel into the stem, away from the crown of the plant. Eventually the stem wilts and dies, reducing production. To control squash vine borers, grow winter squash varieties that borers avoid, such as butternut. On all other squash, cover young plants with a floating row cover until they flower to prevent adults from laying eggs. Remove the cover to allow bees to pollinate the flowers. If you find holes and damage, gently slit open the stem to physically remove the caterpillar. Mound soil over the slit stem so the vine can reroot itself. You can also inject Bt into the stem with a syringe to kill the caterpillars.

Check tomato leaves for leaf blights. There are a number of leaf blight diseases that attack tomatoes in New England.

Prevent bird damage to your strawberries, blueberries, and cherries by covering the row or tree with bird netting or hanging reflective devices around the patch. See August Problem-Solve, Edibles for more tips on repelling birds.

Check raspberry canes for the raspberry tip borer. This insect lays eggs on the tips of raspberry canes and girdles the cane above and below the egg. This causes the cane tip to wilt and die. Although it is not a serious pest, a simple solution is to prune off and destroy the wilted cane tip to remove the egg and insect.

Raspberries and blackberries can be infected with virus diseases transmitted by insects. Insects, such as aphids, feed on wild brambles growing nearby and then spread the disease to cultivated plants. Signs of virus disease include stunted plants, disfigured leaves, and small, crumbly berries. There is no control for viruses once your plants have the

disease, so prevention is key. Always plant certified virus-free plants and remove wild brambles within 500 feet of your planting to prevent its spread.

LAWNS & GROUNDCOVERS

Watch for signs of grub damage on your lawns. These often are the larvae of Japanese and other beetles. Control grubs by following recommendations in June Problem-Solve, Edibles.

Keep weeds under control by mowing at least 3 inches tall to shade them out and growing a lush, thick lawn with no places for weeds to take hold (see September Care, Lawns).

HERE'S HOW

TO CONTROL MOSQUITOES

Mosquitoes can turn a beautiful yard into a nightmare because you can't enjoy it. Also, in New England a number of diseases, such as West Nile virus, have been linked to mosquito bites, so it can be a health issue as well. Mosquitoes like warm, wet weather, so their population changes based on the summer. Here's how to reduce the number of mosquitoes in your yard.

- Female mosquitoes lay eggs in standing water. Remove standing water from your yard in places such as clogged rain gutters, tree holes, discarded cans and containers, and the saucers of outdoor flowerpots.

- Kill mosquito larvae (young) where they live. If you have a pond or water feature, place mosquito dunks in them. This is an organic mosquito control using *Bacillus thuringiensis israelensis* (Bti) to kill the larvae.

- Use screens on outdoor porches and repellents on decks and patios at night, when mosquitoes are most active. Avoid using mosquito lights or zappers. These kill more beneficial insects than mosquitoes.

- Set up bird and bat houses to encourage natural predators of the mosquitoes.

■ *Cucumber beetles attack cucumbers, melons, and the leaves and flowers of squash. Their feeding also spreads bacterial wilt disease. Control cucumber beetles by covering plants early in the season with a floating row cover, setting up traps, and using organic sprays, such as pyrethrum.*

Many lawns can become infested with anthills. Although it's not a major problem on lawns, ant mounds are unsightly and can cause the grass to die around them. Ants are attracted to thin lawns on well-drained soils. To prevent them from taking over, mow high and keep your lawn healthy by practicing good lawn-care techniques (see September Care, Lawns). To rid lawns of existing mounds, try a number of home remedies such as sprinkling hot pepper flakes or orange peels in the area, pouring vinegar or boiling water on mounds, and spreading diatomaceous earth in the mound. A more reliable cure is to mix sugar and borax in a glass jar with small holes poked in the lid. Place the jar near the anthill. The worker ants will be attracted to the sugar and then bring it back to the anthill, where the borax on the sugar will kill the ants. The lid will prevent other animals and pets from eating the borax.

PERENNIALS & VINES

Design your garden to attract beneficial insects and create an ecological balance so you have to use fewer sprays (see the introduction, page 178).

Watch for soft-bodied insects, such as aphids and plant bugs, on your perennial flowers and control them (see Problem-Solve, Annuals).

Control leaf diseases, such as powdery mildew, on perennial flowers.

Decide on a strategy to control tenacious perennial weeds in your flower beds. Goutweed, horsetail, Japanese knotweed, and other weeds are common in New England. These invasive plants can take over a bed quickly if not controlled. The first line of defense is to keep these weeds from invading. Check any new plants you bring in for signs of these weeds, especially if they are pass-along plants from a friend or neighbor. Prevention is a lot easier than removal.

If you see the weeds in your garden, hand dig them when the soil is moist, trying to remove as much of the root system as possible. You'll have to be diligent about weeding regularly for a few years to completely eradicate these invasives. If the weeds have taken over, consider renovating the bed by removing any flowers worth saving and killing the weeds with a herbicide or with plastic laid over the bed. Find a new location to build a new bed. In areas you're trying to reclaim from the weeds, continual mowing will eventually weaken and kill these weeds.

Invasive vines can become a nuisance in our New England landscape. Oriental bittersweet and

TO CONTROL POWDERY MILDEW

Powdery mildew is one of the more common fungal leaf diseases on perennial flowers. It causes whitish growth on the leaves. The leaves eventually yellow and die. Phlox, bee balm, and aster are commonly attacked, but many other perennial flowers, annual flowers, and vegetables also get this disease. Here's how to control it.

- Keep the garden clean, removing diseased flowers and leaves as you see them.

- Plant disease-resistant varieties, such as 'David' phlox and 'Jacob Cline' bee balm. For downy mildew on impatiens, see May Problem-Solve, Annuals.

- Space plants farther apart and thin stems to create more airflow around the plant. Wet leaves enhance this fungal disease.

- Spray *Bacillus subtilis* or baking soda spray (1 teaspoon baking soda combined with ½ teaspoon liquid soap in 1 quart of water) on plants early in the season to prevent this disease from taking over.

HERE'S HOW

TO KILL POISON IVY VINES

First of all, be sure you aren't allergic to poison ivy. If you are, hire a professional to remove the vines for you. Here are steps to remove vines from your yard.

1. Wear protective clothing, including long-sleeved shirts and pants, sturdy boots, and goggles while working around poison ivy. Wash all the clothes immediately after working to remove the oil that causes itching.

2. Cut vines to the ground and grub out the roots, if possible. This should be repeated a few times during the season as new growth appears.

3. Avoid mowing or burning poison ivy because it just spreads the oil.

4. For tough-to-kill vines, use a systemic herbicide while the vine is actively growing. To avoid killing other vegetation, cut vines to within 1 foot of the ground, apply herbicide to the cut stump, and cover with a small yogurt container duct taped to the stump. This will prevent the herbicide from coming into contact with animals and other plants and allow it to be transmitted to the root system.

poison ivy are two of the most prevalent culprits. Cutting these vines repeatedly and grubbing out the roots is the most effective means of control.

ROSES

Watch for blackspot, powdery mildew, and other diseases of roses (see May Problem-Solve, Roses), as well as Japanese beetles (see Problem-Solve, Edibles).

Watch for signs of rabbit and deer browsing and take steps to control it (read more in June Problem-Solve, Perennials).

SHRUBS

Continue to control aphids and other soft-bodied insects feeding on the new growth of shrubs (see Problem-Solve, Annuals).

Watch for scale insects on lilacs, hydrangeas, and other shrubs (May Problem-Solve, Shrubs & Trees has more detail).

Control powdery mildew on lilacs (see Problem-Solve, Perennials). If you see lichens growing on lilac or other tree and shrub trunks, don't worry. The lichens don't harm the plant and actually give it an interesting look in winter.

If your everblooming mophead hydrangeas, such as 'Endless Summer®', *aren't* blooming, follow these steps. 'Endless Summer®' hydrangeas bloom on old and new wood. If the old wood died last winter, then the early flowers won't appear. The shrub may still bloom on the new wood, but that may be late summer, especially in northern sections. If you're applying too much nitrogen fertilizer to the shrub or nearby lawn area, this will cause large, leafy plants with few blooms. This winter, protect the canes with bark mulch (see November Care, Roses).

TREES

Check peach, dogwood, and other tree branches for signs of borers. Look for "sawdust" and holes in the bark. Push a piece of wire into the hole to kill the boring insect. Keep the tree healthy so it can recover.

Watch for spotting of leaves of trees such as maple, ash, and walnut (June Problem-Solve, Shrubs & Trees).

Continue to monitor and spray for apple scab and fireblight on fruit trees and crabapples (May Problem-Solve, Shrubs & Trees). Rake and remove infected leaves on the ground.

August

August is a rewarding time in the New England garden. If all has gone according to plan (if it ever really does), then you should be swimming in vegetables, fruits, and herbs and delighted by masses of colorful flowers blooming in your yard.

August can also be a tough time for watering and keeping up with the harvesting. Many people are on vacation early in this month, and the garden can take a backseat to going to the beaches of Long Island Sound, Cape Cod, or Maine. As in July, before you head out, give your garden and containers a good watering, set up some neighbors or friends to stop by to check on your plants while you're gone, and harvest thoroughly.

This time of year the harvest of edibles can be overwhelming. It's best to keep picking to keep the vegetables coming, but also not to waste the food. It's a time of canning tomatoes, freezing beans, and drying herbs. I find it's a lot more fun to do these chores with family and friends, some lively music, and a glass of wine or beer. Harvesting plums and peaches continues, and even some early apples and pears will be harvested later in the month. Consider donating extra produce to a local food shelf. Check with the food shelf first to see what types of vegetables they are looking for, when to bring them in, and the quantities requested.

Annual flowers are really shining now in the garden, with cosmos, zinnias, and sunflowers leading the way. Cut flowers for your home and give some as a surprise gift to a friend. The more you harvest your flowers, the more the plants will keep producing.

Alas, the pest onslaught continues. Second generations of pests, such as cabbageworms, are hatching and other pests, such as tomato hornworms, are showing up for the first time. Continue to be on the lookout for insect and animal damage and remove diseased plants. This is particularly important for summer-planted flowers and edibles that are still young and vulnerable.

PLAN

ANNUALS

Continue to make note of the annual flowers that seem to be growing and flowering the best in your garden. Note also which ones are duds and should be avoided next year.

Assess your annual flower containers with the same eye toward what's working and what's not. Note which plants are more aggressive and taking over their pots and which are more passive and being overwhelmed. This will help you plan your containers for next year.

BULBS

Catalogs filled with spring-flowering bulbs start showing up in your mailbox now. Take a first look at the offerings and consult your notes from the spring to see what types or which varieties you'd like to order to fill in gaps and replace those that died.

Look for places in your garden to plant fall-flowering bulbs, such as colchicum and autumn crocus.

EDIBLES

Continue to look for open spaces and plant fall vegetables. Pull out spent summer crops of bush beans and lettuce. Scout garden centers and farmers' markets for seedlings of lettuce, Swiss chard, and basil to plant now, or buy extra packets of seed to sow.

LAWNS & GROUNDCOVERS

The beginning of August can be hot and dry. But with tropical storms brewing and winding up in our region, in late August we can see some rain. This will bring lawns back into shape and give you the chance to see the bare spots that will need repairing next month.

Look at your groundcover plantings as well to see where plants have died or need replacing.

PERENNIALS & VINES

August is a good time to check out sales at garden centers. Often perennial flowers will be on sale now, offering an opportunity to redo a section of your garden at a lesser cost.

Make note of vines that are out of control and vow to do a better job of pruning them back in the winter and next spring.

Make note of perennials, such as daylilies, that have finished their main summer flower show for the season while the flower colors and sizes are fresh in your mind. Decide on moving or replacing daylilies that didn't work in the flowerbed.

ROSES

Keep cutting roses for indoor bouquets from hybrid bushes as they continue to flower. Look at the color combinations of roses in a cottage garden with perennials and annuals to determine if you like the look. Sometimes the flower color of a rose or perennial will not be the same as you thought. Weather conditions can cause some flowers to fade (bright sun) or be deeper (more clouds), affecting their look. Your plants may need some shuffling around to get the color combination you like. But also be open to nature's surprises. Often a combination you didn't expect to enjoy can bring great delight in the garden.

SHRUBS & TREES

Now is a good time to see if your shrubs and trees are performing as you expected. Look for shrubs or trees that are outgrowing the space allotted or struggling to survive. Make note of any changes and start looking for sales at garden centers next month for some inexpensive fall shrub and tree planting.

PLANT

ANNUALS

August is a good time to succession plant your flower containers. Some annual flowers, such as coleus and petunias, may be taking over the container right now, crowding out other plants. It's decision time. You can either remove the struggling, overcrowded plants and let the bullies take over, making this into a one-plant container, or you can remove the bullies and replant the whole container for fall. There's really no right answer. It all depends on your wishes and the health of your plants. Whichever way you go, prune back any remaining plants to keep them in bounds and stimulate new branches and flowers for fall.

BULBS

Plant fall-blooming crocus and colchicum later this month. Check garden centers for bulbs or order them through online catalogs. Find a well-drained location in your flower garden or under trees to plant. These fall-flowering bulbs will only send up flowers in fall and will bloom for two to three weeks. They go dormant in winter and will send up leaves next spring, but no flowers. If planted now, they should bloom six to eight weeks later.

Saffron crocus is a type of fall-flowering crocus that you can grow to harvest the stigmas for saffron. It takes a lot of crocus to get enough to eat, but a few dozen bulbs will yield enough for a tasty meal or two. The saffron crocus is only hardy in southern parts of our region.

EDIBLES

Continue succession planting of vegetables in the garden. As the weather cools, especially in northern and mountainous areas, cool-season vegetables such as spinach, peas, radish, lettuce, kale, and arugula can be planted. For fruiting vegetables, such as peas, remember the days are shorter in fall, so plant growth is slower. A variety that normally takes sixty days to produce a crop may need a week or two more. Using your first expected frost date as a guide (see page 180 in the appendix), plant your fruiting crops so you have plenty of time to harvest before the cold settles in. For greens, this isn't an issue because you can harvest leaves anytime after the true leaves form.

LAWNS & GROUNDCOVERS

In northern and mountainous areas, as the weather cools toward the middle and end of August, you can start repairing bare spots in the lawn or renovating an existing lawn (see April Plant, Lawns). In southern and coastal areas, wait until September and October to seed and repair your lawn.

PERENNIALS & VINES

Finish digging and dividing iris rhizomes, keeping only the healthiest ones to replant in the garden (read July Plant, Perennials for tips).

Keep an eye out for that special perennial to fill a hole or a color gap in your late-summer flower border. While the weather may be hot and dry in August, you can transplant mature perennials, especially tough ones, such as hosta and daylilies, now if you keep the transplants well watered.

Look for sturdy perennial vines to fill in a trellis or arbor. While most perennial vines grow best in full sun, for a shady nook, plant climbing hydrangeas. This slow-growing vine has attractive green leaves, exfoliating bark for winter interest, and white flowers in summer. It attaches to a trellis or structure with rootlike holdfasts. Don't let it attach to house siding or it can eventually cause the siding to rot. Prune after flowering (see Care, Perennials & Vines).

ROSES

Continue looking for deals on roses to plant this summer (see April Plant, Roses). Species, shrub, and old-fashioned roses tend to be tough plants and can survive planting in late summer better than hybrid varieties. The more time roses have to establish their root systems before the ground freezes, the more likely they are to survive the cold and windy winters of New England. This doesn't mean if you find a 'Julia Child™' rose you've always wanted, you should not plant it! You just may need to pamper it with plenty of water in late summer and give it some extra care in late fall (see November Care, Roses) to help it survive the first winter.

SHRUBS & TREES

Now is a time to add some mid- to late-summer-blooming shrubs and trees to your landscape. There are probably good examples of these at regional garden centers and public gardens. Make note of the ones you like best and determine if they will fit in your landscape.

Some mid- to late-summer-flowering shrubs to grow include butterfly bush (*Buddleja*), summersweet (*Clethra*), bluebeard shrubs (*Caryopteris* spp.) and panicle hydrangeas (*Hydrangea paniculata*). Some shrubs that will rebloom throughout the summer include potentilla (*Potentilla* spp.), spirea (*Spirea* spp.), and everblooming lilacs (*Syringa*) such as 'Bloomerang®'.

A few trees that have flowers later in the summer include seven sons tree (*Heptacodium miconioides*), Japanese tree lilac (*Syringa reticulata*), and golden rain tree (*Koelreuteria paniculata*). Always check to make sure that the shrubs and trees are hardy for

HERE'S HOW

TO REPAIR BARE SPOTS

1   *To repair a section of your lawn, rake out the dead grass and rake in a layer of topsoil.*

2   *Sprinkle a lawn grass seed variety similar to what's growing in your lawn already.*

3   *Cover the area with straw to preserve moisture in the soil.*

4   *Keep it well-watered for the first few weeks, until the seed germinates.*

Butterfly bushes produce colorful spikes of flowers in midsummer that are the favorite nectar plants for a variety of butterflies.

Hydrangea shrubs make excellent back-of-the-border plants. Many flower from midsummer until fall, providing a colorful backdrop to other summer flowers.

Golden rain tree (Koelreuteria) blossoms attractive yellow flowers in summer. The seedpods that will follow are ornamental as well.

your area and that their ultimate size will fit in the location you have planned.

See tips for selecting a tree or shrub from a nursery in September Plant, Shrubs & Trees.

CARE

ANNUALS

Continue to deadhead flowers, not only removing spent blooms, but also cutting the flower stems back to a side branch or set of vigorous leaves. This technique will serve two purposes. It will clean up the annual flower, and pinching it back stimulates more new growth and another flush of flowers in September and October.

Watch for some self-sown annuals, such calendula and cleome, that may have missed your cultivator. Remove these so they don't overcrowd the bed.

To overwinter favorite geraniums, coleus, fuchsia, and other annual flowers, consider taking cuttings now. Take a stem cutting, 4 to 6 inches in length, from a healthy plant. Dip the cut end in a rooting hormone powder and stick the cutting in a container filled with moistened potting soil. Place the cutting in a bright location, out of direct sunlight, and keep it watered and misted. Your cutting should root within one month, and you can then repot it in a larger container for growing this winter in a sunny window.

BULBS

Cut back the flower stalks of lily bulbs after they finish flowering and the leaves have started to yellow. This will clean up the lily patch and allow you to plant some fall-flowering annuals, such as pansies and snapdragons, in that area.

Stop pinching your dahlia buds. The flowers should be forming starting this month. Stake or cage floppy dahlia plants (see July Care, Bulbs).

Harvest gladiolus flower stalks as they mature for indoor bouquets. Cut the flower stalk when three or four flowers have started to open. Cut the stalk on an angle, above the bottom third or fourth leaf, and place the flower stalk in a vase of warm

TO MAKE NEW BEDS
BY LASAGNA GARDENING

We often would love to expand an annual, perennial, or vegetable bed, or create a bigger shrub island bed, but are intimidated by the amount of sod removal we'd have to do. By using the lasagna gardening technique you can avoid digging sod and still create a new bed or expand an old one for planting next year. It also preserves all the organic matter and humus in the lawn so you have a more fertile bed. Here's how to make a lasagna bed.

1. Mow the vegetation in the area close to the ground with your lawn mower.

2. Spread a layer of black-and-white newspaper three or four sheets thick over the area, wetting each sheet with water as you lay it down so it won't blow away. Colored-ink newspaper is okay, but don't use glossy paper; it contains harmful chemicals.

3. Cover the newspaper with a layer of straw 6 to 8 inches thick. Hay is okay to use if you can't find straw, but it will introduce some weed seeds.

4. Cover the straw with 2 to 3 inches of compost.

5. Let the bed sit all fall and winter. Next spring, plant right into the bed without having to till or turn it.

water immediately. The rest of the flowers should open indoors.

If your amaryllis bulb growing outdoors in a container starts to flower, don't be surprised. These bulbs will send up a flower stalk in response to the shortening days of late summer. Enjoy it. It shouldn't affect the bulb flowering again this winter.

EDIBLES

Keep any seeded crops and young fall transplants well watered and protected from attacks by insect, such as cabbageworms on young kale. Consider placing a floating row cover over newly seeded beds or young transplants. Not only will the row cover protect plants from insects and animal activity, but the extra shade will keep the soil cool and moist and help the seeds germinate better. Many cool-season vegetables, such as spinach, don't germinate well with high soil temperatures.

Thin July-seeded carrots and beets to the proper spacing. Use the thinnings in salads.

Keep harvesting all the summer vegetables, such as tomatoes, peppers, summer squash, cucumbers, and beans, as they mature. Remove diseased and damaged plants, as well as crops that have finished producing, to make room for fall plantings.

Harvest potatoes once the tops yellow and die back. You can leave the spuds in the ground until fall to harvest if you're too busy this time of year, but that increases the chance of rodents, such as mice and voles, finding your potatoes and eating them. When harvesting, carefully use an iron fork or spade to lift the soil, and then handpick the potatoes. Let them cure in a well-ventilated, warm location, such as a garage, for a few weeks. Don't expose the potatoes to light or they will turn green. Although the chlorophyll that forms isn't harmful, it causes an off flavor. Store in a cool, dark basement for winter.

Harvest onions once the tops naturally fall over. Harvest by pulling the bulbs out of the ground and brushing the soil off the bulbs. Harvest shallots when the bulbs form and start to separate. Let both cure in a well-ventilated, warm location, such as a garage, for a few weeks and then store in a cool, dark basement.

Harvest melons and watermelons as they ripen.

To control weed problems in your vegetable garden in the future, try to prevent annual weeds from sowing seeds now in the garden. Annual weeds, such as pigweed, chickweed, galinsoga, and purslane, will drop hundreds of seeds this time of year. These seeds will stay dormant in the soil for years, waiting for the right moisture, temperature, and light conditions to germinate. By removing or cutting back these weeds before they set seed, you'll reduce the amount of seeds in the soil. You can

■ *Cultivate around summer-planted, fall crop vegetables to keep the weeds from taking over.*

■ *Harvest onions when the tops have fallen over. Remove the dried tops and store the onions in a cool, dark, dry place.*

mow weeds along paths or around the perimeter of the garden if you don't have time to weed.

LAWNS & GROUNDCOVERS

Keep lawns watered enough to survive a drought (read more in July Care, Lawns).

Keep groundcovers, such as English ivy, well watered to prevent leaf scorch. Leaf scorch occurs on many plants. The leaves turn brown in response to hot, dry conditions. It's rarely fatal to the plant, but it is unsightly. Remove scorched leaves and, with the cooler weather, the groundcover will recover.

PERENNIALS & VINES

Decide which late-summer-blooming perennial flowers you will continue to deadhead and

on which you'll let the seedheads form. Some perennials, such as black-eyed Susans and coneflowers, have attractive seedpods that can continue to decorate the garden bed into early winter. Also, if you want more of a certain perennial flower, let them drop seed. Many perennials, such as foxgloves, gaillardia, coneflowers, black-eyed Susans, and California poppies, will self-sow readily. Letting these seeds germinate and grow will fill out a flowerbed. However, you'll have to be careful. Often these plants will self-sow too readily and be overcrowded. You'll have to thin out the seedlings, leaving only the healthiest ones.

Don't prune vines that form flowers on new growth, such as trumpet vine. These should be in flower now, and pinching back branches will reduce the number of flowers you'll get.

HERE'S HOW

TO HARVEST MELONS AND WATERMELONS

Some melons, such as cantaloupes, are easy to know when to harvest, while others, such as watermelons, take some practice. Here's what to look for in a ripe melon.

- Harvest cantaloupes when the netting on the skin surface gets more pronounced and turns brown. At this point, gently lift the melons: if the fruit naturally slips off the plant, it's ready. You can also sniff the blossom end of the fruit, which will smell fruity when ripe.

- Harvest honeydews looking for a color and texture change on the fruit skin to indicate when it's ripe.

- For watermelons and melons other than cantaloupes, look at the tendril (curlicue) on the vine closest to the fruit. When it turns brown, that's a sure sign the melon is ripe. For watermelons, check the underside of the fruit for its skin color. When it turns from white to yellow, it's ripe. Also, thump the melons with your fingers, listening for a deep, hollow sound.

TO RENOVATE A STRAWBERRY BED

August is a good time to weed, renovate, and fertilize your strawberry bed after the harvest is finished. Here's how.

1. Chances are your strawberry beds have widened this summer as the plants spread. Till or dig your strawberry rows back to 1 to 2 feet wide.

2. Thoroughly weed the remaining strawberries.

3. Thin the plants to 6 to 12 inches apart, removing crowded plants.

4. Fertilize with an organic 5-5-5 granular product.

5. Water well.

Expand your flower bed using the lasagna gardening technique (see Here's How To Make New Beds by Lasagna Gardening).

ROSES

Continue to enjoy your everblooming roses, cutting some for the table and leaving others to enjoy in the garden. Species and shrub roses should be forming rose hips now. Stop pruning these shrubs so the hips can fill out and provide attractive color, and some food for wildlife (and people!), this fall.

Remove any shoots coming from below the graft union on hybrid roses. On grafted plants the root system is a different variety than the top. If you let the rose branch from the roots form and flower, you'll be surprised to see that it's not what you were expecting. If your rose has no graft union, chances are it's grown on its own roots. Shoots from the roots will be the same variety as the top.

On species and shrub roses, allow the suckers to grow from the base of the plant and root system to fill out the row if you are intending on growing a hedge of roses as a barrier.

Consider tip layering rambling roses now to create more plants (see next page).

SHRUBS

The latest time to trim your evergreen hedges in southern areas is early August. Don't do any major pruning to renovate shrubs this late in the season. Pruning after this time will stimulate new growth when the shrubs should be getting ready for dormancy and winter.

Expand your shrub island bed using the lasagna gardening technique (see Annuals).

TREES

Check for bark damage on tree trunks due to string trimmers and lawn mowers. With a sharp knife clean the wound, remove jagged edges to allow the tree to naturally heal itself. Create mulch rings around these trees to prevent future damage.

Check for stressed trees. Trees that are turning color early or dropping leaves now may have damaged root systems or have suffered from insect

■ *Black-eyed Susans* (Rudbeckia) *are hardy perennial flowers that bloom from midsummer to fall and spread over time. They make great cut flowers.*

TO TIP LAYER A SHRUB

If you have a favorite shrub or rambling rose and want to make more of them to spread around your yard, now is a good time to use a propagation technique called tip layering. It works well for shrubs with drooping branches, such as forsythia, spirea, ninebark, and weigela, and on brambles, such as raspberries and blackberries. Here's how it works.

1. Take a long branch and bend it toward the ground.

2. Where it comes in contact with the ground, remove the leaves. Leave a set or two of leaves at the tip of the branch.

3. With a sharp knife, scar the bottom of the stem coming in contact with the ground, enough to remove the outer bark, but not cutting into the pith.

4. Add some rooting hormone powder to the wound and cover it with a layer of soil 2 to 3 inches deep.

5. Support the part of the stem that is sticking out of the ground with a stake to keep it upright.

6. Keep well watered, and by next spring the tip layer should have rooted. Cut the layered branch from the mother plant, dig up the rootball, and transplant it to a new location.

or disease attacks. Unless the cause of the damage is obvious, such as damage from a mower, consult an arborist about ways to help your tree survive.

WATER

ANNUALS, BULBS & PERENNIALS

Continue to keep annual and perennial flowers and summer bulbs growing strong with regular watering if Mother Nature isn't providing it naturally. Don't let your flowers reach the wilting stage before watering, or it may affect the growth and future flowering of your plants.

Some flowers, such as canna lilies, angel's trumpets (*Brugmansia*), and elephant ears (*Colocasia*), have large leaves that transpire moisture quickly, especially during hot, windy weather. Water these thoroughly and often to keep the soil consistently moist.

Some annual and perennial flowers are naturally drought tolerant, such as California poppies, moss rose, statice, Russian sage, yarrow, and astilbe. Water these plants last when working your way through the flower bed.

EDIBLES

Keep the soil moist for water-loving vegetables, such as squash, cucumber, eggplant, tomato, and beans, with regular watering. Reapply mulch that has decomposed or blown off the soil. Follow the watering guidelines in July Water, Annuals, Perennials & Edibles.

Keep edibles growing in containers regularly watered to keep them producing. Water stress will curtail fruit production.

Check self-watering containers' reservoirs and keep them filled.

■ *Build a mulch ring around a tree or shrub after planting it. Mound the ring so water will accumulate and soak in around the rootball of the plant while the mulch helps control weeds.*

HERE'S HOW

TO RECOGNIZE DROUGHT-TOLERANT FLOWERS

You certainly can research which individual flowers are drought tolerant so you'll know if they will need special attention during hot, windy, dry periods. However, here are some physical clues that will tip you off about whether your flower is drought tolerant.

Fine foliage: the reduced leaf surface means less water lost through evaporation.

Thick or waxy leaves: thick leaves store more moisture and dry out slower.

Hairy or fuzzy leaves: the fine hairs on these leaves keep moisture trapped at the leaf surface so they dry out slower.

■ *Fine foliage: Some plants, such as yarrow, have leaves that transpire less water, making them naturally more drought tolerant.*

■ *Hairy or fuzzy leaves: Lamb's ear (Stachys) is a popular, low-growing perennial that is drought tolerant. The soft, silvery-grey colored leaves feel like a lamb's ear when rubbed.*

■ *Thick or wavy leaves: Moss rose (Portulaca) is a sun- and heat-loving annual flower that tolerates drought. It is low-growing and has flowers in a range of bright colors.*

LAWNS & GROUNDCOVERS

Follow the July Water, Lawns guidelines to keep your lawn watered.

ROSES, SHRUBS & TREES

Continue to keep roses, shrubs, and trees well watered, especially if they're flowering, growing on well-drained sandy soil, or growing during a dry period. Water newly planted shrubs and trees first (July Water, Roses & Shrubs). Everblooming roses and late-blooming shrubs and trees will need more water in order for their flowers to form. Stressed roses, shrubs, and trees will drop their flowers early to conserve moisture.

The same is true for fruiting shrubs and trees, such as such as hollies and firethorn. Lack of water may mean fewer berries will set for the following fall.

FERTILIZE

ANNUALS & EDIBLES

Only fertilize those plants that are newly planted for fall, such as lettuce, spinach, broccoli, pansies, and snapdragons. Fertilize annual flowers that you cut back, such as calibrachoa and petunias, to stimulate new growth. Fertilize vegetables, such as cut-and-come-again lettuce or mesclun mix, that you harvested once and want to regrow for fall.

Continue to fertilize container-grown annual flowers and edibles. These will need a ready supply of nutrients to keep producing into fall.

PERENNIALS & VINES

Stop fertilizing perennial plants, vines, and groundcovers. Fertilizing after July continues to stimulate new growth that will delay the onset of dormancy for winter.

ROSES, SHRUBS & TREES

Finish fertilizing hybrid roses for the season. There should be enough fertility in the soil for them to continue to flower until frost.

Don't fertilize shrubs and trees in August. The plants are moving toward winter dormancy with the shorter days and cooler nights. Any fertilizer now will delay dormancy and make the plant more likely to be injured by an early freeze.

PROBLEM-SOLVE

ANNUALS

Check annual flowers for aphids and spider mites. During hot, dry weather, spider mites will thrive. These small, spiderlike insects are usually not noticed until they're so numerous they form webbing on your plants. By then most of the damage has occurred on your plants. Check leaves regularly during dry weather for stippling and the small mites on the underside of the leaves. Spray the leaves with insecticidal soap to kill this pest.

Continue to clean up spent leaves and blossoms on your annual flowers, especially those growing in containers. Not only will this make the container plants more attractive, it also reduces the likelihood of fungal and other diseases.

BULBS

Continue to watch your gladiolus, canna lilies, and dahlias for signs of insect and disease damage. Periodically remove diseased or insect-ridden leaves to help slow infestation (see July Problem-Solve, Bulbs).

EDIBLES

Continue to monitor for and control insect pests on your vegetables such as cabbageworms, Colorado potato beetle, squash bugs, and squash vine borers (more in June Problem-Solve, Edibles).

Continue to control foliar diseases, such as early blight and *Septoria* leaf spot, on your tomatoes (July Problem-Solve, Edibles).

Watch for powdery mildew developing on your melon and squash leaves. This fungal disease thrives in August with our cooler nights (see July Problem-Solve, Perennials).

Watch for tomato hornworms on your tomatoes and pepper plants. These large caterpillars go unnoticed until you see sections of leaves missing. Looking closely, you can see the 6-inch-long green caterpillar munching away. If you only have a few hornworms, handpick to destroy them. For larger infestations spray Bt on the plants. If you noticed white protrusions on the back of your hornworms, leave the caterpillar on the plant. These protrusions are the egg sacs of a predatory wasp. The eggs hatch, and the wasp larvae parasitize the hornworm. They are actually helping you by killing the hornworms.

Not all problems in the vegetable garden are related to insects, diseases, and animals. Blossom end rot is a physiological problem related to calcium and water in your tomato plants. When tomato plants

■ *Blossom end rot on tomatoes is a common disorder, but isn't a disease. It's caused by fluctuating soil moisture conditions, which create a calcium imbalance in the tomato fruit. Water regularly, discard rotten fruits, and mulch to prevent this condition.*

experience periods of dry weather followed by wet weather, such as a summer thunderstorm, this fluctuation of soil moisture conditions causes a calcium imbalance in the plant. As a result, the cell wall on the blossom end of the fruits begins to break down and rot. This syndrome is particularly evident on plum and elongated varieties of tomatoes, such as 'Roma', and on tomatoes grown in containers. Pick and compost the rotting fruits. To prevent new fruits from getting blossom end rot, mulch around the base of your plants well, water evenly, and in extreme cases apply a foliar calcium spray.

Continue to monitor brambles for borers and viruses (read July Problem-Solve, Edibles).

Many New England gardeners are growing grapes for fresh eating and winemaking. Grapes can have a number of insect and disease problems in our climate, so it's best to consult with your local Master Gardeners about growing them. One prevalent disease is black rot. This fungal disease overwinters on old leaves and grapes around the plant and infects the leaves, stems, and fruits as they grow. It's more prevalent during cool, wet weather. Fungicidal sprays can be used early in the season, but if you are growing just a few vines, as many homeowners do, cleaning up the dropped fruits, cultivating under the vines in summer, and thinning infected leaves and grape clusters will help reduce the disease and allow you to still get a good harvest.

HERE'S HOW

TO CONTROL BIRDS ON YOUR FRUITS

Blueberries, grapes, and raspberries are particular favorites of birds. I've seen flocks of cedar waxwings descend on a blueberry patch and almost clean it out. The best control for birds is prevention. Here are some tips to help.

Netting is a tried and true way to keep birds off your berries. For small plantings, instead of just draping the netting over your plant, build a structure to keep the netting off the shrub. Netting that sits on the blueberry or raspberry plant will be difficult to remove and makes it hard to harvest the berries without damaging the leaves and fruits. Drive stakes into the ground and attach to each a horizontal board, forming a T on top of the stake. Place them so they are just above the plant height. Then drape the netting over the stakes.

Reflective devices help keep birds confused and away. Use holographic tape, aluminum pie plates, and old CDs hung around the berry patch. When the wind and sun hit the devices, they reflect light into the air and scare the birds. Set these up before berries are ripening so the birds get used to not visiting the patch.

While stationary owls don't really work to scare birds (I saw a crow perched on one once), **scare eye balloons** do work well. These balloons mimic the eye of a hawk, a bird predator, so birds stay away. The key is to move the balloon around the patch every few days so the birds don't get accustomed to it.

LAWNS & GROUNDCOVERS

Check groundcovers for signs of disease and remove infected leaves to prevent its spread.

Japanese beetle eggs laid in summer will have hatched by now. The larvae will start to feed on grass roots and can cause lawn dieback. Also, the grubs are a favorite food source of skunks and raccoons. They will visit the lawn at night, making holes as they search for grubs.

Control beetle grubs by spraying beneficial nematodes toward the end of August and into September (see June Problem-Solve, Edibles). This will remove the food source for skunks and raccoons too.

Look for areas on your lawn that are well worn. Sometimes you will make a pathway from a driveway to your house, but the more common path that kids and adults use may lie elsewhere across your lawn. These new paths compact the soil and cause lawn grass to die. Compacted lawn areas are also more likely to have weeds, such as plantain. Solve this problem by working with the flow. Move your path to where people are walking or place steppingstones in the lawn for people to walk on to reduce compaction.

PERENNIALS & VINES

Honeysuckle vines are still flowering strong, but as new growth forms, black aphids are particularly attracted to them. Spray insecticidal soap on the new growth to control the aphids. Aphid feeding causes leaves to yellow. Feeding aphids also excrete a substance called honeydew that can make areas around the vine sticky and messy, especially if they grow on an arbor near a sitting area.

Continue to cut back diseased or insect-infested perennial shoots. Sometimes removing a few shoots will prevent the spread of a disease or insect problem and allow you to enjoy the flowers longer into fall.

Continue to monitor for powdery mildew disease on phlox, bee balm, and other flowers (July Problem-Solve, Perennials).

ROSES

Continue to control adult Japanese beetles on rose leaves (June Problem-Solve, Edibles). Usually the feeding adults will die down toward the end of August. If we've had a hot, dry summer, fewer eggs and larvae will survive, so we should have fewer adults the next year. A cool, wet summer, however, is perfect for Japanese beetle egg and larvae survival.

Watch for spider mites on roses during periods of hot, dry weather (see Bulbs).

Control powdery mildew (July Problem-Solve, Perennials) and blackspot (May Problem-Solve, Roses) diseases on your rose bushes.

SHRUBS

Watch for branch dieback on daphne, ninebark (*Physocarpus*), and other shrubs. It's often not clear what the cause of this sudden wilting may be. Sometimes it's rot diseases invading the roots and blocking the flow of water and nutrients into the branch. The best solution is to cut the wilted branch back to the trunk or main side branch. If severe, this may deform a shrub to the degree that you'll be faced with the decision of replanting or waiting for the shrub to grow back.

TREES

Honey locust (*Gleditsia triacanthos*) is a common landscape tree in yards and parks, but unfortunately it is attacked by a number of insects. Watch for signs of plant bugs, mites, and aphids on honey locust trees. The leaves of heavily infested trees often are deformed and yellow. For small trees and small infestations, use a hose with a strong jet of water to knock the insects off the tree. For larger infestations, consult with your local professional arborist.

Continue to watch for tar spot, anthracnose, and leaf scorch on trees (read more in June Problem-Solve, Shrubs & Trees). Rake up and destroy any fallen leaves caused by these problems. Removing the leaves will reduce the disease in future years.

September

September in New England can be fickle. It often starts with summerlike weather in the early part of the month. We still can be swimming, picnicking, barbecuing, and certainly harvesting flowers and vegetables from the garden. But by the end of September the weather has noticeably changed. Shorter days combined with the cooler nights are really starting to make a difference in plant growth. In mountainous and inland areas, frost is a definite threat. Even along the coast, while frost isn't imminent, the cooler breezes off the ocean hint at the weather to come.

So, this month is all about getting the most from the garden while it lasts. I often set a frantic pace of harvesting vegetables and canning, freezing, and storing them like a squirrel hoarding nuts for winter. And the annual flowers often are amazing this time of year. With vegetables and flowers still doing so well, I have an eye on the forecast almost daily, watching for any hints of cold weather.

Luckily, frosts in September are light, so a simple tarp or floating row cover draped over a patch of cosmos, a favorite tomato plant, or some container geraniums is enough to help them survive. Often if we can avoid that first killing frost, we get what New Englanders have traditionally called an "Indian summer." This means warmer temperatures for weeks into October, allowing us to enjoy our gardens even longer.

Even if you protect your plants from frost, one group of plants that doesn't like even a hint of cold weather are the exotic tropicals you might have been growing in containers in the garden. Mandevilla, canna lilies, elephant ears, and ornamental bananas don't like temperatures even in the 40s Fahrenheit. You can try to overwinter these indoors, or just give them up to nature and start anew next spring.

Toward the end of this month, New England's famous fall foliage colors begin, especially in northern and mountainous areas. It's a good time to enjoy the crispness in the air and the beauty of the garden and natural world.

PLAN

ANNUALS

September is a good time to assess what worked and what didn't in the annual flower garden and your annual flower containers. If you replanted your containers in late summer with cool-season annuals, they should be in full glory come September. For containers that you left with the original plantings, it's good to note which annuals looked good all summer long and which really should have been replaced in mid- to late summer.

Make note of those annuals in the flower garden that are really shining this time of year and where the "holes" are for next year's planting schedule.

BULBS

September is a good time to go bulb shopping. Garden centers will have stocked their fall supply of spring-flowering bulbs, such as daffodils, tulips, and hyacinths. They often get only one shipment of bulbs in fall, so it's a first-come-first-served situation. Go early for the best selection.

When selecting spring-flowering bulbs, keep in mind that size makes a difference. You'll notice different grades and prices on bulbs such as daffodils. Those in bulk bins tend to have lower prices, but those are smaller bulbs. They will usually produce one flower stalk the first year. More expensive bulbs will be noticeably larger and may provide two or three flower stalks. For naturalized plantings of daffodils, go for the small bulbs. They're more cost-effective and in time will produce a nice show. For small groups of daffodils planted closer to the house, spring for the larger, more expensive bulbs. You'll feel more satisfied when they bloom.

Select individual bulbs that are firm and have no noticeable blemishes on them. Don't worry about the papery covering or tunic. That may or may not be in place, but it doesn't matter to the quality of the bulb.

Store spring-flowering bulbs in a dark, cool place until you're ready to plant in early October in northern areas and mid- to late October in

■ *Shop now for spring-flowering bulbs, such as tulips, to get the best selection from garden centers. Choose unblemished bulbs. Plant them in October.*

southern areas. Just remember where you stored them because you might forget and be surprised to find unplanted bulbs in January!

EDIBLES

Now is a good time to plan garlic plantings. Select garlic bulbs from the local garden center or order them online. Choose ones adapted to our area, and *don't* grow garlic bulbs bought in the grocery store. These tend to be California varieties that won't grow well in our climate.

There are two general types of garlic for growing: soft neck and hard neck. Soft-neck varieties, such as 'Inchelium Red' and 'New York White', mature faster and keep longer in storage. They're the ones with strong leaves that are good for braiding. Hard-neck varieties, such as 'Russian Red' and 'Music', are more colorful and, some say, more flavorful than soft-neck varieties. Hard-neck garlic is hardier in cold climates and produces a flower scape in summer that is also edible. We can grow both types in New England, but if you live in a very cold, mountainous area, stick with the hard-necks. As with the spring-flowering bulbs, garden centers will stock garlic in September, so select the largest bulbs of your favorite varieties now. Give them the squeeze test and select bulbs that are solid. Store the garlic bulbs in a cool, dry, dark location and wait until next month to plant.

Plan on growing some cover crops in your garden as well this fall. When cleaning out beds, sow winter rye, winter wheat, oats, hairy vetch, field peas, and other crops to build the soil's organic matter and prevent soil erosion. See Plant, Edibles for more on growing cover crops.

Make plans to protect favorite crops from frost by getting your supply of blankets, tarps, and floating row covers ready to cover plants during chilly nights.

LAWNS & GROUNDCOVERS

Make plans for fall lawn care by buying seed to overseed and to patch bare spots, compost for topdressing the lawn, and fertilizer to boost fertility.

PERENNIALS & VINES

Now is a good time to take a critical look at your perennial flower border. Often in September the colors are not as outstanding as you'd like. It's a good time to plan on incorporating more annuals into the bed next summer or plant more late-summer- and fall-flowering perennials. Some good choices for fall-blooming perennials include Russian sage (*Perovskia*), perennial hibiscus, asters, goldenrod, sedum, monkshood (*Aconitum*), hardy chrysanthemums, and pineapple sage (*Salvia elegans*). Don't forget colorful foliage perennials, such as coral bells (*Heuchera*), hosta, and spurge (*Euphorbia*) too. These plants continue to shine

■ *Shop for perennials now to get good deals on plants left over from the spring. Heuchera has good fall foliage color.*

into fall with their colorful leaves. In fact, they may look even *better* in fall than in midsummer, due to the cooler, rainier weather.

Plan for which of your tropical vines you'll be taking indoors this fall to overwinter. Mandevilla is a popular tropical that won't survive our winters. Move this warm-weather lover indoors at the first hint of cool nights.

ROSES

Make note of which of your shrub and species roses have the best and most attractive rose hips. Rose hip colors include yellow, orange, and red. Some rose varieties have better hip colors and production than others. Not only do the hips provide fall color along with the everblooming rose flowers, they're good for making jams and teas as well.

SHRUBS & TREES

Fall sales on shrubs and trees are starting soon. Make notes about which trees you need for your yard and start shopping around. Look for the healthiest tree in the garden center to tag and bring home when you're ready to plant.

PLANT

ANNUALS

Cold-hardy annual plants, such as pansies, violas, primroses, snapdragons, and flowering kale, fill

■ *Russian sage* (Perovskia) *is a colorful, late-summer perennial with silver-green leaves. The plant is drought tolerant as well.*

garden centers in September. It's a good time to spruce up your containers with these annuals or supplement your flower gardens. Look for areas in your annual and perennial flower borders that have little color and pop some of these cool-weather lovers into the garden. Plant in groups of three, five, or seven to get the most dramatic effect. Plant these annuals at the same depth as they were planted in their pots at the proper spacing suggested on the plant tag.

HERE'S HOW

TO PLANT COVER CROPS

1 *Dump all of the seed packages into a big bowl to save time opening packages later. Planting will go faster.*

2 *Broadcast the seeds and cover them with 1 inch of soil. Water the seeds daily until they sprout, then water every four or five days.*

BULBS

Although it's too early to plant spring-flowering bulbs, it *is* a good time to prepare their soil beds. Clean out spent annuals and cut back perennials that have faded. Amend the soil area where you'll be planting a whole bed of bulbs with compost. Wait to add additional fertilizer until you actually plant the bulbs.

EDIBLES

Plant your last crops of cold-hardy greens, such as mesclun mix, spinach, hardy lettuce varieties ('Winter Density'), and kale, in early September. If you're growing in a cold frame, you can keep sowing until later in the month. The limitation for growing vegetables in fall in New England often isn't the air or soil temperatures, but rather the day length and light intensity. Days are getting too short for lots of growth, so plants grow slowly. Luckily, with greens you can harvest at any stage after germination to have a tasty, fresh treat.

Wait to plant garlic until October. Planting too early will encourage the bulbs to start growing in fall. This can lead to winter injury because the bulbs aren't dormant.

Decide which herbs from your garden you'll be trying to overwinter indoors. Chives, parsley, rosemary, and sage are all good choices. Cut them back, dig the herbs from the garden, cut back their rootball, and plant them in a container with fresh potting soil. Place these potted herbs in a partly sunny location to acclimate them to being in the pot, and keep them well watered. Toward the end of the month, move them indoors. Some herbs, such as chives and rosemary, will survive growing indoors all winter. Parsley, however, is a biennial and will send up a flower stalk in late winter and eventually peter out. But you can still enjoy the leaves in dishes into next year before it ends up in the compost pile.

For large herb plants you'd like to overwinter indoors, save space by taking cuttings and root these plants. Sage, rosemary, and mint are easy to root by taking a 3 to 4-inch stem cutting from healthy plants. Remove the bottom leaves and dip the cut end in a rooting hormone powder. Stick

HERE'S HOW

TO PLANT A SALAD BOWL

1. *Purchase wide, shallow pots to plant salad bowls. If you have an old plastic salad bowl, you can drill holes in the bottom and plant it. Fill the bowl about halfway with potting soil.*

2. *Plant the lettuce bowl with lettuce transplants. For extra taste, plant some bunching onions in the center of the bowl and a dill plant or two on the edges. Fill in potting soil around the plants and water them. On hot days, move the bowl into some shade. On cool days, move the bowl into the sun. If temperatures are forecast to drop below freezing, bring the bowl into the garage.*

HERE'S HOW

TO DIVIDE AND TRANSPLANT A PEONY

Peonies are long-lived, favorite perennials in New England. However, over time they can stop flowering due to increased shade from trees or being overcrowded. Dividing peonies also allows you to make more plants for yourself and others. Here's how.

1. Cut back the foliage on peony bushes, even if it's still green.

2. Dig up the bush, knock off the excess soil, and examine the root system. Look for ideal places to remove sections from the roots. Each division should have three eyes on it for the plant to grow best.

3. Find a new location in full sun. Dig a hole larger than the rootball. Amend the hole with compost.

4. Plant so the eyes on the roots are no more than 1 to 2 inches below the soil level. If you plant too deep, a peony may not flower. Keep well watered and mulched.

the cuttings in a pot filled with moistened potting soil. Keep the container out of direct sun, but in a warm location. Once the cuttings have rooted, transplant them into individual pots and grow in a sunny window all winter.

Plant cover crops now as beds open up. Cover crops are a grain or legume that is sown in fall to hold soil in place. They're tilled or turned under in early spring as soon as the soil can be worked to add valuable organic matter to the garden. The best combination of cover crops is a grain and legume mix. Select grains such as winter rye, winter wheat, and oats, and legumes such as field peas, hairy vetch, or clover to sow in your bed. Prepare the soil as you would for sowing vegetable seeds. Broadcast the seed on the bed and lightly cover it with soil. Keep the bed well watered. In cold areas, sow winter rye and hairy vetch because these cover crops can germinate in cool soil conditions.

LAWNS & GROUNDCOVERS

Fall is a good time to do some lawn seeding and renovation. Many gardeners want to avoid spreading harmful herbicide and chemical fertilizers on their lawn, yet still want a green lush lawn all summer. Here's how to get started.

HERE'S HOW

TO GROW A LAWN ORGANICALLY

The key to preventing weed, disease, and insect attacks organically is to have a healthy lawn grass with deep, thick roots. To achieve this, you'll need to build up the fertility of the soil under your lawn.

1. Aerate existing lawns to provide space for air, water, and fertilizer to reach the roots. Rent a core aerator from the local rent-all company or, for small lawns, use an iron (or other metal) fork (see more in April Care, Lawns).

2. Topdress lawns each fall with a ¼-inch-thick layer of compost (2A) raked into the grass (2B). This translates into about 1 yard of compost per 1,000 feet of lawn. The compost will feed the grass roots slowly and provide a good base for the grass to grow thick and lush.

3. Overseed lawns with grass seed adapted to *your lawn's* growing conditions. Select a mix high in Kentucky bluegrass for sunny spots and one high in fescue for part-shade locations. Even if your lawn looks healthy, overseeding by spreading the grass seed over existing grass will enable even more grass to grow and thicken the grass in thin areas.

4. Fertilize with a granular organic product (also see Fertilize, Lawns).

Now is a good time to transplant and spread groundcovers around your landscape. Look for healthy patches of desirable groundcovers such as vinca, pachysandra, and lily-of-the-valley. Thin these patches by digging up random plants and moving them to locations with similar conditions under trees, in a perennial garden, or on a bank.

PERENNIALS & VINES

September is a good time to divide and transplant spring-blooming perennial flowers such as peonies.

Plant chrysanthemums in your annual and perennial flower gardens. Plant as you would any container perennial. However, most of these varieties are not hardy in our area. In protected spots in southern New England you can get them to return in spring, but they don't reliably regrow in most other areas. (See Care, Perennials for more on overwintering mums.) Look for hardy chrysanthemum varieties, such as 'Sheffield Pink', to be a more reliable perennial in our climate.

ROSES

While planting hybrid roses is chancy in September, shrub, species, and old-fashioned varieties can still be planted. Planting earlier in the month is better for these shrubs. Follow the planting guidelines found in April Plant, Shrubs.

You can dig up root suckers on species roses such as rugosa rose and transplant these now. Get as much of a root system as possible when digging and keep the transplants well watered.

SHRUBS & TREES

Fall is a *great* time to plant deciduous shrubs and trees purchased from a nursery or garden center. Evergreens are best transplanted as soon as possible, especially in northern areas, so they can establish their root systems before the ground freezes. Follow the planting guidelines in April Plant, Shrubs & Trees.

While transplanting existing trees and shrubs this time of year can be risky, it is a good time to prepare the plants to move in spring. Root pruning will help create a strong rootball so next spring when you dig up and move your plant it will have a better chance to survive. To prune roots, use a sharp spade to slice into the soil around the tree or shrub at the drip line. Don't remove the soil—just sever the roots. This will stimulate more root branching where the rootball is located.

CARE

ANNUALS

For frost-sensitive annual flowers, such as marigolds, zinnias, and petunias, you have a choice in September. If frost threatens, you can cover these plants so they will survive a few more weeks. Or you can just let them die. One way to decide

is if the annual flowers are still growing strong and have more unopened flower buds, then they are worth saving. If, however, they are looking ragged and tired, it's probably best to let them go.

When covering flowers, use lightweight blankets, tarps, and floating row covers to protect them. Remove the covering once the temperatures are above freezing again.

HERE'S HOW

TO SELECT A TREE OR SHRUB

When selecting a tree or shrub from a nursery in fall, take a close look at the plants to be sure you're getting a healthy specimen.

- Avoid trees or shrubs with obvious broken branches, wounds on the trunk, and broken rootballs.

- For container shrubs and trees, check the roots to see if they are still white and actively growing. See if the container soil is still moist.

- For trees and shrubs that have been balled and burlapped, rock the plant back and forth to see if the rootball moves with the trunk. If it moves independently, the roots aren't well established in the ball. Select another plant.

■ *Fall is a good time to plant shrubs and trees. Select plants that are in good health and are not root-bound.*

Move containers close to a house if a light frost is predicted. For heavier freezes, move them into a shed or garage or the house. By moving them back and forth depending on the weather you'll be able to save plants for weeks.

To overwinter prized annuals, you can take cuttings, root them, and grow the young plants as houseplants all winter. You can also transplant small specimens into pots and bring those indoors. Quarantine the plants and check for insects for a few weeks after bringing them inside. Spray with horticultural oil or insecticidal soap to kill most common insects that hitched a ride. Grow these plants in a sunny window and keep the soil barely moist all winter.

Geraniums can be saved another way. Cut back the foliage by one-half. Dig up the plants, remove the soil, and bring them indoors. Store geraniums in perforated plastic bags filled with slightly moistened peat moss. Place the root systems in the bags and place the bags in a dark, cool room in the basement. Geraniums should stay dormant until early spring, when they will start leafing out. Pot up the plants at that time and grow them in a sunny window until they can be planted outdoors.

BULBS

Cut back the foliage on your amaryllis bulb that has been growing outdoors. Move the container and bulb indoors into a dark, cool basement. Stop watering and let the bulb go dormant for six weeks. See January Care, Bulbs for more on forcing amaryllis bulbs into bloom.

EDIBLES

Protect tender vegetables and herbs from frost. As with annual flowers, look at those plants that are still producing or have immature fruits that might still ripen if given a few more weeks. Those are the priority to save.

You can encourage some vegetables to ripen fruits sooner by removing new growth, young flowers, and immature fruits. Tomatoes, peppers, Brussels sprouts, winter squash, and melons are some of the vegetables on which you can snip off the growth point and remove flowers and young fruits that

won't have time to mature before frost. This will send more energy into ripening the larger fruits on the plant.

Tomatoes can be coaxed into ripening if you wait to harvest them once they show some color. Bring fruits indoors into a warm room, out of direct sunlight. Wrap them individually in newspaper or paper towels and let them sit in a tray. Check every few days for any rotting fruits (compost those). Of course, totally immature or green tomatoes make an excellent relish or stir-fries, so don't give up on them either.

To extend the growing season even further, buy or build a cold frame. A cold frame can have an elaborate or very simple design. The idea is to protect young plants from the cold and wind and provide sunlight for them to continue to grow. You can seed mesclun mix, lettuce, spinach, radishes, and kale in cold frames now to grow into early winter.

Harvest apples and pears as they ripen. Apples should be firm, crisp, and juicy, with the right color for that variety. They will continue to ripen after picking, so when in doubt, pick early. Harvest pears before they mature on the tree. If allowed to ripen fully on the tree, the pear's flesh will have a gritty texture and may even start rotting. The ripe fruits should change from a dark green to a lighter green for most varieties. Pick when they are still firm and they will continue to ripen indoors.

LAWNS & GROUNDCOVERS

September is prime lawn care month in New England. It's a good time to aerate lawns, overseed with grass seed, and topdress your lawn with compost (also see Plant, Lawns).

Moss is often a problem on lawns growing in part shade. Moss grows because the lawn grass isn't getting enough sun, the soil pH is too low, or the soil is thin because of underlying rocks or ledge. You can correct some of these conditions to eliminate the moss and bring lawn grass back in those areas. First, rake out the moss. Then, based on a soil test, add lime to raise the pH to between 6.5 and 7.0. Prune tree branches to allow more light into the area and topdress the lawn with compost. Sow grass seeds, and hopefully the lawn will grow in thick.

Mow the leaves on your lawn and let them be. The shredded leaves feed earthworms and soil microbes, which break them down quickly to improve the soil structure and fertility of your lawn.

Protect fall vegetable and herb plantings with a floating row cover. This cheesecloth-like material lets water, light, and air in and keeps the plants protected from a frost.

Moss isn't all bad. If you have a moist area under evergreens, moss may be the perfect groundcover solution. Moss looks inviting, but it isn't as sturdy as grass, so don't plan on walking on it much.

PERENNIALS & VINES

Start cleaning up the perennial border, cutting back to the ground any plants that have yellow leaves and are naturally dying back. This will make the border look better in fall and allow room to plant bulbs next month.

Decide which perennials you'll want to leave for the attractive seedheads and which you want to prevent from self-sowing. Astilbe, coneflowers, and baptisia look attractive in the fall garden even after their flowers have faded. Although they will drop seeds to germinate, usually their seedling numbers are manageable. Other perennials, such as yarrow, black-eyed Susans, and oat grass, can have attractive seedheads in fall too, but they self-sow readily and can become weeds in the garden. If you have enough of these plants, deadhead the flowers once they pass their prime. You can collect seeds of many of these perennials to sow in the garden next year. That way you'll be planting the seeds where *you* want and not just where they dropped.

Protect perennials growing in containers from cold weather. Perennials in containers won't survive the winter outdoors, so decide now whether to move the container to a warm garage or basement come October or to transplant the perennial into the garden now and mulch it well.

Move tropical vines, such as mandevilla, into a warm spot for winter. Some gardeners treat mandevilla as an annual vine and buy new ones each year. If you want to try to overwinter your container mandevilla, cut back the vine, spray for any hitchhiking pests, such as whiteflies and aphids, and move the plant into a sunny window. Keep it barely moist all winter and cut back the vines as they grow leggy.

ROSES

To allow roses to properly harden off this fall, stop deadheading now. On many bushes, rose hips will form. Hip formation helps the rose change from growth mode to dormancy mode and get ready for the cold weather ahead.

Move miniature roses into containers if you intend on keeping them indoors as houseplants in winter. Acclimate them to the change by potting up the roses and growing them outdoors for a few weeks in a partly shaded location. Spray for insects and then move the pots to a sunny window indoors.

SHRUBS

Start cleaning up dropped leaves of shrubs, especially those that had foliar diseases this summer. This will reduce the amount of fungal spores around the plant and make it less likely they will get the disease next year. Compost the leaves in a hot compost pile (see October Care, Edibles).

TREES

Toward the end of September, the fall colors are starting to show in mountainous and northern regions. Enjoy the show! No matter what we plant in our yards, nothing compares to what Mother Nature does in the New England forest.

Begin mulching fallen leaves as they drop from early shedding trees. See October Care, Trees for more on what to do with the leaves.

WATER

ANNUALS

Except for the occasional remnants of a tropical storm or hurricane, September can be a dry month. Keep containers well watered as they put on their final flower show for the season.

Mulched annual flower gardens usually won't need much extra water in September. But if we have a classic early September heat wave, water thoroughly to soak the soil. You may only have to do this once or twice in early September to keep the soil moist for plants.

BULBS

Stop watering amaryllis bulbs to get them ready for dormancy (see Care, Bulbs).

Keep dahlias well watered. Often September is when they put on their best show, so be sure they have enough moisture to keep the flowers coming.

EDIBLES

Keep newly transplanted or seeded fall crops well watered. Because of the shorter days and cooler nights, most mature vegetables and herbs won't need much supplemental water unless we have a hot spell.

Keep cover crops well watered for best germination.

LAWNS & GROUNDCOVERS

Water newly sown lawns to ensure the grass grows in thick and lush. Once the grass grows in, reduce watering.

PERENNIALS & VINES

Keep newly transplanted perennial flowers and vines well watered. Mulch will help preserve the soil moisture, so watering once or twice after transplanting may be enough to keep the roots happy.

SHRUBS & TREES

Keep newly transplanted shrubs and trees well watered. Fill the moat around the base of the plant a few times a week to keep the roots moist. Another option is to use "gators" around trees to slowly moisten the soil (read more in July Water, Roses, Shrubs & Trees). Shrub and tree roots will actively grow into fall, so it's important they have enough moisture to survive.

FERTILIZE

ANNUALS

There's little need to fertilize in-ground annual flowers. In containers, add a highly soluble fertilizer, such as fish emulsion, if new transplants need a boost of nitrogen.

BULBS

Fertilize existing bulb plants with a bulb fertilizer. Fall is the time that spring-flowering bulbs are putting on new root growth, so fertilizing them now will help form stronger roots and, hopefully, more flowers next spring.

Fertilize new bulbs as you plant them (see October Plant, Bulbs).

EDIBLES

Give newly planted greens a dose of a highly soluble liquid fertilizer, such as fish emulsion, if the plants have yellow leaves.

LAWNS & GROUNDCOVERS

If you are only going to fertilize your lawn once a year, now is that time. Fall lawn fertilization helps build strong grass root systems without stimulating lots of top growth. So you won't have to mow more often and you'll have a strong lawn going into winter.

The best fertilizer for lawns is slow release. I usually recommend an organic granular fertilizer with a 3-1-2 ratio. This ratio is nitrogen to phosphorous to potassium. It slowly feeds the grass roots as needed. In areas near waterways, some communities and states have banned the use of phosphorous fertilizer on lawns because phosphorous can easily leach out of lawns into waterways and contribute to pollution. Look for no-phosphorous lawn fertilizers if you live in these areas. Follow the application directions on the bag.

PERENNIALS & VINES

Compost is usually the only fertilizer recommended for perennial flowers and vines in fall. As you begin to clean up the perennial border, remove weeds and add a layer of 1 to 2 inches of compost. This will add to the soil fertility and help mulch the roots for winter.

ROSES

Avoid fertilizing roses in fall. Also, if your roses are growing close to the lawn, don't fertilize the lawn with a high-nitrogen fertilizer. It can leach from the lawn grass into your rose bed and stimulate new growth. Roses need to be shifting from growth mode to dormancy mode this time of year.

SHRUBS & TREES

Only fertilize existing shrubs and trees if you notice a nutrient deficiency based on the plant growth and a soil test. Wait to fertilize any newly planted fall trees and shrubs until next year.

PROBLEM-SOLVE

ANNUALS

Clean up annual flower garden plants that are fading to reduce the amount of disease in the soil. Rake out or pick off diseased leaves and dispose of them.

Watch for powdery mildew on flowers this time of year. It usually is in full force! Pull out plants that are severely infected. It's probably too late to bother spraying to save them.

HERE'S HOW

TO FERTILIZE USING A DROP SPREADER

1 *Fall is the best time to fertilize your lawn. Using organic fertilizers, such as compost and bone meal, you'll feed the grass roots and slowly feed the plants to create a lush, healthy lawn.*

2 *Use a fertilizer spreader to apply an organic granular fertilizer to your lawn.*

3 *Following the label's direction, fill the spreader half-full with fertilizer so that it's easier to push.*

4 *Spread the fertilizer evenly over the whole lawn, trying not to overlap paths. Shut the fertilizer hopper when making turns so as not to dump too much fertilizer on one spot.*

BULBS

When removing summer bulbs such a gladiolus, canna lilies, and dahlias from the garden after they've finished producing, inspect the plants carefully. Don't try to store diseased bulbs, corms, or tubers. Only select the ones that are solid to the touch and have no visual signs of damage. Compost the rest.

Make plans to thwart squirrels and mice from eating the spring-flowering bulbs that you'll be planting in October. Get your supplies and products in line to prevent damage to these bulbs (see more in October Problem-Solve, Bulbs).

EDIBLES

Continue to remove disease-laden plants, such as squash with powdery mildew and blighted tomatoes. Avoid composting diseased plants because even in a perfectly made compost pile, some disease spores may survive to reinfect your garden next year.

LAWNS & GROUNDCOVERS

Continue to control grubs in your lawn until the middle of the month in northern areas and throughout September in southern areas. This will reduce damage to your lawn grass and reduce the population of Japanese beetles and other adult beetles attacking your plants next year. (Refer to June Problem-Solve, Edibles for more details.)

Rake and remove diseased leaves from groundcovers as they start to die back. Too many leaves left in the groundcover bed can contribute to overwintering fungal diseases that will infect new growth next year.

If mushrooms start popping up in your lawn due to the cooler, wet weather, don't worry. Other than being unsightly, they don't harm the lawn grass. They're fruiting because there are some old tree trunks, branches, or wooden debris buried in the soil that is rotting. Simply mow them down if you don't like the look.

PERENNIALS & VINES

Weed perennial beds as you cut back perennials that are dying off. Remove perennial weeds, such

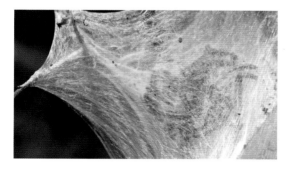

■ *Watch for tent caterpillar nests this time of year in cherry, plum, apple, and other trees. Destroy the nest with a wooden stick or* Bacillus thuringiensis *(Bt) organic spray.*

as dandelions and plantain, to the roots. A little weeding now will make for much less work in spring.

Cut back severely infected perennials, such as asters or bee balm with powdery mildew, to clean up the garden and reduce the amount of disease spores in the area.

ROSES

Now is a good time to assess the amount of pest damage on your roses. Roses that were heavily attacked by Japanese beetles, blackspot disease, or animals may be weakened enough that they won't survive the winter. Pamper these prized plants, providing adequate water this fall and mulching them to ensure they survive (see November Care, Roses).

As with the perennial and annual flower gardens, weed now to reduce the amount of work you'll have to do in spring.

SHRUBS & TREES

Watch for fall webworm nests being formed in fruit trees, especially apple, pear, and crabapple. These caterpillars feed on leaves and form white, webbed nests. Although not a serious pest in most cases, for small- to medium-sized trees the feeding webworms can cause some defoliation and weakening. To control fall webworms, physically remove the nests by pruning off the branches where they reside. For larger infestations, or if pruning will severely deform the tree, spray Bt on the nests. This organic pesticide will kill just the caterpillars and not harm other insects, birds, wildlife, or pets.

Rake up and remove leaves that are dropping early due to powdery mildew, anthracnose, and other foliar diseases. Most of these diseases are commonplace in the environment, so composting these leaves is fine. The severity of these diseases depends on the weather each year. However, by removing them from around the tree or shrub you'll slow the onset of the disease next year.

Weed out seedlings of maples, elm, box elder, and other trees that have sprouted in the garden. The seeds that dropped in spring have germinated and rooted by now. It will be a lot easier to pull out these seedlings now, when they're young, than next year when they're older and larger.

October

There is no more spectacular sight than New England in October. People travel the world to see our magnificent fall foliage colors. The combination of short days, cool nights, and moisture brings out leaf pigments that have been masked by green chlorophyll all summer. The result is a spectacular and artistic display of yellow, gold, orange, red, and purple leaves.

While gardeners can't take responsibility for this amazing color show, we certainly can bring it into our yards. Now is a good time to do a little planning for shrubs and trees that will provide the colors we love in October. Maples (*Acer*), sweet gum (*Liquidambar*), sour gum (*Nyssa*), Japanese zelkova (*Zelkova*), mountain ash (*Sorbus*), gingko (*Gingko*), serviceberry (*Amelanchier*), birch (*Betula*), beech (*Fagus*), and ash (*Fraxinus*) are some of the more colorful fall foliage trees around. We are looking not only for types of trees and shrubs that consistently turn a brilliant color, but specific varieties as well. Some great tree varieties to consider planting for fall color include 'October Glory' maple, 'Red Sunset' maple, 'Greenspire' ash, 'Coral Fire' mountain ash, and 'Miss Scarlet' sour gum. For shrubs with good fall foliage colors try staghorn sumac (*Rhus typhina*), 'Mt Airy' fothergilla (*Fothergilla*), 'Velvet Cloak' smokebush (*Cotinus*), and high bush blueberries (*Vaccinium*). Working these into your landscape will complement the brilliant show Mother Nature is providing.

With all the cleaning up to do in the yard, you'll probably have a lot of organic matter. Fallen leaves, old garden plants, weeds, and cut-back perennials all can be used to make a compost pile that will feed your gardens for years to come. Fallen leaves have many uses in the yard. You can shred and leave them to feed the lawn, collect and make leaf mold piles, add them to your compost pile to help balance your nitrogen and carbon materials, or simply till them into annual flower and vegetable gardens to add organic matter directly to the soil.

October is the time for planting spring-flowering bulbs and garlic. But it's also for enjoying the end of the growing season. Don't rush! Take some time to enjoy it.

PLAN

ANNUALS

October is a good time to look and see which annuals are still in their full glory and which should have been pulled a while ago. Some annuals, such as cosmos, alyssum, and marigolds, look great right up to a frost and sometimes beyond. Frost-sensitive annuals, such as impatiens, begonias, coleus, and moss rose (*Portulaca*), will give up the ghost at the first hint of cold weather. Make note of these annuals. Next year you can have a mix of cold-hardy and frost-sensitive annuals that look good even into October.

BULBS

Check out websites, catalogs, and magazines for ideas on designing with spring-flowering bulbs in the landscape. Since you'll be planting bulbs now, getting creative with how you plant can lead to a more dramatic effect in spring. Look for ways to plant bulbs with complementary colors together. Think of bulbs that will bloom in succession to extend the color season. Look for places and ways to naturalize bulbs in your lawn or under trees. Think of bulbs that will complement your spring-blooming perennial flowers.

Note where existing bulbs are planted and be careful not to disturb them when planting more bulbs in your garden.

EDIBLES

Take note of those vegetables that are still looking good and producing in October in your neighbor's garden. These fall beauties include leeks, spinach, peas, radishes, broccoli, cauliflower, and lettuce. Plan to incorporate these into *your* vegetable garden next summer so you can have a bountiful crop of edibles late into the season.

LAWNS & GROUNDCOVERS

Now that you have time to really look at your lawn, assess the weed situation. Identify those areas that have more than 50 percent weeds; they will need renovating in spring. Look for patches of creeping Charlie and ajuga that are running through your lawn. Make note to remove these next year as well.

PERENNIALS, VINES & ROSES

Notice which perennial flowers offer some fall color and interest and think about planting more of these in spring. Hosta and balloon flower (*Platycodon*) leaves turn yellow in fall. Sedum flower heads still have a burnt red color, even when their flowering season has gone by. Perennial geraniums have a reddish leaf color. These can be used to complement the colors of fall foliage shrubs and trees in your yard.

HERE'S HOW

TO PLANT LOTS OF BULBS

1 *Remove the soil to the proper depth so that the bottom of the bulbs will be three to four times as deep as the width of the bulbs. Incorporate any needed soil amendments, including organic matter, fertilizer, and bone meal.*

2 *Toss the bulbs into the garden. Even out spacing as needed, but avoid straight planting lines. Make sure the bulbs have their basal plate facing down, pointed side up.*

3 *Cover the bulbs with soil and water well.*

SHRUBS & TREES

When researching shrubs and trees for your yard, use fall foliage, berry, and bark colors and textures as other criteria. Yes, you should certainly purchase shrubs and trees whose ultimate size will fit your location and which will get the right amount of sun and shade, are hardy in your area, and are easy to grow. But also think of shrubs and trees that will provide colorful berries, leaves, and bark in fall and winter. Remember, we have about six months when deciduous plants won't have leaves, so we need to think of ways to make the yard look attractive during this off season.

Purchase tree protectors from garden centers to be wrapped around prized young trees in November (November Care, Shrubs & Trees).

PLANT

ANNUALS

Collect seed from self-sowing annuals, such as cleome, flowering tobacco (*Nicotiana*), and California poppy. While these annuals may have already dropped seed around them in the garden, by collecting seed now you can play garden designer as well. Sprinkle seed in areas where you'll want these annuals to pop up in spring. This can be in the perennial flower garden, under trees, or elsewhere in the annual flower garden. Write down what you sprinkled—and where—so you will be on the lookout for the seedlings in spring.

BULBS

October is prime time to plant spring-flowering bulbs. Starting in early October in northern areas and mid- to late October in southern areas, plant daffodils, tulips, crocus, hyacinths, scilla, and snowdrops.

Bulbs grow best in well-drained, loose soil amended with compost. The planting depth of the bulbs is important. If planted too shallowly, they may be injured by the cold. If planted too deeply, they may not flower. Generally, plant bulbs at a depth of two to three times their height. You can plant a little deeper in sandy soil and a little shallower in clay soils. Refer to the following graphic for the proper planting depth for each type of bulb.

Add fertilizer to your bulb planting holes (see Fertilize, Bulbs).

Protect bulbs to keep rodents, such as mice, voles, and squirrels, from eating them in the ground (see Problem-Solve, Bulbs).

HERE'S HOW

TO LAYER MIXED BULBS FOR AN EXTENDED DISPLAY

If you have a small area and want to get the most bang from your bulb planting, consider layering the bulbs in one hole. By layering different bulbs that bloom at different times in the same hole you can extend the bulb flower season by weeks. Here's how.

1. Select three or four different type of bulbs that bloom in early, mid-, and late spring. Include large (daffodil), medium (tulip), and small (crocus) bulbs in the mix.

2. Decide on a design. Do you want all one or two colors? Do you want colors that will be complementary? Select different varieties of the types of bulbs to achieve your color goals.

3. Dig a hole about 10 inches deep and as wide as you have room for the number of bulbs purchased. You'll be placing the bulbs almost touching in the hole to get the best visual effect when they bloom.

4. Amend the hole with compost and bulb fertilizer.

5. Place the largest bulbs (daffodils and hyacinths) in the bottom of the hole so the bulbs are about 8 inches deep.

6. Cover those bulbs with soil and plant the next layer with medium-sized bulbs (tulips and small daffodils) in the hole about 4 to 6 inches deep.

7. Cover this layer with soil and plant the final layer with small bulbs (crocus, snowdrops, scilla) about 1 to 2 inches deep. Cover with soil and water well.

If you didn't do so in early summer, dig up bulbs that didn't flower this past spring and replant them in new holes amended with compost. Mark the area so you know where to look for these bulbs next spring.

Buy some bulbs to force indoors this winter. Most spring-flowering bulbs will need a chilling period of twelve to sixteen weeks before they can start growing and flowering. Paperwhite narcissus is the exception (see January Plant, Bulbs). Now is the time to pot up some bulbs and place them in a cool (between 40 and 50 degrees Fahrenheit) and dark basement until midwinter. Select all one type of bulb per container, such as daffodils, or repeat the layering technique for outdoor bulbs in a different container. Water them well.

Planting bulbs in containers filled with moistened potting soil is the best way to force bulbs. It allows the bulbs to grow roots in fall and be ready to sprout in winter. However, some gardeners don't have the proper space or cool location to chill their bulbs. The solution is to place the bulbs in paper bags in the refrigerator, away from any vegetables, for a chilling period. Pot them up in midwinter. They will be slower to flower, but this technique will still work.

EDIBLES

It's time to plant garlic.

Plant cover crops if you haven't already in September (see September Plant, Edibles). Select cover crops, such as winter rye and hairy vetch, that will germinate better in the cooler October soils.

Take cuttings of herbs to grow an indoor herb garden in winter (read more in September Plant, Edibles).

Pot up perennial herbs such as rosemary and sage that you plan on bringing indoors to overwinter in a sunny window (see September Plant, Edibles).

Sow seeds for an indoor greens garden. Most likely you won't be able to grow greens in a sunny window due to our shortened days in fall. However, you can grow greens under grow lights to harvest as additions to salads.

LAWNS & GROUNDCOVERS

If the weather stays warm, especially in southern regions, you can still lay sod and sow grass seed to patch bare areas and renovate larger swatches of lawn. (Read more in April Plant, Lawns.)

HERE'S HOW

TO PLANT GARLIC

Garlic is one of the few vegetables planted in fall. While spring-planted garlic may form bulbs and cloves, by planting in fall you'll get the biggest and best-quality bulbs. Plus, there are fewer chores to do in fall, so you'll have more time to plant. Here's how.

1. Select varieties adapted to your area. Hard-neck garlics that produce flower scapes in spring include 'Russian Red'. Soft-neck varieties that are good for braiding include 'New York White'. You can try elephant garlic, which produces baseball-sized bulbs with a mild flavor.

2. Prepare a raised bed in your garden: remove rocks and old plant debris, and amend the soil with a 1 to 2-inch layer of compost.

3. Rake the bed flat and smooth and plant individual cloves 4 to 6 inches apart in rows spaced 6 inches apart. Plant them 1 to 2 inches deep.

4. Water well and cover with a layer of straw 4 to 6 inches deep to protect the cloves from heaving out of the ground during winter's freeze-and-thaw cycles.

Ornamental cabbage turns a brilliant color with the cool weather of October. Even though the leaves are edible, most gardeners grow these cabbages for their fall beauty.

PERENNIALS & VINES

Early in the month, finish digging and dividing peonies (see September Plant, Perennials).

Although it's not ideal, in the beginning of October you can still move hard-to-kill perennials such as hosta and daylilies. Dig the whole clump and remove the rootball, getting as much of the root system as possible. Divide into wedges 1 to 2 feet in diameter and replant in compost-amended soil. Keep well watered and mulch well this first winter to help it survive. These plants are tough and should be able to make it and grow again next spring.

ROSES

Early in this month, finish moving species roses and transplanting miniature roses into containers (see September Care, Roses).

SHRUBS & TREES

Finish planting any trees and shrubs purchased this fall, following the guidelines for planting in April Plant, Shrubs & Trees.

If planting evergreens this late in fall in northern areas, protect the needles from drying out over the winter by protecting them with a burlap windscreen (see November Care, Shrubs & Trees). Another way to prevent moisture loss in winter is spraying evergreens with an anti-desiccant spray. This spray creates a waxy coating over the needles and prevents excess moisture loss. Spray when temperatures are above 40 degrees Fahrenheit on a calm day (see January Care, Shrubs & Trees). Deciduous trees are not a problem because they have no leaves in winter.

In northern areas, mulch over the ground after planting shrubs and trees to help keep it warm later into the season. Tree and shrub roots will continue to grow even at 40 degrees Fahrenheit, so keeping the soil warm longer allows them to get better established.

CARE

ANNUALS

By the end of October, frosts are more frequent throughout most areas except perhaps along the coast. It's time to decide how much longer you'll want to keep annual flowers growing in the ground and in containers. If you protected them from an early frost in September, you bought some time. Frost-tolerant annuals, such as snapdragons, kale, and violas, can take temperatures into the 20s Fahrenheit and bounce back to flower during warm spells, so these are worth leaving in the garden. Cut back the rest of the annuals, or dig them up and compost them. Containers can be kept growing longer because of their ease of maintenance, so they *may* be worth the effort to stretch into November.

Edge annual flowerbeds now in order to have less work in spring (see Care, Perennials & Vines).

BULBS

Dig and store tender bulbs, such as canna lilies and dahlias, after a frost. After cutting back the foliage and digging up the bulbs, knock off most of the soil. Cure them in a warm, well-ventilated garage or room for a few days (a few weeks for gladiolus). Then move them into a basement or room at 40 to 50 degrees Fahrenheit. Store the bulbs in slightly moist peat moss in perforated plastic bags. This will keep the bulbs moist enough in winter, but not so moist that they rot. Gladiolus can be stored without peat moss in onion bags hanging in the room.

Keep amaryllis bulbs in a cool, dark location (with no water) until November.

HERE'S HOW

TO OVERWINTER TENDER BULBS

1 *After the leaves have been killed by frost, loosen soil with a garden fork and gently lift bulbs out of the soil, being careful not to damage them.*

2 *Shake off most of the soil and trim off all but an inch or two of the stem.*

3 *Let the plants dry for a few days until the stems shrivel, then trim the stems off completely.*

4 *Put the bulbs in a plastic bag ideally packed with dry wood shavings, peat moss, or shredded leaves. Label the bag and store the bulbs in a cool area away from frost.*

EDIBLES

Harvest winter squash and pumpkins before a killing frost early in the month in most areas. If you plan on saving these squash for cooking in winter, frost will weaken the skin and cause rot to occur faster. After harvest, cure winter squashes and pumpkins in a warm, well-ventilated garage or barn for two weeks. Clean the skin with a 10 percent bleach solution before storing for winter at 40 to 50 degrees Fahrenheit in a basement or root cellar.

Harvest Halloween pumpkins but wait until close to the holiday to carve them. To have your ghoulish carved pumpkins last longer, rub Vaseline on the cuts to prevent them from drying out so quickly.

If you haven't had a killing frost yet, harvest the last of your warm-season vegetables, such as tomatoes, peppers, eggplants, and beans. Cool-season vegetables, such as spinach, broccoli, peas, radishes, carrots, and beets, can take a frost and still survive.

TO BUILD A COMPOST PILE

A good way to use all the leaves and plant material being cut back and dug up from your gardens is to make a compost pile. A compost pile is a mix of high-nitrogen materials (green) with high-carbon materials (brown). Some common green materials to add to your pile include fresh, untreated grass clippings; trimmings from flowers and vegetables; and kitchen scraps. Avoid adding disease-infested plants, pernicious weeds such as quackgrass, and any meat or bones. Some common brown materials include dried leaves, hay, or straw. Here's how to build your pile.

1. Find a convenient location close to your garden to build the pile.

2. Make a freestanding pile, or contain it with wooden pallets, high-gauge wire, or boards. The ideal size of a compost pile is 3 feet wide by about 5 feet tall. This will be large enough for the pile to heat up, but not so large it will be difficult to work.

3. Place a layer of brown materials on the bottom of the pile. Then layer green and brown materials alternately until you fill the bin. Water each layer as you add it.

    Cover the pile with a board or tarp when finished so it doesn't get too wet. A wet pile will go anaerobic, meaning it will start to smell and only slowly decompose. A dry pile may decompose very slowly too.

4. Once the pile heats up, turn it by mixing the outer materials with the inner materials. Wet it again if it needs moisture and let it heat up.

5. If you have more materials than will fit in the pile, build a holding pile. Once you have enough materials, build a second pile.

6. Once the material looks and feels like soil, even if some of the organic matter is still visible, your compost is ready to use. This may take weeks or even months depending on the conditions.

Cover these crops when temperatures are expected to dip into the 20s Fahrenheit. Continue to harvest cool-season crops as needed.

Continue to clean up the vegetable garden, removing and composting old plants that were not infested with disease or insects.

Based on a soil test, add lime to raise the soil pH or sulfur to lower the pH. Add other rock-based minerals, such as greensand and granite dust, as well in fall. This will give these organic fertilizers time to break down and influence the soil before planting next spring. (See Fertilize, Annuals also.)

HERE'S HOW

TO USE FALL LEAVES

Here are some creative ways to use your leaves this fall.

- If you only have 2 to 4 inches of leaves on the lawn, simply run your mower over the leaves to chop them up. They will quickly decompose, feeding your lawn grass. Some research suggests that sugar maple leaves, in particular, will help prevent dandelion growth in lawns too.

- For larger piles of leaves, collect them and make a leaf mold pile. Simply pile the leaves up, contain them with flexible wire fencing, and let them sit. After a few years you'll have usable compost.

- Collect excess leaves and place them in your annual flower or vegetable gardens. Till them in and they should be partially decomposed by spring.

- Use chopped leaves to protect tender roses, perennials, and groundcovers. Whole leaves will mat down and retain moisture next to the stems, causing rot. Chopped leaves have more air spaces and tend not to mat down.

- Have *fun*. Make a leaf pile to jump in with your kids. Use some leaves to make scarecrows for Halloween.

LAWNS & GROUNDCOVERS

Continue to clean up deciduous groundcover patches as the leaves die back. If you have an evergreen groundcover, such as vinca, weed the area thoroughly so the weeds don't get a jump on you in spring.

Mow for the final time of the season toward the end of October or when the lawns stop actively growing. Mow a little lower than normal to remove more of the grass growth. This will help prevent thatch buildup and fungal disease from occurring in spring.

PERENNIALS & VINES

Finish cleaning up the perennial flower gardens, cutting back herbaceous perennials to 4 inches above the ground.

Finish weeding the perennial bed, digging out tough perennial weeds such as dandelion and horsetail.

With a spade, edge the beds. Cut down into the lawn grass about 4 to 6 inches deep along the edge at an angle and remove the sod and soil. A clean edge will prevent weeds from encroaching on the flower bed and make a cleaner line between the bed and the lawn. Add a 2 to 3-inch layer of mulch to the edged section. Edging the beds now means less work in spring. (Use the edging sod in the compost pile as one of your "brown" ingredients.)

Remove plant supports, such as peony rings and stakes, and store them in a dry place for winter. They will last longer if they're not stored outdoors, exposed to the elements.

If you have container perennials that you want to overwinter, move them into an unheated basement or garage where temperatures will stay barely above freezing. If you expect the temperatures to dip below freezing in their storage area, place the container in a cardboard box and fill it with hay or packing materials for added insulation. You can also bury a plastic container in the middle of a mulch pile. The added protection from the mulch should help the roots survive. Don't try to bury ceramic or clay pots or they will break from the freezing and thawing cycles.

Now that the leaves have dropped, it's a good time to check plant ties and supports on climbing perennial vines, such as clematis and climbing hydrangea. It's easier to see which may need replacing. Replace worn supports and reattach vines to the support for winter.

Add lime and minerals as needed, based on a soil test (see Care, Edibles).

ROSES

In southern and coastal areas, finish planting species and shrub roses. Protect these new transplants with a thick layer of bark mulch placed around the base of a plant. This will slow the freezing of a rose bush, giving the plant's roots more time to get established before winter.

Wait to protect your hybrid roses until November (see November Care, Roses). Placing winter protection on the roses too soon, before mice and voles have found winter homes, can encourage them to reside in mulch pile around your rose, providing them not only with a home but food (rose stems) for winter as well.

SHRUBS

Protect any shrubs planted in containers by moving them to an unheated garage or basement. Container shrubs won't survive the low winter temperatures outdoors. (Also see Care, Perennials & Vines.)

Continue to clean up dead leaves around the base of shrubs to remove areas where disease may overwinter and infect plants next spring.

Do one final weeding and edge the mulch rings and island beds (see Care, Perennials & Vines). It will be one less job to do next spring.

TREES

By the end of October, the leaves are starting to pile up. Don't look at all these leaves as a problem: they are a solution to many garden chores.

Weed and edge the mulch ring around your trees (see Care, Perennials & Vines).

WATER

ANNUALS

Pansies, snapdragons, chrysanthemums, ornamental cabbage, and ornamental kale that were planted in the ground or in containers need supplemental watering during dry periods. Even though fall weather is cool and the soil dries out slower, we still can get dry spells.

BULBS

If the weather stays dry, deeply water new plantings of spring-flowering bulbs. Usually one or two waterings in October will be enough.

EDIBLES

Check fall-planted spinach, lettuce, kale, peas, and other cool-season vegetables. Water when the soil is dry at a depth of 2 to 4 inches.

LAWNS & GROUNDCOVERS

Keep fall-planted lawns well watered with at least 1 inch of water a week. Reduce watering once the lawn grass seed germinates and starts growing strong.

PERENNIALS & VINES

Water mandevilla and other container vines you'll overwinter until the water seeps out of the drainage holes.

Water container perennials that you'll be saving one last time before they go into dormancy in a cool, dark basement or garage.

ROSES, SHRUBS & TREES

Water fall-planted roses, shrubs, and trees if you aren't getting soaking rains weekly. Their roots will need the water to keep growing into fall and will help the plants survive the winter.

FERTILIZE

ANNUALS & EDIBLES

Now is a good time to take a soil test of your gardens. In fall, soil laboratories are less busy so you can get your results back sooner. You also have time to add soil amendments, such as lime and sulfur, to correct deficiencies. Contact your state land grant university (home of the Extension Service) or a soil lab. You can also use a private laboratory or a home test.

BULBS

You only need to add fertilizer to the planting hole of newly planted bulbs. For established bulb

HERE'S HOW

TO TAKE A SOIL SAMPLE FOR A LAB

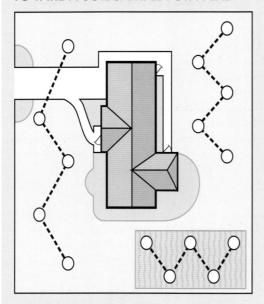

While adding compost to your annual flower and vegetable garden is always a good idea to keep the soil healthy, sometimes you need to supplement compost with other fertilizers. But before you just spread a general fertilizer on your soil, take a soil test. This will give you a snapshot to see exactly which nutrients you need. Here's how to take a soil sample to send to a soil lab. The lab will analyze the results and send you a report.

1. Take separate samples for each type of garden. For example, don't mix lawn, vegetable, and fruit tree soil samples together.

2. With a shovel, dig 6 inches deep into the soil and place a small sample of the soil in a bucket.

3. Repeat this technique in about ten different locations in your garden. The more locations you sample, the more accurate the results will be.

4. Mix the samples together and take a sample of the sample (about a small baggie full) to send to the lab.

HERE'S HOW

TO TEST SOIL PH AT HOME

1 Add soil to the kit from the area of the garden that you want to test. Then add water according to the instructions.

2 Add the indicator powder to the water in the container and shake the container to mix the soil, water, and indicator powder. (The indicator powder usually comes in a capsule.)

3 Hold the container against a piece of white paper so that you can check the color of the water against the color key on the container. The color of the water will match one of the colors in the key on the container. The reading will tell you what is happening in the soil—acidic (low pH) or basic (high pH) soil, low nitrogen levels, or high phosphorous levels. After testing, you'll know what to add (or not add) to the soil.

plantings, sprinkle a granular bulb fertilizer around where they grow (see September Fertilize, Bulbs).

LAWNS & GROUNDCOVERS

Finish fertilizing your lawn if you didn't already in September (also see September Fertilize, Lawns).

PERENNIALS, VINES & ROSES

After you finish weeding, cutting back, and moving your perennials, add a layer of compost 1 to 2 inches thick on your perennial beds and around vines and roses. If you have healthy soil, this will be enough fertilizing. Keep compost away from the trunks of vines and roses to prevent crown rot.

PROBLEM-SOLVE

ANNUALS

Although pests are rarely a problem this late in the season, keep an eye out for aphids, whiteflies, and mealybugs that have hitched a ride indoors on geraniums and other annual flowers you'll be overwintering in a sunny window. On a warm day, spray these outside with an insecticidal soap.

BULBS

Prevent damage to spring-flowering bulbs, such as tulips, crocus, and hyacinths, from mice, voles, and squirrels. These critters love to dig around freshly turned soil in your bulb patch and will feed on most spring-flowering bulbs, except daffodils and fritillaria. To prevent damage, add sharp sand, crushed eggshells, or crushed seashells to the hole when planting. As the critters tunnel to find the bulbs, they will encounter the sharp materials and be deterred. Another method is to plant bulbs they don't prefer, such as daffodils, around and in between tulips and other preferred bulbs as a buffer zone. For severe infestations you can lay netting down on the bulb bed to stop them from digging. In small areas, consider buying or building a bulb cage. Sink it in the ground and plant bulbs inside the cage. This wire cage should have holes big enough for root and shoot growth, but small enough to keep the critters out.

EDIBLES

Watch for rabbits and other animals looking for a fall snack in your newly maturing fall spinach, lettuce, or Swiss chard bed. Cover the bed with a floating row cover to keep it warm and prevent animal damage.

LAWNS & GROUNDCOVERS

Control moss and mushrooms in lawns as needed (also see September Care, Lawns, and Problem-Solve, Lawns).

PERENNIALS & VINES

Finish weeding perennial flower beds. Apply a layer of bark mulch to protect the roots of tender perennials and provide a weed barrier for next spring. It will be one less chore to do then.

Now that the leaves have dropped on perennial vines, such as climbing hydrangea, check the bark for scale insects. Scale will be easier to notice without the distraction of the leaves. Look for small white, brown, or black bumps on the stems that can be easily flicked off with your fingers. Spray horticultural oil on the branches to coat, suffocate, and kill these insects.

ROSES

Review what you're using as deer repellents and controls to protect rose branches this coming winter. Deer will start browsing on roses especially once their normal food sources start dying off. Consider using repellent sprays and protective devices to keep them from deforming your shrubs (see January Problem-Solve, Roses).

Purchase the materials you'll need for winter rose protection—such as bark mulch—now, before the supplies are low in garden centers. You'll be applying these materials next month (see November Care, Roses).

SHRUBS & TREES

Finish raking and removing any diseased leaves that dropped from your shrubs and trees. Most of these leaves will have fungal diseases that are common each year on trees. You can compost these leaves without concerns about reinfecting your trees next year.

Continue to watch for and control fall webworm on your trees (see more in September Problem-Solve, Shrubs & Trees).

November

Winter is right around the corner and may even be knocking at your door in some mountainous areas of New England. November can be pleasant along the coast, where the warm ocean moderates temperatures. We can also have significant snow in mountainous and inland areas. Whatever your weather, November's the time to wrap up the outdoor garden.

Animals are starting to find winter homes and looking for food this time of year as their natural food sources dry up. Knowing when to mulch for protection is key because you don't want to create a winter home for mice and voles right next to your prized roses or shrubs. Protect your trees and shrubs from mice, rabbits, and deer before the ground freezes and snow comes to stay for a while.

November is also a good time to clean the garage, basement, and garden shed. If you're like me, the rush of work in spring, summer, and fall means I often just toss old plastic pots, tools, and stakes into the garage. This not only leads to a messy workspace, it also creates crowding. I invariably lose a tool or two in the process. Now is a good time to organize. Create a system to store garden hand tools after they've been cleaned and sharpened for easy access. Assess your plastic garden pots and decide which and how many you should keep. Recycle the rest. Save plant labels and make note of where you planted each plant. If you're short on space, look for ways to hang garden tools and products, making room for winter.

Early November is a good time to finish chores such as cutting back perennial flowers, harvesting the last of the cold-hardy vegetables, raking up excess leaves, and finishing weeding and mulching.

Later in the month, it's time to shift to winter protection of your plants. It's good to know which perennial flowers, shrubs, and trees may be borderline hardy for your area. These are plants that will need extra protection from the winter's cold and winds. Do a little research now that you have some indoor "gardening" time.

PLAN

ANNUALS & PERENNIALS

While the garden is still fresh in your mind, start noting the varieties and types of annual and perennial flowers you enjoyed in your garden. As you finish cutting back perennial flowers and pulling out annual flowers, make note of which you want to keep for next year or grow again. Write your thoughts down. Often we have a clear idea of what we'd like to move or change after gardening is done in early winter, but come spring we forget exactly what that was.

■ *When naturalizing bulbs in your yard, select bulb types, such as crocus, that spread easily. Plant them in swaths or groups in areas where you won't mow often, such as under tall trees.*

BULBS

Look for more places to plant your spring-flowering bulbs in the yard. As long as the ground doesn't freeze, you can plant bulbs right through November.

Consider naturalizing bulbs in woodland areas, under trees, along the edge of a forest, or even in your lawn. Small bulbs that naturally spread, such as scilla, grape hyacinths, crocus, and snowdrops, are good choices for these areas. To get a natural look, simply toss the bulbs in an area and plant them where they fall. If planting in the lawn, remember that you will have to wait until the bulb foliage yellows in spring to be able to mow it down. This might mean the lawn will look a little shaggy in early summer, so plant them where this won't be a visual distraction.

Make one last purchase of spring-flowering bulbs from garden centers to force into bloom this winter indoors. Pot these up now and start the chilling process (see October Plant, Bulbs).

EDIBLES

Plan to protect cold-tolerant vegetables such as leeks, carrots, parsnips, and kale from freezing night temperatures. November can be fickle. It can be 60 degrees Fahrenheit one day and 20 degrees Fahrenheit the next. By covering edibles with row

■ *Save seeds from your favorite annual and perennial flowers now once they have dried on the plant. Remember that seeds saved from hybrid varieties won't come true to color or form as the mother plant.*

covers you can extend the harvest into winter. Remove the covers once warmer weather turns (for more, see Care, Edibles).

LAWNS & GROUNDCOVERS

It's time to wrap up the mowing and lawn-care season. If you haven't already, mow one final time, leaving the lawn about 2 inches high. Make plans to protect your lawn from snowplows by driving stakes along the driveway and sidewalk. This will lessen the chance of a snowplow ripping up the turf.

Inventory your supply of de-icing salts and research alternatives to traditional de-icers that will be less damaging to lawn grass roots (see January Care, Lawns).

ROSES

Gather the materials you'll need to protect hybrid roses and tender varieties from winter's cold, which include bark mulch, rose cones, stakes, and animal repellents (read more in Care, Roses).

SHRUBS & TREES

Inventory your supply of tree wraps, hardware cloth, fencing, repellents, and other materials needed to protect your shrubs and trees from animal damage this winter. Properly discard old containers of repellent sprays that have been sitting

■ *Plant berry-producing shrubs, such as beautyberry* (Callicarpa), *in your yard to give your fall garden some bright color and food for birds.*

■ *Firethorn* (Pyracantha) *is an easy-to-grow tree that produces bright red berries in fall. The color shows well against a large, white wall like this one.*

around for years in your garage and purchase new ones. These will be more effective and safer to use.

Make note of which trees and shrubs had particularly attractive fall foliage color this year. Consider planting more of that variety in your yard in the future.

Looks for shrubs and trees that feature beautiful berries in fall to add to your display. The most popular plants are hollies (*Ilex*). There are evergreen and deciduous types of hollies. Both have separate male and female plants, so you should get some of each in order to get berries on a female plant. The deciduous types are more cold tolerant and better for northern sections of our region. Bonus: The berries stand out better because the leaves drop in fall. Some good deciduous holly varieties for fall berry color include 'Winter Red', 'Winter Gold', and 'Aurantiaca' (orange berries). Some good evergreen holly varieties include 'Blue Prince' and 'Blue Princess'. Other shrubs that produce colorful berries in winter include American cranberry viburnum (*Viburnum trilobum*), American beautyberry (*Callicarpa americana*), firethorn (*Pyracantha*), and gray dogwood (*Cornus racemosa*). Some native shrubs, such as the red osier dogwood (*Cornus sericea*), also have colorful red or yellow stems in winter that can be cut for decorating or enjoyed as a nice contrast to the white snow.

Dig a hole now if you plan to plant a living holiday tree in the yard after Christmas. Remember the ultimate size and shape of the tree before deciding where to plant. Prepare the holes as you would for any tree (March Plant, Shrubs & Trees). Save the soil from the hole in a warm garage or shed where it won't freeze solid in December. You'll need it to backfill the hole when you plant later this year.

PLANT

ANNUALS & PERENNIALS

Planting season is finished for annual and perennial flowers. But you can still collect seed from favorite flowers, such as coneflowers, black-eyed Susans, and calendulas, that are still standing in the garden.

A little plant genetics: seed saved from hybrid varieties will not come "true to type." This means that next year's offspring may look different and have a different flower color than the original parent plants. If you don't mind a little experiment, go ahead and save those seeds to sow in spring. Make note of what happens. Seeds from old-fashioned or open-pollinated varieties will be similar to their parents, so these you can collect, save, and sow in spring; you should get a similar-looking flower.

BULBS

Keep planting spring-flowering bulbs, especially in warmer coastal areas. Even in cold, mountainous areas, it's better to plant them late than to wait until next spring to plant. I even planted tulip bulbs I had forgotten in December one year and they bloomed the following spring. Spring-flowering bulbs rarely survive the winter if stored indoors. They will shrivel and dry out.

If you haven't already, pot up some spring-flowering tulips, hyacinths, and crocus for forcing this winter. Place them close together in a shallow pot filled with moistened potting soil. Place them in a dark basement or room at 40 degrees Fahrenheit for twelve to sixteen weeks. Bring them out in March and let them start growing in a sunny, warm window (see October Plant, Bulbs).

■ *To force bulbs this winter, pot some in containers, placing them so that they almost touch. Cover the bulbs with soil, moisten them, and leave them in a cool, dark basement for twelve to fourteen weeks to chill.*

Pot some purchased amaryllis bulbs toward the end of the month for forcing and blooming around Christmas. Use a container one size larger than the bulb, filled with moistened potting soil. Plant the bulb so its top is above the soil line and keep it well watered in a sunny, warm window.

EDIBLES

Move all your potted herbs and cuttings of herbs that you plan on growing indoors this winter to a sunny window indoors. Start more herbs from seed to grow under grow lights or in a sunny window. Some good choices include chives, parsley, and mint. These grow well with the lower light levels of winter. If you're growing herbs from seed indoors under grow lights, you can expand the choices to include thyme, sage, oregano, and basil.

If you don't have a sunny window or space to grow herbs or greens under grow lights in winter, plant microgreens. These are herbs and vegetables such as radish, sunflower, bean, lettuce, mustard, and alfalfa that are harvested just after germinating to be added to salads. See more on growing a microgreen indoor garden in December Plant, Edibles.

LAWNS & GROUNDCOVERS

While November tends to be too late to successfully sow lawn grass seed, you still can overseed your lawn to help fill in thin areas and create a lush lawn. (Read more in September Plant, Lawns.)

Heel in groundcovers growing in containers that you didn't plant—that is, temporarily plant them in a mulch pile or soil pile in a protected location, out of direct sun. The mass from the mulch or soil will help the roots overwinter.

ROSES

Protect unplanted roses in containers similar to groundcovers. Bury the container in a soil or mulch pile and cover the top as described in Care, Roses.

SHRUBS & TREES

Finish planting any deciduous trees and shrubs purchased this fall, following the guidelines in April Plant, Shrubs & Trees. Don't purchase or try to plant any evergreens this late in the year. The roots won't have enough time to get established in the soil before the ground freezes. Water won't be able to reach the branches, which increases the chances that leaves or needles will dry out due to lack of moisture.

■ *Finish fertilizing lawns this month as long as the weather stays warm.*

Protect shrubs and trees that you can't plant this fall as described in Plant, Lawns & Groundcovers.

CARE

ANNUALS

Check on annuals such as fuchsia and geraniums (*Pelargonium*) that you brought indoors to grow in a sunny window. Reduce watering, cut back errant growth, and watch for any hitchhiking insects.

Drain and move soaker and water hoses indoors for winter. If not drained they might crack during winter's freezing and thawing.

Move stakes, plant supports, water timers, and other plant accessories indoors. Clean these well first by removing soil and plant debris.

BULBS

Bring amaryllis bulbs out from their six weeks of cold storage to start growing later this month. If you start growing them now, you may have open flowers by the December holidays.

Check summer bulbs, such as canna lilies, dahlias, and gladiolus, that you have in winter storage. Discard any rotting bulbs. For dahlias and cannas, if the bulbs are shriveling, mist them with water so they don't dry out.

For spring-flowering bulbs that you just got around to planting, mulch to keep the soil warmer for longer into fall. This will give the bulb roots more time to establish before they stop growing due to the ground freezing. Lay bark mulch, wood chips, or straw over the bulb area. This mulch also keeps the ground frozen once winter hits so there is less freezing and thawing. Freezing and thawing soil can heave perennials and bulbs out of the ground, where they will die due to the cold winds.

Snow is an excellent insulator for bulbs and perennial flowers. In exposed areas where you planted late, or for tender perennials, layer over with evergreen boughs such as spruce and pine.

When it does snow, it will collect on the boughs and insulate the plantings below.

EDIBLES

Continue to protect fall crops of leeks, spinach, carrots, parsnips, and kale. Floating row covers are the best materials to use to protect these from cold snaps in November. Look for the winter blanket type of row cover that will protect vegetables from temperatures into the low 20s Fahrenheit. Remove the cover during our occasional warm spells.

Ventilate a cold frame over a fall crop of greens on sunny days. Even on cold days, the bright sun can overheat a cold frame, killing the plants.

Store root crops, such as carrots, beets, and parsnips, in a cold basement in slightly moistened sand or peat moss. Another way to store these roots, especially if you don't have room in your home, is in the ground. Mulch the root crop bed heavily with hay or straw. A layer 1 to 2 feet deep should be enough to keep the soil from freezing solid in winter in most areas. You probably can use less mulch along the coast. Hold the material in place with a floating row or bird netting until it gets wet enough to stay in place. During winter, dig through the mulch to harvest roots as needed.

Cover garlic plantings if you didn't already when you planted (see October Plant, Edibles).

Cover strawberry beds with a layer of hay or straw 2 to 4 inches thick to prevent these shallow-rooted plants from heaving out of the ground in winter.

■ *Grow vegetables, such as lettuce, mesclun mix, and spinach in cold frames in the winter. Protect plants by closing the tops during the cold evenings, but prop them open during sunny days.*

TO CARE FOR GARDEN TOOLS

Now is a good time to clean and sharpen garden tools.

- Inspect tools for cracked handles or broken parts and fix or replace them.
- Take apart movable parts of pruners and hedge trimmers. Clean and oil them well.
- Clean blades of hoes, cultivators, and shovels. Remove dirt and rust with a wire brush.
- Sharpen blades of pruners, shovels, hoes, hedge trimmers, and cultivators. You can use a metal file or purchase a blade sharpener for hand tools.
- Sand and oil wooden handles of shovels, hoes, and cultivators with linseed oil to protect them from cracking and breaking.

Do a final weeding in blueberry and bramble patches and mulch with wood chips or bark mulch. You'll have fewer weeds to contend with in spring.

Continue building your compost pile, adding layers of green and brown materials and watering each layer (see October Care, Edibles).

LAWNS & GROUNDCOVERS

Finish raking excess leaves and use them in the garden and yard (see October Care, Lawns).

Once you're finished mowing the lawn for the season, clean your mower, removing old grass, dirt, and debris. These can contribute to the metal rusting and weakening. Either prepare the mower for spring now by sharpening the blade, changing the oil, and checking the filters, or wait until later in winter (see February Care, Lawns).

Clean and store blowers and string trimmers. If you use battery-operated lawn equipment, store the battery in a basement or in a room where temperatures don't go below freezing. This will extend its life.

PERENNIALS & VINES

Finish adding a light topdressing of compost and mulch to your perennial flower gardens (see October Fertilize, Perennials). Mulch over the crowns of tender plants in your area, such as butterfly bushes (*Buddleja*) in the north, or ones planted in fall. This will help protect their roots and prevent frost heaving in winter.

Snow is an *excellent* insulator. For beds in windy locations, erect a snow fence so snow accumulates where the perennial flowers or tender low shrubs are planted. Remove the snow fence in early spring.

ROSES

Species roses, such as *Rosa rugosa*, and old-fashioned hardy roses, such as 'Madame Hardy', rarely need any winter protection. These are tough plants. Even if their branches die back during a severe winter, they still will grow new shots from their roots and survive.

HERE'S HOW

TO PROTECT TENDER ROSES

The best way to protect these roses is to wait until after a few freezes and then mound a pile of bark mulch or wood chips over the crown of the plant.

1. Pile the mulch about 1 to 2 feet deep over the crown. This will be enough to protect the crown in winter. Avoid using materials that will mat down and hold moisture close to the branches, such as whole dead leaves.

2. Don't worry about the branches that are sticking out of the mulch pile. These may or may not survive the winter, depending on where you live and the weather. They will be pruned in spring anyway to remove winter-injured branches and to trim the rose bush into the proper shape.

3. For smaller rose plants and miniature roses planted in the ground, you can use rose cones. Prune these roses in fall so you can fit the cone over the shrub. Secure it to the ground with stakes so the cone doesn't blow over.

4. Hardy climbing roses won't need protection, but climbing roses that are marginally hardy will. To protect them, cut back the side branches to within 1 to 2 feet of the main branches. Cut the main branches back to about 6 feet tall. Remove the branches from their trellis. Wrap the branches with burlap and carefully bend them down to the ground. Secure them with ground stakes and cover with bark mulch. Unwrap and reattach them to the trellis come spring.

For hybrid tea, floribunda, grandiflora, and tender shrub roses, you'll need to protect them from cold temperatures, drying winds, and salt spray (in coastal areas) to ensure their survival.

Move potted miniature roses indoors to overwinter in a sunny window. Watch for hitchhiking insects (see Problem-Solve, Annuals).

SHRUBS

Protect broadleaf evergreen shrubs that are in exposed areas or marginally hardy for your area with a burlap windscreen.

Panicle hydrangea (*Hydrangea paniculata*) varieties, such as 'PeeGee' and 'Pinky Winky®', produce beautiful flowers in late summer. Often these flowers will start out white and turn a rustic pink color with age. These flowers dry naturally on the shrub in fall and can be used as dried flowers indoors. Harvest the flowers anytime in fall to be included in arrangements or holiday decorations.

Ideally shrubs should be grown outside of the drip line of your house's gutters. That way they will receive natural rainfall and not be crushed by snow or ice falling off your roof. However, shrubs may

HERE'S HOW

TO PROTECT BROADLEAF EVERGREENS

Broadleaf evergreens, such as rhododendrons, pieris, and mountain laurel, are beautiful landscape plants that add greenery year-round. However, in windy, exposed locations, and in areas where they are marginally hardy, these plants can be easily winter injured. Often the drying wind or salt spray from the ocean causes more damage than cold temperatures. The result is brown leaves in spring and a deformed shrub. Here's how to protect these evergreens from the elements.

1. Select hardy varieties of broadleaf evergreens for your area and plant them in protected locations for the best results.

2. To protect existing plants, drive four wooden or metal stakes into the ground around the shrub before the ground freezes.

3. Wrap chicken wire around the stakes to enclose the shrub. Attach it to the stakes with plant ties or metal staples. The chicken wire forms a sturdy frame that stands up well to snow.

4. Wrap burlap around the chicken wire to provide the windscreen.

5. Make sure the burlap doesn't touch the leaves. The burlap can wick moisture away from the leaves, adding to the damage.

grow into the drip line and will need protection in winter. Flat-topped shrubs, such as yews, junipers, and globe arborvitae, are most susceptible to limbs and branches breaking from falling snow. To protect these shrubs, build a wooden teepee that can be placed over them. This should be strong enough to divert the snow and ice away from the shrub and prevent limb breakage.

When temperatures stay above 40 degrees Fahrenheit, spray an anti-desiccant to protect evergreen leaves from drying out in winter. This spray creates a waxy layer on the leaves that prevents moisture loss (see more in January Care, Shrubs), but it must be reapplied a few times in winter to be effective.

TREES

Protect small, tender evergreens such as dwarf Alberta spruce from cold winds by creating a burlap windscreen as described in Care, Shrubs.

Place trunk protectors around young trees whose bark might be eaten by rabbits, mice, voles, or deer. Avoid using paper tree wraps; use plastic trunk guards or hardware cloth around the trunks instead. Place them about 1 to 2 inches below the soil line and high enough up the trunk to be above the normal snow line for your area. Remove these in spring.

For multistemmed small trees, such as tall junipers and arborvitae, which are easily damaged by snow buildup on their branches, wrap the branches together with bird netting to help prevent breaking.

For small evergreen trees along a road or the ocean, wrap them with bird netting as described above, and then wrap the netting with burlap to prevent salt-spray damage.

Instead of cutting down old, dying trees around your property, consider leaving them as wildlife trees. First, make sure the limbs of these trees won't fall on your house, power lines, or buildings as they decay. Any trees left to naturally decompose in the forest or a clear area create habitat for many insects, birds, bats, and animals. These trees are also used by birds, bats, and animals for nesting. Insects

that infest the rotting branches are a good source of food. Once the branches and trunk fall to the ground, if not unsightly, leave the branches to rot. They provide more food for ground dwellers, and the bark rots into organic matter for the forest soil.

WATER

ANNUALS
Water geranium, fuchsia, and other annual flowers you brought indoors for winter sparingly. These plants will not be growing much in November, so water only when the top few inches of soil are dry.

BULBS
Keep amaryllis and paperwhite narcissus that you are starting to force indoors well watered. Water until it drains out of the drainage holes in the bottom of the pot. Use a saucer to collect the water and prevent stains on furniture.

EDIBLES
Check cold frames regularly, and water any late-fall greens when the soil is dry.

Water overwintering root crops, such as carrots and parsnips, in the garden before harvesting; it makes them easier to pull without breaking the roots.

LAWNS & GROUNDCOVERS
Lawn watering should be finished for the season. Usually we get enough fall rains to keep the soil moist for newly seeded lawns and sod. Remove lawn sprinklers and have automatic watering lines and sprinklers cleaned out and checked this fall before turning them off for the season.

PERENNIALS & VINES
Check container vines, such as mandevilla, that you are overwintering indoors. If in a sunny window and actively growing, water as you would houseplants or annual flowers brought indoors.

SHRUBS & TREES
Keep newly planted shrubs and trees watered right up to when the ground freezes. Shrub and tree roots will continue to grow in temperatures down to the low 40s Fahrenheit. Water deeply and infrequently.

Move hoses and watering cans indoors for winter. Drain the hoses of water and hang them in a garage or basement where they will be out of the way. Remove water from watering cans and hang them on a wall for storage.

FERTILIZE

ANNUALS & EDIBLES

Lightly fertilize any annual flowers and edibles actively growing under grow lights indoors. Any plants growing in sunny windows won't need fertilizer this time of year.

Continue to add organic matter, such as chopped leaves and untreated grass clippings, to annual flower gardens and vegetable beds. These materials will slowly decompose in winter and early spring, adding valuable organic matter to the soil.

Store granular fertilizers for the season in a cool, dry location. These fertilizers can last for years, as long as they don't get wet. Place them in a safe location where pets and kids can't find them.

Store liquid fertilizers away from children and pets in a location that stays above freezing. Cold temperatures will make your liquid fertilizers less effective.

Dispose of any old pesticides and fertilizers properly at your local hazardous waste drop-off center.

Add lime to raise the pH of garden soils for next year. Most soils in New England tend to be on the acidic side, but some patches of high-alkaline soil exist as well. Add sulfur to lower the pH on these soils. Add sulfur regularly to blueberry soil to keep the pH below 5.0. A sign that your blueberry soil pH is too high is chlorosis on the leaves, meaning the leaves will be green with yellow veins. Simply lowering the pH is usually enough to correct this problem.

BULBS

If you're still planting spring-flowering bulbs into this month, remember to fertilize the bulbs as you plant (September Fertilize, Bulbs).

LAWNS & GROUNDCOVERS

Finish topdressing lawns early in November with compost (see September Plant, Lawns).

Early in the month, you can still amend the soil with lime or sulfur to alter the pH to get to the optimum range of 6.5 to 7.0 for lawns. Based on a soil test, add these minerals to the soil. They will slowly break down during winter and spring and affect the pH by next year. If your soil test shows you need to add magnesium to the soil, apply dolomitic limestone (which contains this element).

Save ashes from your wood stove if you burn wood for heating. Wood ashes are a good source of potassium and can raise the soil pH too. Use a fireproof, metal container to save your wood ashes and store them in a safe place (see February Fertilize, Annuals).

Add a layer of compost 1 to 2 inches thick to groundcover beds if you haven't already.

PERENNIALS & VINES

Watch for yellowing leaves on tropical vines, such as mandevilla, that you brought indoors. This is more a function of low light levels than lack of fertilizer. Lightly fertilize only once new growth appears.

■ *Watch for hitchhiking insects, such as whiteflies, on any plants you decide to bring indoors for winter. Spray these insects with insecticidal soap to kill them.*

PROBLEM-SOLVE

ANNUALS

Control insects, such as aphids, whiteflies, and mealybugs, on the leaves and stems of annual flowers you brought indoors (geraniums, for example). Use insecticidal soap to kill large infestations. Spray a few times a week to kill hatching eggs. For small infestations of mealybugs, dab the bugs with a cotton swab dipped in rubbing alcohol. It will kill them instantly.

Control fungus gnats on any forced bulbs, container flowers, or herbs you brought indoors (see January Problem-Solve, Perennials).

BULBS

Watch for damage in your bulb beds from tunneling chipmunks, squirrels, and voles. (Read more in October Problem-Solve, Bulbs.)

EDIBLES

Watch for any tunneling and damage from mice and voles in cold frames. As the weather gets colder, they're looking for warm places to spend the winter. Your cold frame provides warmth and food at the same time. Trap them or place hardware cloth around the cold frame, dug down 6 to 10 inches into the soil, to prevent them from entering.

Check indoor herbs and vegetables growing under grow lights for mealybugs, aphids, and whiteflies (see Problem-Solve, Annuals).

PERENNIALS & VINES

Finish cutting back and removing any diseased or insect-infested stems of herbaceous perennials to prevent them from attacking your plants as they emerge in spring.

ROSES, SHRUBS & TREES

Protect shrubs and trees from deer damage. Fencing is usually the best method. Wrap young trees and shrubs in a cylinder of wire that stands 6 to 7 feet tall so the deer can't browse the branches. Secure the cylinder to the ground with stakes.

For larger shrubs and trees, protect the trunks with trunk guards (see Care, Trees). Protect the young

■ *Protect young trees from mice and voles this winter by placing a cloth tree wrap around the trunk. Put it about 1 inch below the soil line and as high as the normal snow line for your area.*

branches with repellent sprays. There are many home remedies and commercial sprays on the market. It's best to choose three or four different types and rotate their use through the winter. This way the deer won't get used to any one smell. Scent-based sprays work better than taste-based sprays. Try sprays containing rotten eggs, cayenne pepper, blood, and garlic to repel deer.

Prevent woodpecker and flicker damage to your trees as soon as you see activity. Their pecking will create holes that provide an entryway for insects and disease. To deter them, place visual devices such as aluminum flashing, Mylar tape, and old CDs on the tree. When the sun hits these reflective materials it shines light that disorients the birds.

As the weather turns colder, many gardeners stock up on firewood for winter. With the outbreaks of exotic insect pests, such as emerald ash borers and Asian long-horned beetles, on trees in our region (see page 12 in the introduction), it's important to help stop their spread. One way to do that is to not transport firewood between states or even into different communities. Even if the firewood looks insect-free, you might inadvertently move these invasive pests into a new area.

December

It's the holiday season, and although gardening activity is grinding to a halt, there are still many garden-related holiday activities you can do at this time of year. First, of course, is getting a holiday tree. While artificial trees dominate the market, I still like an old-fashioned, freshly cut tree. My family's holiday tradition is to go out a week or so before Christmas to cut our own tree from a tree farm.

Christmas trees aren't the only way to use native and landscape plants for the holidays. Now is a good time of year to make your own wreaths using trimmed greens from your fresh-cut tree and mixing in berries, pinecones, colorful branches, and other evergreen boughs. If a full-on wreath feels like too much work, there're also swags, or just display a bucket full of cut evergreen boughs and branches in water (like a bouquet). I especially like placing balsam boughs close by a door. Every time I pass by I rub my fingers against the needles to release that classic balsam holiday aroma.

Other plants are well known for the holidays too. Rosemary and lavender smell heavenly, and of course there are all the traditional potted holiday plants, such as poinsettia and holiday cactus.

Since December is also gift-giving time, it's good to take an inventory of gardening supplies and accessories that might need replacing. Perhaps your spouse or a favorite gardener in the family needs a new pair of gloves, a better pruner, or some plant markers?

While outdoors can be brown or white, depending on the year and where in New England you reside, there is still some activity in the garden. Deer that survived hunting season are out looking for food. Vegetables that you are protecting are waiting for harvest. Plants that you left for winter interest, such as ornamental grasses, are dancing in the winter wind. With all the work you've done this year, it's also good to just sit back with a cup of hot coffee and gaze out the window at all the subtle beauty of the season.

PLAN

ANNUALS

Inventory the herbs you dried from the past summer (see July Care, Edibles). Many of these make excellent gifts as part of floral arrangements. You can also use dried lavender, rose leaves, and rosemary in potpourris and sachets. The beauty of dried herbs as a gift is that they will last much longer than cut flowers or even some holiday potted plants.

Take some of your dried culinary herbs and make the cook in the family their own personal dried herb collection. Instead of giving him or her individual herbs in jars, make a blend, such as herbes de Provence, which includes oregano, rosemary, thyme, and marjoram.

BULBS

Look in your local garden center for flowering bulbs as gifts for the holidays and to decorate your house. Paperwhite narcissus and amaryllis are the most popular types. You often have the option to buy a kit with a pot and soil included. However, there's often a better selection of bulb varieties if you buy just the bulb and create your own planting of these holiday favorites. You can experiment with different varieties of amaryllis with differing colors and flower shapes. Some unique varieties include 'Rosado', with its red, orchidlike, narrow-leafed flowers; 'First Love', with its pink and white, curly, double flowers; and 'Misty', a slightly fragrant, trumpet-shaped, rose-colored variety. Be aware, though: the more exotic the variety, the more costly the bulb. But amaryllis can be saved from year to year (see Care, Bulbs), so with some care it may rebloom for many years.

EDIBLES

Make plans to keep growing microgreens growing indoors to harvest fresh herb and salad greens to supplement your meals. Make sure you have plenty of seed and soil and pots available to have a continual harvest throughout the winter (see Plant, Edibles).

LAWNS & GROUNDCOVERS

Purchase or collect wooden or metal stakes to be used as guides for snowplow drivers. Pound these into the ground at the edge of your driveway and sidewalk before the ground freezes. This will help the driver know where your driveway ends and lawn begins, reducing the amount of damage to your lawn. Also, this is a good way to guide where you want them to push the snow. Try to keep from piling snow on woody plants that might break under the weight.

PERENNIALS & VINES

Look at your climbing vines and note ones with berries that can be used in holiday decorating. American bittersweet (*Celastrus scandens*) is a native version of the invasive Oriental bittersweet that is growing rampantly throughout New England. *Don't* use Oriental bittersweet (*Celastrus orbiculatus*) berries for decorating because they can drop or be eaten by birds and spread in your landscape. If you didn't plant the bittersweet in your yard, there's a good chance it's the invasive one. Other vines that produce attractive berries for decorating include Boston ivy (*Parthenocissus tricuspidata*) and Virginia creeper (*Parthenocissus quinquefolia*). However, these black berries are favorites of birds, so it may be hard to find many left in December.

December is gift-giving time, and it's good to think of gifts that the flower gardener will appreciate. A good pair of pruners is always a nice idea. Look for bypass pruners and ones that will fit your gardener's hand well. Don't forget a pruning holster to hold the tool while they work. You might just have to give them a gift certificate and let them pick it out because it's important that a hand pruner fits well in the user's hands. Some other nice gift ideas are plant stakes and support rings to help keep tall perennials vertical, a kneeling pad to ease the pain of weeding and planting, and plant ties and markers so your recipient can keep track of what variety is planted where.

ROSES

When decorating, don't forget rose hips. These seedpods can be orange, yellow, or red. By December, the hips may be shriveled, but they are still colorful for adding to a wreath or dried floral arrangement.

When looking for a live plant gift for the holidays, remember the miniature rose. These are often available in garden centers in December and make nice indoor plants until it's time to plant them in the garden in spring (see April Plant, Roses).

SHRUBS & TREES

If you have a good stand of evergreens, such as pine, spruce, cedar, or juniper, you can harvest some of the branches for use in swags and wreaths. It's okay to prune some sprigs now. Just make sure you don't deform the tree or shrub in the process.

Use cuttings and berries from native shrubs and trees, too, to decorate holiday wreaths, swags, and trees (see November Plan, Shrubs & Trees).

When selecting a fresh evergreen holiday tree, it's good to know the different types available and how they compare. Check your local Christmas tree farm to see what types they grow. Below are some of the more common trees in our region.

Don't just think of evergreens in terms of holiday trees. With limited indoor space, creative gardeners decorate rosemary or lavender potted

HOLIDAY TREE OPTIONS

TYPE OF TREE	CHARACTERISTICS
Balsam fir	Dark green needles with a pleasant fragrance. The needles hold on the tree a long time.
White pine	Soft long, bluish-green needles. The needles hold well on the tree, but the branches are weak and don't hold heavy ornaments well.
White spruce	Stiff, short, green needles and strong branches. Good tree shape, but the needles have an off smell when crushed.
Blue spruce	Sharp, blue-gray needles on a classically shaped tree. It has good needle retention.
Scotch pine	The most common holiday tree type, its bright green needles hold on the tree even when it has dried.

herbs as tabletop trees. These are often sold at the holidays pruned into a Christmas tree shape. Even houseplants, such as ficus or tropical hibiscus, can be decorated and used as holiday trees. It's still festive, even if it's not traditional.

PLANT

ANNUALS

A nice way to display holiday plants without taking up much room is to create an open-air terrarium. Many garden centers now sell tiny versions of popular holiday plants such as poinsettia, kalanchoe, and cyclamen. These approximately 1-inch-diameter container plants can be planted in a shallow planting tray or bowl. Cover the soil surface with ferns or moss, and decorate the area with holiday ornaments, stones, or wood. You can mix and match foliage houseplants, such as polka dot plant, to add more color. To make it even lower maintenance, keep the plants in their pots and just hide the pots in the bowl with sphagnum moss. The best part of this type of display is that you can create different themes, such as holiday and desert plants. It's creative for kids and others to get involved, and the plants are inexpensive. That makes it easier to toss them into the compost when the show is over.

BULBS

If you haven't already, move your amaryllis bulb from the cold, dark storage area into a sunny,

■ *For a fun winter project, consider growing a terrarium with your kids. Select plants that like the humid conditions and add wood pieces, stones, and other decorations as well.*

bright window for forcing (see November Care, Bulbs). However, even if you start in early December you probably won't have open flowers for Christmas.

Pot up some paperwhite narcissus (see January Plant, Bulbs) or some newly purchased amaryllis

HERE'S HOW

TO GROW MICROGREENS

Select a variety of different vegetables, herbs, legumes, and even flowers to grow as microgreens. Since you'll be harvesting these greens soon after they germinate, the ultimate size of the plant doesn't matter. It's all about taste, color, and texture. You can make your own mix, or purchase premixed selections from seed companies.

1. Use a shallow plastic container, such as a prepackaged salad greens box, with drainage holes.

2. Fill the bottom of the plastic container with 2 inches of moistened potting soil.

3. Press down the soil with a pre-cut piece of cardboard that fits in the container.

4. Sprinkle your microgreen mix or individual varieties on the soil surface. Press the seeds into the soil with the cardboard.

5. Place the container on a shallow tray with water so the microgreens will be watered from the bottom.

6. Place the container in a sunny window or under grow lights. If your microgreens look long, leggy, and not very green, they probably need more light.

7. Keep moist and harvest in seven to ten days. Snip off the microgreens at the soil line and add to green shakes or salads.

8. Continue to plant containers of microgreens to harvest crops continuously in winter.

bulbs (see November Plant, Bulbs) now for a January show.

EDIBLES

Continue to plant microgreens indoors, either under grow lights or in a sunny window.

Start a windowsill herb garden if you haven't already (see November Plant, Edibles).

Start sprouting seeds indoors to add to your salads and meals (more in February Plant, Edibles).

LAWNS & GROUNDCOVERS

While the lawns and groundcovers have gone dormant for the season, there is some grass to grow indoors. If you have a cat, it will appreciate a little holiday gift of fresh greens. Plant a grass garden for your kitty (also see February Plant, Edibles).

SHRUBS & TREES

If you plant a live Christmas tree in your yard, do so right after the holiday (see November Plant, Shrubs & Trees). Move the tree from an unheated garage into the house for decorating a few days before the holiday. Leave it indoors no longer than one week, preferably in a cool room so the tree won't come out of dormancy. Keep the rootball well watered. After the holiday, move it back into an unheated garage for one week and then plant it in the previously dug hole. (See more on how to dig a hole in March Plant, Shrubs & Trees.) Use the unfrozen soil you stored in a protected location to backfill the hole and water well. If the tree is in an exposed area, erect a burlap windscreen around it to prevent the needles from drying out. (Read more in November Care, Shrubs & Trees.)

CARE

ANNUALS

Check annual flowers, such as geraniums, that are growing in sunny windowsills. There shouldn't be much new growth with the low light levels this time of year. Feel free to pinch off any errant branches. The same is true for any rooted annual flower or herb cuttings that you have saved from the garden.

BULBS

Check the saved amaryllis bulb that you brought up from the cool, dark room to start growing. You should be seeing signs of new growth coming from the center of the bulb. Some amaryllis bulbs will send up new leaves first, and then they'll send up a flower stalk. Others will be the opposite.

Place overwintered amaryllis bulbs or newly planted ones in a sunny window. You may have to rotate the pot if the flower stalk starts to lean toward the light. You may also have to stake the flower stalk to keep it from flopping over. Many new varieties of amaryllis can have up to six flowers per stalk, making them heavy. As individual flowers fade, pinch them off to keep the flower stalk looking neat. Once all the flowers have faded on the stalk, cut the flower stalk back to the bulb. Let other flower stalks or leaves take over.

Check overwintering bulbs in the basement for signs of rotting or shriveling. Remove and compost rotted canna lily or dahlia bulbs. If bulbs start to shrivel, mist them to keep them moist.

EDIBLES

Pinch branches and leaves of herb plants, such as chives and parsley, that you're growing under grow lights or in a sunny window for eating.

Rinse any seeds you're sprouting for eating twice a day to prevent mold buildup and help with germination.

LAWNS & GROUNDCOVERS

Protect your lawn areas along walkways and sidewalks from de-icing salts. There's not much you can do if your town is spreading de-icing salts along the sidewalk right next to your lawn. However, in your yard, remove the snow first before adding the salts. This will prevent shoveling the salts onto other areas of the lawn. Try using alternatives to traditional de-icing salts, such as sand or kitty litter. Water the lawn areas well along these walkways and sidewalks as soon as the snow melts to help dissolve the salts and cause less damage to grass roots.

Don't walk on frozen lawns that don't have a snow cover. Walking on the frozen grass blades can break them and cause dieback in spring.

■ *Mulch over tender perennial plants with pine boughs that will help collect snow on top of them. Snow is an excellent insulator.*

PERENNIALS & VINES

Use extra evergreen boughs from your fresh holiday tree as mulch over tender perennial flowers or ones just planted this fall in your garden. The boughs themselves won't add much protection, but they will collect snow on top of the perennials. Snow is an excellent insulator and will protect your flowers from heaving and thawing during warm winter periods. New England gardeners living in colder areas that have consistent snow cover from December through March often have better success overwintering tender perennials than gardeners in warmer parts of our region where the snow cover comes and goes all winter. If you don't have fresh evergreen boughs, use straw or hay to help collect snow on these plants.

ROSES

Finish adding winter protection to your roses if you didn't get to it in November (see November Care, Roses). If we get an early snowstorm, remove the snow and mulch with bark or wood chips. Chances are the snow will melt and the roses will need the extra protection.

Keep potted miniature roses in a sunny window and away from cold drafts.

SHRUBS & TREES

Check tree guards, burlap wraps, and other winter protection placed on your shrubs last month (see November Care, Shrubs & Trees). We sometimes can get wet, heavy snowfalls in December that will collapse a burlap windscreen or protective deer fencing. Once the storm passes and the ice or snow melts, carefully fix the damage.

Prune broken branches after a storm to remove any dangerous limbs that might injure a person or damage a building or landscape feature. Prune the branches back to a side branch or the main trunk. For large broken limbs, follow the tree pruning recommendations in February Care, Trees.

'Tis the season for outdoor holiday light decorations. There's nothing more heartwarming than attractively displayed lights on snow-laden shrubs and trees. Lights should never be left on trees or shrubs through the winter, however. Loosely drape them over branches; don't secure them to the branches with ties. Also, don't secure the lights tightly to the trunk of trees or branches. Although it may look attractive, the light strand can girdle the tree if not removed early in spring. Remove the lights during a warm spell in winter or wait until spring. Don't try to remove lights frozen to the leaves or branches or you can damage the plant.

Keep live Christmas trees protected from extreme cold and drying out by placing them in an unheated garage or shed until you're ready to move the tree indoors.

WATER

ANNUALS

Water any indoor annual flowers lightly in December. Wait until the soil is dry a few inches deep in the pot before watering thoroughly. You can use the finger test to decide when to water. If you can stick your finger into the potting soil down to your knuckle and the soil is still dry, water.

If you forget to water for a period of time, a plant will start wilting. Instead of just watering from the top, place the container in a tub with a few inches of water and let the water soak slowly into the dried rootball through the container's drainage holes. This will thoroughly revive a potted plant. If you just water from the top, the rootball might

have shrunk as it dried, so the water will just run down the sides of the pot and out the drainage holes without moistening the soil.

BULBS

Keep amaryllis bulbs that are actively growing well watered. The bulbs often are potted in small containers with little soil. The soil dries out quickly and can affect the growth of the flower stalk and length of time the flowers bloom.

If forcing bulbs, such as paperwhite narcissus, indoors in a vase of water, make sure the roots are always in contact with the water to ensure continuous growth.

Check the moisture level of stored summer bulbs, such as dahlias, in their storage area. The peat moss medium should be damp but not wet. It should be moist to the touch, but not so moist that you can wring water out of the medium when you squeeze it. If it's too wet, open up the plastic bag and let it dry out. If it's too dry, mist the peat moss with water.

EDIBLES

Keep microgreen containers well watered. The soil will need to be continually moist for good germination and growth. However, don't overwater until the soil becomes soggy. This will cause damping-off disease (see January Problem-Solve, Edibles), which can wipe out a planting. The same is true for greens you're growing under grow lights. It's always best to bottom water, if possible, to avoid disturbing the top growth (see February Plant, Annuals).

PERENNIALS & VINES

Check potted perennials and vines, such as clematis, that you're storing in containers indoors in a cool, dark area. Only water the soil in the containers if they are very dry. A sign of extreme dryness would be not only soil that is dry to the touch, but also that the soil rootball has shrunk and there's space between the pot and the soil. Add enough water to moisten the soil so it's damp but not wet.

For tropical vines, such as mandevilla, that are overwintering indoors in a sunny window, water when the soil is dry a few inches deep. It's better to thoroughly water the container, enough so water runs out the drainage holes, *infrequently* than to lightly water frequently.

ROSES

Water miniature roses grown as houseplants in winter only when the soil is dry at a depth of 2 to 3 inches.

SHRUBS & TREES

Check container shrubs or trees being stored in an unheated garage or shed. Water only if the soil is very dry. Cover the soil rootball with mulch to help preserve the moisture and you shouldn't have to water much all winter.

If warm temperatures continue into December and the ground isn't frozen, water fall-planted shrubs and trees well.

FERTILIZE

ANNUALS & EDIBLES

Annual flowers, vegetables, and herbs growing indoors in a sunny window are not growing much this time of year and so don't need fertilizing. Wait until new growth appears to start fertilizing again. The exception is plants growing under grow lights. Apply light doses of an all-purpose, indoor plant food when you water.

Store fertilizers in a cool, dry location. Keep them out of reach of children and pets.

BULBS

If you intend to keep amaryllis bulbs after they finish flowering, you'll need to keep the green leaves growing strong, so apply light doses of an indoor plant food every month when you water.

PROBLEM-SOLVE

ANNUALS

Check overwintering annual flowers for outdoor pests that hitched a ride inside. These include whiteflies, aphids, mealybugs, and scale. Bring your plant into a warm garage or basement to

spray with insecticidal soap or Neem oil to thwart whiteflies and aphids. Dab small infestations of mealybugs with a cotton swab soaked with rubbing alcohol. Spray Neem or horticultural oil to suffocate scale insects. You may have to reapply these sprays every few days to kill newly hatching insects and control an infestation.

Make sure any sprayed plant is not within close range of kids and pets. Even though the plant itself may not be harmful if it's ingested, the pesticide spray may be a danger.

Check holiday plants growing indoors to see if they're poisonous to pets. Cats and dogs love to munch on a variety of leaves to add roughage to their diets. They can be harming themselves. It's important to keep potentially poisonous plants out of reach. The table on the next page lists the plants that are most toxic if ingested and how they can harm your pet.

BULBS

If your amaryllis bulb didn't rebloom, it might be due to a number of factors. Amaryllis bulbs need to rejuvenate themselves after being forced into flower indoors in winter. The small soil mass in most containers doesn't provide enough fertility to replenish the bulb. Once flowering ceases, start fertilizing with an indoor plant food

■ *To keep the humidity high around houseplants in winter, fill a pebble tray with water and place your houseplant pot on top of it. The water will evaporate, keeping the humidity levels higher than normal.*

DECEMBER

to keep the leaves growing strong. Then, fertilize every month through the summer. Keep the container well watered too. Drought will stress the bulb.

Another factor affecting whether amaryllis bulbs rebloom is their dormant period. These bulbs need

■ *Keep poisonous holiday plants, such as mistletoe, out of reach of kids and pets.*

six weeks of dormancy in order to flower. If they don't get enough dormant time, they may not flower. (Starting in September, you should have stopped fertilizing and watering. Let the foliage naturally die back and place the container in a cool, dry, dark location.)

Even after growing your bulb well and giving it a dormant period, it still may not rebloom. Give it a try, but if it's not blooming, compost it and buy another.

EDIBLES
Check your microgreens, indoor herbs, and any edibles growing under grow lights for damping-off disease (see January Problem-Solve, Edibles).

Watch for aphids, whiteflies, mealybugs, and spider mites on your young plants (see Problem-Solve, Annuals).

Check for fungus gnats on any potted indoor flowers, herbs, or vegetables, and control them (see January Problem-Solve, Perennials).

Keep outdoor vegetables protected from the cold. Brussels sprouts, kale, and spinach can take temperatures into the 20s Fahrenheit and still be

POISONOUS HOLIDAY PLANTS	
PLANT	DANGER
Poinsettia	It's commonly believed this is extremely poisonous to kids and pets, but it's not. However, the milky white sap can cause mouth and stomach upset.
Mistletoe	This favorite, romantic holiday plant is very toxic to pets. It can cause a quick drop in blood pressure, breathing problems, and even seizures.
Holly	Holly leaves and berries can cause vomiting and diarrhea.
Daffodil	If you're forcing daffodils, such as paperwhite narcissus, keep your dog and cat away. The bulbs are particularly toxic.
Lily	Although considered a traditional Easter plant, potted lilies can also found at Christmas time. Lilies are very toxic to cats. Even a small amount can cause stomach upset and convulsions.
Amaryllis	Like daffodils, the bulb is most toxic to dogs and cats, but eating the leaves and flower stalk can also cause vomiting, diarrhea, and lethargy.
Holiday cactus	This plant has low toxicity to pets.
Christmas tree	These are generally nontoxic to pets, but don't let your pet drink the water from the fresh tree basin. It might contain harmful mold, bacteria, or fertilizer.

edible. Use thick floating row covers to keep the temperatures warm. Secure them to the ground with stakes, stones, or boards. Not only will this make a warmer environment, it will also help keep hungry rabbits and mice away.

If the hay or straw placed over your overwintering carrot bed keeps blowing off, lay bird netting over the straw. Secure it to the ground with stones or boards to keep the insulating hay in place.

LAWNS & GROUNDCOVERS

Look at areas of your lawn that you seem to be reseeding each year because of snowplow damage or damage from deicers. Think about ways to prevent the damage. This might include growing a different plant in that place, such as annuals. If you create an annual flower bed along a walkway or driveway you can flush out the salts and repair the soil damage in spring before planting. Sometimes substituting grass with bark mulch is the simplest solution to not having to repair that same spot every year.

PERENNIALS & VINES

While most herbaceous perennials have died back for the season, woody perennials, such as lavender and candytuft (*Iberis*), may need some extra protection from rabbits and mice. Either cover these woody perennials with a thin wire mesh to create a barrier or spray smell-based animal repellents on them now, before the snow flies. Use the same technique on woody vines that might be attractive to deer.

ROSES

Miniature roses growing indoors are very susceptible to spider mites in winter. Spider mites love the dry conditions that occur indoors in New England homes this time of year. Unfortunately, you don't notice the damage until a web forms on the leaves. If you look closely you'll see small mites scurrying around. The leaves will have a stippled and bronze appearance. The best prevention for spider mites on roses is to mist the plant regularly to keep the humidity levels high. You can also group roses with other houseplants in a tray filled with pebbles and water. The plants and the evaporating water will increase the humidity

levels and discourage the mites. Once you have spider mites on your plants, spray roses in a warm basement or garage with horticultural oil.

SHRUBS & TREES

Check fencing and reapply animal repellents, rotating the types you use to keep deer confused and away.

Attracting birds to your yard is a great idea for any garden. While you can feed birds to enjoy their presence, you can also grow trees and shrubs that provide food, shelter, and nesting for them in your yard. There are many types of shrubs and trees that provide spring nesting and summer and fall food for birds. But you should also consider winter habitats. Some overwintering birds, such as chickadees, and early returning migratory birds need safe places to hide and food to eat. Look at your landscape and evaluate if you have a good mix of evergreens and berry-producing shrubs and trees to attract birds in winter.

Look for evergreens, such as Robusta juniper (*Juniperus chinensis*), that provide berries in winter and a place for small birds to hide. Northern bayberry (*Myrica pensylvanica*) is a broadleaf evergreen that's hardy in most areas of New England. It produces edible berries that hold onto the shrub into December. Even large evergreen trees, such as white pines, produce abundant amounts of pinecones that birds can feed on while being sheltered from winter storms.

When selecting berry-producing deciduous trees and shrubs that will provide food for birds, look for varieties that hold their berries a long time. Crabapples are popular for this reason, and varieties such as 'Sargentii' and 'Harvest Gold' are known to hold their fruits into winter. Rose hips on shrub and species roses are also a good choice for this reason. Low-growing shrubs, such as cotoneaster, have red edible berries for birds and make a nice, low plant to grow near the house. Other deciduous shrubs and trees that have persistent berries include chokeberry (*Aronia*), hackberry (*Celtis*), hawthorn (*Crataegus*), holly (*Ilex*), firethorn (*Pyracantha*), and sumac (*Rhus*).

New England Gardening Resources

The listings in this section will help further your gardening education and offer some inspiration and ideas on what to grow in your landscape. By no means is this list complete, but it's a great starting place to make you a better gardener. I divided the listings by state, but since the climate and growing conditions are similar throughout much of New England, feel free to look at other states in our region for information and inspiration.

MASTER GARDENER ASSOCIATIONS

Master Gardeners are home gardeners who have attended a series of workshops, often taught by university professors, to increase their knowledge of gardening and horticulture. In exchange for having participated in these workshops, they volunteer their time back to the community, answering home gardeners' questions (often through a phone hotline) and working on special gardening projects with kids, seniors, and others in their community. They are a great resource for a novice gardener. You might also get inspired to take the class and become a Master Gardener yourself.

SOIL TESTING LABORATORIES

I mention soil testing as a good first step to determining the health of your soil before you plant. You can purchase home soil test kits from garden centers. For a more scientific analysis, you can send soil samples to private laboratories to be tested. Some of these labs are located at state land grant universities, and the basic test often costs less than $30.

CONNECTICUT

Home and Garden Education Center
www.ladybug.uconn.edu

University of Connecticut
Leslie Alexander
State Master Gardener & Education
    Program Coordinator
leslie.alexander@uconn.edu
1380 Storrs Road, Unit 4115
Storrs, CT 06269
(806) 486-6343
www.ladybug.uconn.edu/mastergardener/
    index.html

Soil Nutrient Analysis Laboratory
6 Sherman Place, U-102
University of Connecticut
Storrs, CT 06269-5102
www.soiltest.uconn.edu

MAINE

Home Gardening News
www.umaine.edu/gardening/
    maine-home-garden-news

University of Maine Cooperative Extension
Master Gardener Volunteers
extension@maine.edu
5741 Libby Hall
Orono, ME 04469
(207) 581-3188
www.umaine.edu/gardening/master-gardeners

Analytical Laboratory and Maine Soil
    Testing Service
5722 Deering Hall
Orono, ME 04469
(207) 581-3591
www.anlab.umesci.maine.edu

MASSACHUSETTS

Home and Garden Information Center
www.ag.umass.edu/home-lawn-garden-information

Massachusetts Horticultural Society
Master Gardener Program
Steve Shaw
Training Course Coordinator
sgshaw@aol.com
900 Washington Street
Wellesley, MA 02482
(617) 933-4929
www.massmastergardeners.org

Western Massachusetts Master Gardeners
wmmga10@yahoo.com
66 Rural Lane
East Longmeadow, MA 01028
(413) 525-6742
www.wmmga.org

Soil and Plant Tissue Testing Lab
West Experiment Station
University of Massachusetts
682 North Pleasant Street
Amherst, MA 01003
(413) 545-2311
www.soiltest.umass.edu

NEW HAMPSHIRE

Education Center and Information Line
www.extension.unh.edu/Gardens-Landscapes/
    Education-Center-Information-Line

University of New Hampshire
    Cooperative Extension
Rachel Maccini
Statewide Program Coordinator
rachel.maccini@unh.edu
200 Bedford Street
Manchester, NH 03101
(603) 629-9494
www.extension.unh.edu/Master-Gardeners/
    How-do-I-become-Master-Gardener-Volunteer

University of New Hampshire
    Cooperative Extension
Soil Testing Program
Spaulding Life Science Center, Room G28
38 Academic Way
Durham, NH 03824
www.extension.unh.edu/Problem-
    Diagnosis-and-Testing-Services/
    Soil-Testing

RHODE ISLAND

Gardening RI Information Center
www.gardeningri.com

University of Rhode Island
Vanessa Venturini & Kate Venturini
Cooperative Extension Master
    Gardener Coordinators
vanessa@uri.edu
kate@uri.edu
3 East Alumni Avenue
Kingston, RI 02881
(401) 874-7142
www.uri.edu/cels/ceoc

VERMONT

Information Fact Sheets
www.uvm.edu/mastergardener/
    ?Page=VermontResources.htm

University of Vermont
Heather Carrington
Master Gardener State Coordinator
heather.carrington@uvm.edu
63 Carrigan Drive
Burlington, VT 05405
(802) 656-9562
www.uvm.edu/mastergardener

The University of Vermont
Agricultural and Environmental Testing Lab
219 Hills Building, UVM
Burlington, VT 05405
(802) 656-0285
www.uvm.edu/pss/ag_testing

Frost Maps

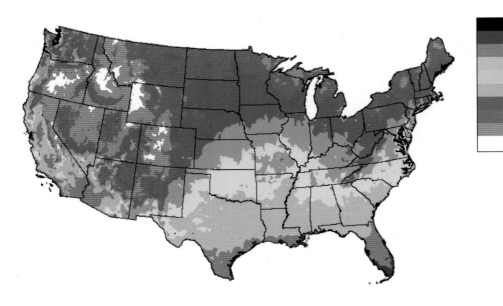

	Median
	Rare or no freeze
	Jan 1–Feb 28
	Mar 1–Mar 31
	Apr 1–Apr 15
	Apr 16–Apr 30
	May 1–May 15
	May 16–May 31
	Jun 1–Jun 30
	Jul 1–Jul 30

FIRST FALL FROST MAP

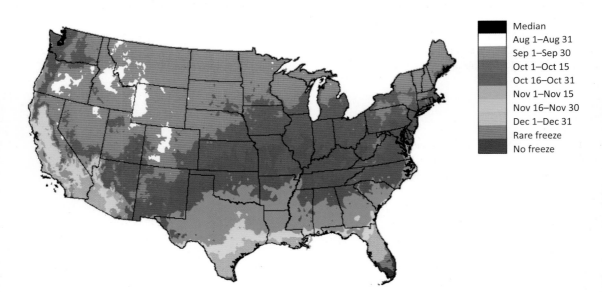

	Median
	Aug 1–Aug 31
	Sep 1–Sep 30
	Oct 1–Oct 15
	Oct 16–Oct 31
	Nov 1–Nov 15
	Nov 16–Nov 30
	Dec 1–Dec 31
	Rare freeze
	No freeze

Maps courtesy of the National Climatic Data Center, NOAA Satellite and Information Service,
www.ncdc.noaa.gov/cgi-bin/climaps/climaps.pl

Soil and Mulch Calculator

GARDEN SIZE (SQUARE FEET)	CUBIC YARDS OF MATERIALS NEEDED 1 INCH DEEP	CUBIC YARDS OF MATERIALS NEEDED 2 INCHES DEEP	CUBIC YARDS OF MATERIALS NEEDED 4 INCHES DEEP	CUBIC YARDS OF MATERIALS NEEDED 6 INCHES DEEP	CUBIC YARDS OF MATERIALS NEEDED 8 INCHES DEEP
100	0.3	0.5	1.25	2	2.5
200	0.5	1.25	2.5	3.5	5
300	1	2	3.5	5.5	7.5
400	1.25	2.5	5	7.5	10
500	1.5	3	6	9	12
600	1.8	3.5	7.5	11	15
700	2	4	8.5	13	17
800	2.5	5	10	15	20
900	2.75	5.5	11	17	22
1,000	3	6	12	18.5	25

Another way to calculate how much mulch, soil, or compost you'll need is to calculate the garden length times its width times the desired depth (in feet).

Convert this measurement from cubic feet to cubic yards by dividing by 27 (the number of cubic feet in one yard). For example, if you have a 10-by-20-foot garden area (200 square feet) and you want to add 3 inches of compost, then you'll convert 3 inches into feet (0.25 feet). Then multiply 200 × .25 = 50; now divide by 27. The total amount of compost you'll need is 1.85 cubic yards.

MULCH GUIDE

There are a variety of mulches and each has benefits for your plants. Use this guide to help determine the best mulch for your landscape situation.

- **Bark mulch:** This common mulch comes in bags or in bulk. The options range from bark chunks to shredded pieces of bark. The chips and chunks last longer in the landscape, but the shredded bark is easier to spread.

- **Wood chips:** Wood chips are a mix of various woods, leaves, and stems from arborists (depending on the job they were doing). Often it's inexpensive or even free depending on the arborist. Wood chips aren't as evenly colored and decorative as bark and have a mix of chip sizes, but this mulch is very economical.

- **Straw and hay:** Straw (made from wheat, rye, or barley) is more expensive, but has fewer weed seeds than hay. Commonly used in vegetable and annual flower gardens, hay and straw break down quickly within one growing season and can be tilled into the soil as a soil amendment.

- **Stone:** Crushed stone or volcanic rock is used as decorative mulch under house drip lines and around trees and shrubs. It preserves soil moisture and helps weed control. However, it doesn't build the soil through decomposition the way bark mulch, straw, and hay will.

- **Plastic and landscape fabrics:** Black or red plastic mulch is used in vegetable gardens to warm the soil for warm-season crops such as melons and tomatoes. While it suppresses weeds and conserves soil moisture, it's best to run a soaker hose under the mulch to ensure plants are getting adequate water. Landscape fabric is a geo-textile that lets water and air through, but suppresses weed growth. It is often covered with bark mulch or stone to be more decorative.

Index

Photo Credits

Heather Claus: 23

Tom Eltzroth: 75 (both), 121 (middle, bottom), 133 (bottom), 159 (right)

Katie Elzer-Peters: 10, 11 (all), 12, 39 (all), 60 (both), 61 (all), 63 (bottom right), 76 (all), 77 (all), 83, 85 (right), 87 (all), 93 (bottom), 94 (both), 95, 98 (both), 106, 107 (left), 108, 110, 120 (all), 125, 133 (top), 134 (both), 135 (both), 137, 154 (right, all), 160, 175

Bill Kersey: 8, 17, 24 (bottom), 38 (both), 45, 49, 51, 52, 78 (top), 79, 82 (bottom), 101, 104, 154 (left)

Troy Marden: 74

Elizabeth Millard: 93 (top)

Charlie Nardozzi: 128

NOAA, Northeast Regional Climate Center at Cornell University: 180

Jerry Pavia: 6, 32, 53 (top)

Shutterstock: 13 (all), 14, 15, 18, 22, 25, 27, 28, 31, 42, 53 (bottom), 54, 56, 57, 67, 72, 88, 93 (top left), 96, 100, 102, 107 (bottom right), 111, 112 (both), 113, 114, 116, 121 (top), 123 (both), 124 (both), 126 (all), 127, 130, 132, 139 (both), 143, 144, 148, 149, 156, 158 (right), 159 (left), 162, 166, 168, 171, 173, 176

Neil Soderstrom: 35, 105, 109, 158 (left), 163, 164

Susan Weigel: cover

Meet Charlie Nardozzi

Charlie Nardozzi is a nationally recognized garden writer, speaker, and radio and television personality. He has worked for more than twenty years bringing expert gardening information to home gardeners through radio, television, talks, the Internet, and the printed page. Charlie delights in making gardening information simple, easy, fun, and accessible for everyone.

Charlie is the author of *Vegetable Gardening for Dummies, Urban Gardening for Dummies, Northeast Fruit and Vegetable Gardening, New England Getting Started Garden Guide,* and *Foodscaping* (the last three for Cool Springs Press). He writes and produces *Vermont Garden Journal* on public radio, hosts gardening tips on the local CBS television affiliate in Vermont, and is the former host of the nationally broadcast PBS *Garden Smart* television show. Charlie is a widely sought-after speaker for flower shows, Master Gardener groups, and garden clubs across the country.

For more information, check out Charlie's website at www.gardeningwithcharlie.com.